IN SEARCH OF THE INFINITE

RELATED BOOKS PUBLISHED BY ATTAR BOOKS

Where Do I Go When I Meditate? Keith Hill

Prophecy on the River Judith Hoch

The Lantern in the Skull Hugh Major

The Luminous Nun Kerryn Levy

The Matapaua Conversations Peter Calvert and Keith Hill

The Bhagavad Gita: A New Poetic Version Keith Hill

IN SEARCH OF
THE INFINITE

A meditator's journey of spiritual discovery

ATHAN EAST

First edition published in 2022 by Attar Books

Copyright © Athan East 2022

The right of Athan East to be identified as the author of this work is asserted according to Section 96 of the Copyright Act 1996.

Paperback ISBN 978-0-9951333-6-5
Hardcover ISBN 978-1-99-115700-3
Ebook ISBN 978-1-99-115701-0

All rights reserved. Copying and distributing passages excerpted from this book for the purpose of sharing and discussing is permitted on the condition that the source of each excerpt is fully acknowledged, and such excerpts are not onsold. Otherwise, except for fair dealing or brief passages quoted in a newspaper, magazine, radio, television or internet review, no part of this book may be reproduced in any form or by any means, or in any form of binding or cover other than that in which it is published, without permission in writing from the Publisher. This same condition is imposed on any subsequent purchaser.

Cover photograph by Linda Ooi, Melbourne, Australia

Attar Books is a New Zealand publisher which focuses on work that explores today's spiritual experiences, culture, concepts and practices. For more information visit our website:

https://attarbooks.com

Dedicated to
BHAI SAHIB
my beloved Luminary of Life,
an epitome of Wisdom, of Humility, and of Love,
who taught me the way to The Infinite.

Above all,
and with all-consuming veneration and praise,
this book is also dedicated to
THE INFINITE
The Creator of all Life,
known by various names
enshrined in all the World's Scriptures.

∞

CONTENTS

	Introduction	9
1	The Promise to Write	13
2	The Early Days	23
3	My Working Life	32
4	Raising a Family	43
5	Plunging into Cult Practices	46
6	Experiential Cosmic Awakening	57
7	The Core Values of VCM	68
8	Careers, Marriage, Children, Trauma	84
9	Food, Death, Karma, Service	98
10	Accepting the Unexpected	115
11	On Spiritual Growth	119
12	On the Departed Souls of Dear Ones	127
13	Cleansing Victimised Souls	144
14	On Salvation	164
15	The Guru	170
16	Meditation	192
17	Conclusion	219
	References	225
	Further information / Contacts	226
	To the Reader	227

INTRODUCTION

IN 2005, AFTER MY WIFE AND I had been practising Vibrant Celestial Meditation (VCM) for over two and a half decades, I was directed to write about my spiritual experiences and share them with humanity. I was initially reluctant to do so. I have never enjoyed openly sharing my experiences, whether regarding personal growth or spiritual matters, even with close friends. I found the thought of truthfully revealing events of my personal life embarrassing, while views on religious and spiritual matters can be sensitive, even if they are experiential truths.

An inner struggle then ensued, between the sublime call to write and my rational mind telling me to ignore it. Lack of confidence generated negative thoughts, such as, "You don't have any writing experience," and "You don't have money to publish." Trying my hand at revealing my Guru's and The Infinite's messages to the public just felt too great a burden.

At the same time a void formed within me, haunting me with the feeling that my purpose in this lifetime would remain unfulfilled if these experiential truths were not shared. Accordingly, I felt I had to pull myself together and complete this onerous writing task, even if it meant leaving its publication to someone else, perhaps after my death. I eventually overcame my self-doubts and, slowly but surely, started writing. Even then my progress suffered repeated starts and stops. That explains why it has taken me almost fifteen years to complete this project!

I suppose the Creator was aware of my doubts, because my eldest daughter surprised me one day with a reminder that this book must not only be written, but published. A text message she sent me on 8 May 2014 reads: "According to Bhai Sahib, the book that is going to be written by you is one of your biggest successes and a big favour to God and to Bhai Sahib." Bhai Sahib, or Sri Bhai Sahib Ji, refers to my Guru, who returned to the Creator in November, 2011. My eldest daughter is blessed to occasionally receive messages and guidance from Bhai Sahib. That particular message was enough for me to overcome the inertia that had stopped me writing for a number of years.

This book has two parts. The first part outlines my reluctance and struggles as I followed my often acrimonious path towards learning about the truth. The second part aligns my journey with that of Bhai Sahib, describing the spiritual path he presented to the world.

The book begins by depicting my unending struggle and the anguish I felt from early childhood, which led to the growth of a defiant streak in me, along with an unrestrained temper. My earliest days were also bloated with negatives, which formed a vicious cycle as I plodded into adulthood. This psychological damage subsequently affected all spheres of my life, including my livelihood, health, marital relationship, and the way I managed my family. Not finding any satisfactory answers for my troubles within my mundane surroundings, as a last resort I turned to the supernatural.

My journey into the supernatural became even more urgent following the birth of my youngest daughter. During delivery, her neck was entangled by her umbilical cord. That caused asphyxia, which resulted in cerebral palsy and triggered infantile spasms. My adamant refusal to accept that there is no known cure led me on an all-out search for God. I supposed that only a God-Force would provide the answers I needed. I wanted my daughter to have a normal life, and I wanted to know why this had happened to me and my family. However, my visits to various temples and mediums proved totally ineffective, as they mainly offered talk laced with empty promises, providing only a false sense of reassurance.

My search at this time ended with my deciding that there is no God, as there was no evidence to support His existence or whereabouts. From then on my mind became totally shut to anyone who preached anything about God to me.

Years later, a friend challenged me to attend a seminar on Vibrant Celestial Meditation. I took up the challenge only because he agreed to give me a full refund if I was not satisfied with the meditation course. VCM

INTRODUCTION

practice turned out to be a massive turning point in my life. It led me to realise that spirituality of the highest level must involve the Creator, The Infinite. I realised this understanding can only and wholly be obtained through His grace and blessing, as a result of one's relentless and profound prayers of supplication and benediction. It dawned on me that the realisation of The Infinite involves authentic spirituality of the highest order. This book is titled *In Search of The Infinite* to emphasise the all-important need to be aware of The Infinite in every moment of our life.

> The Infinite refers to the Supreme Creator, Supreme Soul, who is formless, and is known by the various names enshrined in all the world's scriptures. The Infinite is Omniscient (All-Knowing), Omnipotent (All-Powerful) and Omnipresent (Present Everywhere). The Infinite is the same before, now and after, and always shall be.
>
> The Infinite is the cause of you, of me, and of everything there is. The Infinite, therefore, is the Supreme Cause of All Things. All things are possible and revolve around The Infinite, who is also described as The True One, Creator, Supreme Intelligence, and Who is beyond the understanding of humanity, including the prophets of old, and, for that matter, any intelligent extraterrestrial beings, whatever they may be, and wherever they may be located in the wide expanse of the universe (or multiverse).

Chapter One

THE PROMISE TO WRITE

"THE BOOK! ... THE BOOK! ... I CANNOT DIE! God! I can't die now! I'm sorry, God! Please give me another chance. Let me complete the book that You have commanded me to write. I'm sorry! I'm sorry!"

I had been lobbing a shuttlecock during a game of badminton when my vision of my friendly opponent started to blur. I had to stop when the waves of dizziness got stronger and my vision went fuzzier. I exited the hall to catch the night air, hoping the cool breeze would stop both the spinning and the pain that was slowly creeping into my head. It did not. Wave after wave of excruciating pain, escalating in intensity, washed through my body, putting increasing weight on my head, which I was forced to support with both hands.

I tried fending off the pain by vigorously bending my head and upper torso in a repeated up and down motion, like a slave humbly bowing to the master, begging for the pain to stop. Breathing as rapidly as I could, I hoped to raise my oxygen levels to counter what I thought was my brain being starved of oxygen.

Strange, circuit-like images began sliding across my perception, like a black and white television screen trying to latch onto a channel. Then an ancient, yellow-tinged scroll inscribed with unfamiliar writings appeared in my vision. Was it what they call the Akashic Records? Wanting to be aware of every moment of this experience, even if I was trudging through the valley of death, I attempted to read what was written on the scroll, but the image retreated further each time I focused on it.

With the pain not abating, I rushed back into the badminton hall where I knew I could find help. I barely managed to call out to my badminton teammates to send me to a hospital before I collapsed into a crouching position, unable to maintain a dignified upright position any more.

At the hospital, after I had been strapped with all sorts of wires and devices, the doctor discovered I had suffered a heart attack. The coronary angiogram revealed that three of my heart arteries were obstructed: two were totally blocked, the third was 80%. A stent was immediately guided through one of the arteries, but the procedure failed as the blockage was too calcified.

Later I was transferred from the ICU to the High Dependency Ward. The same medical officer who had treated me at the emergency ward was on duty. He noticed I was awake and walked straight to where I was to whisper: "You're lucky to be alive!" After saying that, he left just as quickly. I was subsequently referred to the National Heart Institute where, a week after my heart attack, open-heart surgery was successfully carried out.

Yet I did not really comprehend the severity of this life-threatening episode until after my discharge. Sometimes a person receives warning signs before a major health impairment. Very often the signs are not taken seriously or are dismissed. For several weeks prior to this incident, I experienced a persistent sense that prompted me to be concerned regarding my body's blood circulation. I sought the advice of an older badminton teammate on which supplement would improve blood circulation. He recommended a Chinese Mok Yee (black fungus) concoction. In the meantime, lethargy set in, hanging over me like a dark grey cloud for days on end. When I looked in the mirror, an unusually dark and dull-looking face with a cadaverous pallor stared back at me.

On the fateful Sunday morning of 13 April 2014, hours before playing badminton, I walked past a pharmacy. As if working on foresight, I went in and consulted with the pharmacist.

"What herbs would you recommend me to take for blockages?" I asked nonchalantly.

"That would depend on what sort of blockages you are referring to," replied the pharmacist, a little smugly.

"Well, blockages that would affect the circulation of blood," I responded somewhat boringly.

"Again, that would depend on the cause of the blockages, whether it is caused by high blood pressure or high cholesterol," explained the pharmacist, as if talking to a child.

"I don't have any high blood pressure, but my cholesterol is slightly above the normal range," I said, quelling my rising annoyance.

The pharmacist then put on her sales pitch and rattled off her recommendation of Omega 3 Fish Oil. I took the bait and paid RM 147 for a bottle of 120 capsules. I left the pharmacy feeling somewhat relieved I had found a solution.

Despite my spontaneous action that morning, it was too late to stop the heart attack, which, like a shadow, stealthily crept up on me that evening. On reflection, I wondered if I could have warded off the heart attack if I had taken heed of the impulse and dosed up with the black fungus concoction and fish oil capsules two weeks prior to the fateful day. Over the years, I had been more concerned about my liver, for which I had been taking herbal supplements. I felt confident that my heart was strong; I could engage in rather vigorous physical exercises and feel none the worse for it. I was never so wrong! Several days before the operation to treat my heart, I had a precognitive dream.

I am standing on top of a hill, beside a perfect-looking new bus. I am looking, unafraid, at a scene of two tigers roaming freely down the hill in the distant valley. They seemed to be on the lookout, hunting for prey. The tigers eye me and start ambling in my direction. Arrogant as ever in the face of a challenge, I deduce from a quick mental calculation that I would be safely locked inside the bus before the tigers could get anywhere near me.

The scene changes. I am taken aback as I find myself holed up in a small old rickety bus. The door is too misaligned to be properly latched to the main frame. There is a small hole in the roof. One of the tigers leaps up onto the roof, while the other encircles the bus, waiting for its prey to succumb out of sheer exhaustion. The tiger on the roof peers through the small hole, scheming to find a way to get at me. It squeezes its forefoot in and, shoulders straining, starts pawing vigorously in the air, reaching down as far as it can, like a pussy cat trying to hook its prey. In the melee, I had the audacity to raise my fingers to touch the edge of the claw and examine its sharpness.

The frightful awareness of my horrifying impending death woke me rudely from the dream. My hand was still outstretched and hovering in the air. I wasn't sure if it was from touching the claws, or if I was trying to push the thought of a hideous death away.

SELF-REFLECTION

As a VCM practitioner, I should have heeded my inner prompting by seeking a proper medical checkup, rather than continuing to be overly confident of my health. In my dream, this was symbolised by the big nice-looking bus. In truth, the small rickety bus was an actual reflection of my poor health: death was glaringly imminent, as symbolised by not one, but two, tigers. One tiger of death was waiting patiently for my poor health to eventually break down, and the other was looking for a quicker path, like a heart attack, to get at me. That inner prompting clearly emanated from my higher mind. Interference from our conscious mind, along with its ego counterpart, tend to obstruct our receiving sublime inner promptings.

Bhai Sahib had always stressed that in order to receive the desired guidance, we need to be in a totally calm, relaxed and surrendered mode, and with total humility submit to the Divine within. We also need to draw on the power of discernment, which is inherent within us. In this instance, it would have helped if I had been able to first discern then heed this repeated inner prompting by going for a full medical examination, rather than being overly confident and therefore lackadaisical.

I guess my destiny has not yet been fulfilled, and for that reason I was able to strike a bargain, a covenant, with God. God is different from man. The situation did not involve an eye for an eye, but whether I perceived I had lived my life to its fullest worth, or whether I had lived it nonchalantly, as is normal for the majority of us.

With this new lease of life, I prayed it would provide me with the final impetus I needed to complete writing my story, after having made several determined, but interrupted, attempts since 2005. Or so I thought.

ANOTHER SHATTERING WAKE-UP CALL

On 7 August, 2018, I entered my sixty-fifth birthday without any fanfare. A few days later, I had a biopsy done on a tiny mole on my nose. Prior to that, I had embarked on a tour with a group of childhood friends in a van. We travelled through Haadyai in southern Thailand and along the east coast of Peninsular Malaysia . On the fifth and last day, on our way home, I received a call from the hospital to meet the skin specialist. I knew it was not going to be good news. I was proven right: the test result confirmed that the mole on my nose was basal cell carcinoma.

I kept thinking of the unfulfilled promise I had made to God as part of my bargain in 2014, after I suffered the heart attack. I was less concerned about the cancer. The unfulfilled promise weighed more heavily on me! Not long after the carcinoma surgery, I had a dream:

I am walking along the corridor of a row of shops. I am looking at a shop that sells household appliances. The shop is fully stocked. Appliances are stacked from the floor level to the top of the shelves. Several rat-cage traps are displayed at the very top. I can see a live rodent in a cage trap. I am shocked, and rudely awakened by the sight of that rodent.

I instantly knew that the dream was about myself, since a shop building also symbolises one's physical body. The live rodent probably symbolised a serious disease. Since the rodent was confined in a cage trap, I interpreted it as telling me that if it was a disease, it should not have spread to other parts of my body. Additionally, it was probably located somewhere above my neck, as indicated by the live rodent being located near the ceiling. I suspected that it was most likely another serious disease, since the dream came after I had successfully undergone surgery to remove the basal cell carcinoma.

I then decided to go for a check-up, as I was not comfortable with a spot located at the soft palate of my mouth. On 17th August 2018, the biopsy results revealed it was again cancer positive, but a type different from the one located on my nose. This was squamous cell carcinoma. A full body PET scan confirmed my dream. The cancerous tumor was located between the soft palate and the entrance to the right nostril. Other parts of my body were not affected. The cancer's location at the roof of my mouth, which is at the higher part of the body, was symbolised by the cage trap being located near the ceiling.

THE NEED FOR INTROSPECTION

Since my heart attack in 2014, and the subsequent promise I made to God that I would write this book, I realised I had not only failed to do so, but had also allowed the ego-self to continue its reign over me. I then recalled a message received from the departed Bhai Sahib, through my eldest daughter, approximately two years prior to the heart attack. I share an extract from that message:

"Athan, hear carefully what I am going to tell you. Starting from now, stop eating outside food. MSG (monosodium glutamate) will kill you, especially when you reach middle and old age. I ask you to eat healthy foods like vegetables, fruits, etc. Consume all the types of food that I have taught you in the VCM course. Organic food, preferably. I am not saying you are going to get cancer. I just want you to stay healthy always. If not, you will easily get tired and get sick. I know you are a nice person. I know what I see in you, Athan. I see you lacking confidence in yourself. When are you going to start writing? Didn't God ask you to write? Where is it?

"Athan, love God, love yourself, love family, love God's children. Contribute more in taking care of your children. (God told you this in His earlier messages.) Don't always leave your wife to do your part. She has done this over the past few years. God said He gave man and woman (parents) children and He expects both to do their duties as father and mother. Men always take their wives for granted, leaving the wife to do the man's part in bringing up the children, making excuses that they are busy with breadwinning duties. To God these are all excuses.

"All the contributions we make, when we ask God for things, He takes account of what we do with what we ask for. This is an obstacle to receiving further blessings. I may not communicate with you for a long time after this. God said I have revealed too much already."

The warning fell on deaf ears. I had assumed my health would be fine again after I had survived the heart attack. I also did not take the message seriously because I thought I would not contract any more serious diseases. Then two types of cancer were detected in me. I had even forgotten that my health was at a low, as was symbolised by the small rickety bus in my dream of 2014, just after my heart attack.

Reading the message again made me realise that Bhai Sahib had actually tried his best to warn me. He had even mentioned cancer when he warned me about consuming the wrong type of food. Although I had removed pork from my diet since 1994, I did not pay attention to the other unhealthy foods that have a high content of fat, MSG, and preservatives.

I learned much earlier that everyone has to walk their own path in life. As a consequence, God forbids fortune-telling and disclosure of what one's future will be. Bhai Sahib himself was warned not to reveal too much about my life to me. Although I was quite capable of reading between the lines of his message, I had failed to heed his advice, instead allowing my ego-self to interfere with my assessment.

Once, while alone in meditation, I spontaneously understood that I had overwhelmed myself with numerous pent-up grudges and negative feelings, including the uncontrollable temper that had stuck to me for so long. I realised the connection between negative emotions and the growth of cancer, which I had brought upon myself. Besides the consumption of unwholesome foods, negative emotions were a major cause of me being struck with cancer.

I was also able to understand why Bhai Sahib had, in that same message, advised me to love God, to love myself, my family, and God's children (our fellow human beings). I must confess that I had never known how to express love in any meaningful way.

Meanwhile, a fellow VCM practitioner had lent me a book titled *Fresh Vegetable and Fruit Juices*, written by N. W. Walker, Doctor of Science. The author states that one of the most insidious causes of ulcers and cancer is long-time resentment nursed by the victim, often from childhood. Unless resentments are completely resolved, they can frustrate otherwise effective attempts to help the patient. The book confirmed my intuition regarding the direct connection between cancer and powerful negative emotions. Even though I had received a great deal of goodness, in terms of spiritual knowledge and experiences, during two decades of VCM practice, I was still challenged by the various resentments I had accumulated since childhood.

Out of the blue, I spontaneously and unexpectedly had the feeling that I needed to forgive those who I felt had hurt me, let go of old grudges, and change for the better. I began by telling myself that it did not matter at all whether I was right or wrong over whatever had happened in the past. What I needed was to dislodge those negativities to allow emotional detoxification to take place.

With that, I began the process of self-healing. I apologised to my wife and all my children for my shortcomings as the man in the family. I called my siblings and apologised to them for my behavior. I apologised to my former employer and his family members involved in the affairs of the company over my conduct during my tenure of employment. I called for a meeting with fellow VCM practitioners where I openly apologised for my past behavior.

Meanwhile, I was informed by the doctors that my heart was functioning at only 38% of its capacity. When my cancer treatment was in progress, the hospital authorities had made me sign a special additional indemnity, in case of any serious complications. I almost failed to complete the entire cancer treatment, but managed, over a period of seven weeks, all 35 cycles of radiotherapy and five out of the seven cycles of chemotherapy treatment. On reaching my 27th round of radiotherapy, the oncologist told me that they were deciding if treatment should be terminated. I was then losing weight fast, down from 83 kilograms to 64. The specially-made protective facial mask worn during radiotherapy session was beginning to lose its fit, due to bodily shrinkage caused by weight loss. Low blood count was also unfavourable for the further administration of chemotherapy.

Alone in my bedroom, and with severe pains, I broke down and uttered aloud: "That's it, God! It's all over. I'm sorry. I've failed you again and again. I've failed Bhai Sahib. I'm sorry I didn't write the book. I don't deserve another chance. I don't think I can make it. Just let me go. I'm sorry."

I had resigned myself to the idea that I was going to fail. I could not consume any solid food due to a swathe of ulcers at the right underside of my tongue, in the gums, on the inside wall of the mouth, and across my entire neck. They were the side effects of radiotherapy. Besides my serious drop in weight, I suffered constantly from extreme bodily pain, dry mouth, severe constipation and sleep deprivation. I also had to endure the heavy morning traffic as I struggled to stay focused while driving myself from home to hospital every weekday for the treatment.

Being totally exhausted, I felt as if I was hanging by a thread to the life force within. While it was like living hell, I could still remain quite calm and fearless as I watched myself experiencing the seemingly endless pain and discomfort.

At this point in my treatment, the oncologist was considering ending further treatment. Then, just when I thought it was all over, the oncologist introduced a topical pain-killer patch to replace pain-killer tablets and the liquid morphine that had been given to me earlier. My pain became more manageable, and I began to consume some solid and powdered food. My weight stabilised around 65 kilograms, until the completion of the 35th and final round of radiotherapy. However, at the end of the last week of the seven-week treatment period, only five out of the planned seven rounds of chemotherapy were administered.

A scan done in February 2019, three months after the completion of my treatment, showed a tiny light spot. The oncologist was quietly confident that it was probably inflammation caused by the effects of chemotherapy treatment. Another scan done six months later, in August 2019, confirmed I was cancer-free.

My cancer treatment was tougher to bear than the heart attack I suffered in 2014. Recovery was also much more difficult. Instead of allowing myself to be affected by the constant pain and discomfort, I shifted my focus to writing this book. I asked God for another chance, silently uttering,: "God, I am starting to write again. Please hold on." Due to my weakened body, I felt that time was not on my side. The good news is that this shattering wake-up call drove me to complete writing about eighty percent of this book. Not long after, I had a dream:

I see a long stretch of bumper-to-bumper traffic that is at a standstill on a long and winding paved road. Running alongside this road is an undulating, sandy-surfaced road. I am on the sandy-surfaced road, on a journey. I am skateboarding ahead effortlessly, despite the road surface being like that of a sandy beach on a bright sunny day.

The dream refers to the route I am taking in my journey of life, as opposed to the route that is commonly taken by most fellow humans in their life journey. In the dream, the vehicles and paved road symbolise material comforts and physical needs that the vast majority of humans strive for and are overwhelmingly engrossed with. In contrast, the skateboard and the sandy surface road symbolise bare necessities. Ironically, the long queue of stalled traffic on the paved road symbolises the majority of humanity taking a more difficult path, seemingly engrossed in striving for material comforts.

In a humble way, I was being reassured that my life journey was right and bright, symbolised by my ability to skateboard effortlessly, despite my lack of material comforts. My dream confirmed to me that I am on the right path as I work on my spiritual quest, even if it is a challenging path. A message received during one of our VCM meditation sessions was similarly reassuring: "Do not think of what your body needs. Think of your soul."

With this Divine inspiration, I felt uplifted as I attempted to complete my writing task.

Chapter Two

THE EARLY DAYS

EARLY ONE MORNING I WAS WOKEN by my heavily pregnant mother's groans. "Son, leave the room now," she urgently called out to me from the far end of our bedroom. My mother was in labour with my youngest brother. She grimaced in pain as she struggled to stand, one hand pressed against the wall, the other clutching at her loose sarong to keep her modesty. The year was 1958. I was five years old.

This scene, of my mother suffering labour pangs, is deeply etched in my memory, as are recollections of the experiences that followed. From this moment physical abuses were hurled on me like a bucket of icy water thrown into my face, awakening my child's innocence to the stark realities of what life had in store for me. I have no recollections of tenderness and love from that time. Through my five-year-old eyes, it seemed life was all about physical and emotional pain and mental torture. The experience shaped the rest of my life.

A DIFFICULT UPBRINGING

To escape communist control and the extreme poverty that had descended on mainland China, my parents emigrated to Singapore, along with some of their fellow villagers, neighbours and relatives. I was born in Singapore. A year after my birth, my parents broke rank with their fellow countrymen to settle in a small village at the southern tip of what was then Malaya. This is where they lived for the rest of their lives, working their farms day and night to put food on the table. Having been born into a life of peasantry, their view of life was that it consisted of suffering and abject hard work.

There were more than a dozen mouths to feed back in China. They included my three older brothers, one of whom was born of a different mother. My mother was the first wife. Polygamy was not an uncommon practice in the Chinese culture then, and perhaps even now. I was told by my late mother that my father took a second wife at the behest of my paternal grandmother, during one of his trips to visit his village in China. Many different dialects are spoken among the Chinese people. My paternal grandmother was adamant that she wanted to have a Hakka lady as a daughter-in-law, in order to propagate and ensure the continuity of the Hakkas. Filial piety, a virtue greatly emphasised by Chinese culture, ensured my father submitted to the will of his mother and took a Hakka woman as his second wife. His first wife, my mother, was Cantonese.

With the exception of my eldest brother and my paternal grandmother, who eventually escaped to join us in Malaya, the rest of our family remained trapped in China, as by then communism had taken control and had isolated the country from the rest of the world. My parents regularly sent used clothing, Chinese herbs, and foodstuffs such as dried meat and lard, to my older brothers in China. Those items would be sent by ship via Singapore, through shipping agents whose offices were housed in pre-war buildings.

It was clear to me that my parents, especially my father, had very strong feelings of guilt for having left behind my older brothers in China. It was probably one of the main reasons he was obsessed with money, having to support so many family members. As far as I knew, my father spent very little on himself.

My parents usually took me along whenever they travelled to Singapore to dispatch food and clothes to China. They would stay for several days with my mother's relatives, who lived on a hill slope. Most of the houses were made from wood, with asbestos roofing. Residents drew on a common well for water. Their toilets sat across a narrow stream, on a gentle slope. Pigs were allowed to roam around freely: I had to learn fast to differentiate between pigs' feces and soil, to avoid stepping on the former. I recognised Singapore then by the sight of trishaws, which were a common means of transport. There was also the nauseating smell of the terribly polluted Singapore River, its waters dark and dirty. Before my father returned home from Singapore, he would often buy a whole roasted duck, at a cost of three dollars. The roasted duck would be divided into three meals for our family.

In my father's Southern Malaya rural village, he rented half the ground floor of a shop house, from where he ran his retail business, selling traditional Chinese medicinal products. He also rented one of the four rooms on the first floor, which was used as a bedroom for all members of my family. In the backyard, my parents reared poultry and planted vegetables for food. A common well located at the back of the shop house served two adjacent houses as a source of water. A bucket-styled toilet and a bathroom were shared by about a dozen occupants.

Even at a tender age, I wondered why life had to be so miserable and tough. My father was a hot-tempered man. He often became aggressive. I often painfully witnessed my mother being scolded or chased out of the shop house by my father. Sometimes, my mother would go off alone to stay with her relatives in Singapore. Whenever that happened, I felt lonely and cried incessantly.

Recalling another incident, I clearly remember watching my mother standing at the far end of an overhead bridge that spanned the railway lines. She was carrying my youngest brother, who was then an infant. My mother had just been chased out of the house by my father. My other younger brother was standing next to me with his mouth agape, as he watched helplessly. A group of onlookers who were attracted by the commotion were also watching the drama.

Not long after that incident I asked my mother, "Ma, why did Pa chase you out of the house?" "I will tell you when you become a grown man," my mother replied.

I never did ask my mother when I was an adult, and neither did she tell me the reason. I often overheard neighbours whispering about the ruckus caused by my parents, which at that young age I could not understand.

LIFE WITH MY FATHER

It was also common to see my father conversing noisily and dogmatically with others. His only pastime was listening to the radio, a German-made Grundig brand. He derived extreme pleasure from listening to Chinese political propaganda. It was ironic that he would always sing the praises of China, yet had chosen to abandon that country.

For all his repulsive behavior, I noticed that my father had to tolerate his nemesis, another man who lived in the same shop house. A primary school teacher, he was a member of the family who were the chief tenants. He appeared to be suffering from a mental aberration, as seen in his erratic behavior. One moment he would appear calm, in the next he was verbally attacking my father. Eventually, a decade later, his eccentric outbursts drove my father to move to another less strategically located shop house.

The temperamental chief tenant had a passion for weight-lifting and badminton. Very early each morning he religiously carried out breathing exercises in a standing position. Pressing both his palms against his stomach region, he exhaled through his mouth, his body and head bowed slightly. I recall being told that he learned the practice from a quack doctor.

This particular man deserves special mention because I was told of a paranormal incident that befell him decades ago. As a child, I met this man's fiancée, a petite lady with a dull complexion of a sickly whitish hue. She died of an illness before they could marry. Her spirit appeared to him late one evening. I shall elaborate on this incident in a later chapter.

Coming back to my early childhood, a typical daily routine involved my father making me sit behind the shop counter from morning till night. He often tied one of my hands with a rope, which he fastened to one of the many drawers that stored Chinese herbs. He then prepared several arithmetic sums for me to practise. These included multiplication questions that involved several digits. I was then only four to five years of age, so of course was unable to solve them. My father would then cane me on my back, hands and fingers. On reflection, only a gifted child would likely have met his expectations. Other than this, I was not exposed to any educational activities. Years later, I received a surprise telephone call from one of the erstwhile tenants. She was then already in her eighties. During that phone conversation, she sympathetically reminded me of the arithmetic exercises and the punishments that my father had repeatedly meted out to me.

Whenever I was given a break, I was only allowed to move about within a confined space of about twenty feet square. This was inside the house, where my father could keep a watchful eye over me. I was rarely allowed to play with the neighbourhood children. I was taught to recognise predetermined spots that my father designated boundary points, and was not permitted to go beyond them.

During one of these breaks, I was playing with a bunch of keys that belonged to my father. I was merely inserting each key into the keyhole of every drawer. It did not last for long, as I realised my father had been staring fiercely at me. I interpreted that what I was doing was wrong. I stopped doing it immediately.

Later in the day, my father was having a discussion with several men who were seated near the counter. He then wanted to retrieve certain items from one of the drawers, but he could not see the bunch of keys. I watched him searching vainly for them. The next moment, he turned and stared angrily at me. He then started swearing, accusing me of being the culprit. He immediately reached for the bunch of canes and began hitting me furiously. I still clearly recall how my mother had to apply a yellow medicinal solution on my back and hands, treating my bleeding welts.

A while later, my father found the bunch of keys. It was in one of the pockets of his new pants. He had worn them earlier, and had unwittingly placed the keys in one of the side pockets. He then folded the pants and put it back in his closet, along with the keys. Did my father regret or apologise for what he had done to me? The answer is decidedly, "No!"

When I was about eight years old, I was asked to help carry a kettle of boiling water from one point to another, a distance of about one hundred meters. I was wearing large, adult-sized wooden clogs. On the way, while walking down a short, steep slope, I slipped and fell. The boiling water splashed on my body, especially on my stomach. I screamed loudly in pain, scratching myself vigorously. The skin just peeled off, leaving a big patch of raw white flesh on my abdomen.

Despite this incident, my father, who had been out of town for several days, had no qualms about using the cane on me. Similarly, even though I had contracted chickenpox, I was caned when a man complained to my father that I had hurt his son in a fight.

To my father, spewing verbal abuse on a daily basis was an acceptable means of communication. He was always shouting, swearing, scolding, criticising or condemning something or other. I remember struggling with nervousness, and quivering visibly whenever he called for me, even if just to address an envelope that required the use of the Roman alphabet. Not only did my father fail to see the damage he was doing to me, he seemed to derive sadistic satisfaction from staring angrily at me. Over lunch or dinner, he would hit me if I held the chopsticks in a way that he thought was incorrect, or if I spread my arms too far apart against the table. I was taught table manners the hard way.

Writing using my left hand also invited caning on my fingers. I was born left-handed. Physical punishment was repeatedly meted out until I succeeded in writing with my right hand. While I use my right hand for writing purposes now, I still use my left hand when holding a racquet or carrying a heavy item. From my observation, those who use their right hand to write, and their left to perform tasks that require strength, were generally disciplined to do so during their childhood.

There were other incidents of punishment. My father would storm into the bathroom to cane me whenever he felt that I had taken too long to bathe. He would also sneak up on me to regularly check on what I was doing. The cane was again used if he considered what I was doing was wrong. This might include playing with toys or spiders, which were common pastimes for boys during those days. Never a day passed without him wearing his trademark expression: the angry stare.

MY EDUCATION AND CHILDHOOD

Like my father, during my primary school days some teachers used threats of punishments or the cane to get pupils to do assignments. My arithmetic lady teacher carried a long stick to control the class, even though pupils were generally well-behaved. I had the impression that she was eccentric, as she would force boys to strip in front of the class for not being able to recite a given multiplication table. As for the girls, she would lift up their skirts and spank their bottoms in full view of the rest of the class.

I also recall a short, male teacher who was a pervert. He appeared to be more like a gangster than a teacher to me. A day never passed without him scolding or meting out physical punishment to pupils. Once, he made a long cardboard tag attached to a piece of string and hung it over the neck of an Indian boy. On the tag was written, 'I am a donkey'. He made that poor pupil walk along the corridors of the entire school building wearing the sign. He also regularly and aggressively attempted to persuade pupils to attend his private tuition classes. He charged three dollars per month for a weekly lesson, which lasted an hour. However, I also note that except for the few overly strict teachers, the others were kind.

In terms of academic achievement, I consider myself an average student. The best class position I achieved was second, in Primary Four. It was my happiest moment, but was short-lived, lasting less than a day. I was badly shattered when my father remarked that the teacher must have made a mistake marking my test papers, having given me more marks than I deserved. My sense of achievement was completely neutralised.

Despite these early traumas in my life, I developed a sense of propriety and justice. When I was in Primary Five, I remember an incident where a Chinese teacher criticised a Malay teacher during a lesson. The victim was Mr. Hashim. I felt it was wrong of the Chinese teacher to have done so, so I wrote a letter to Mr. Hashim expressing my disappointment. Mr. Hashim read the letter, then put it in his shirt pocket. He did not utter a word, but he did turn towards me and nod in appreciation.

By the end of my primary education, I had grown increasingly rebellious. I was beginning to fight back when my father physically and verbally abused me. My eldest brother, who was twelve years older than me, treated me no better. On several occasions I fought against my father and my eldest brother at the same time. My eldest brother died at the age of 69. I shall relate more about him after his death in Chapter 12.

My difficult childhood caused me to become an increasingly problematic child. Even my relatives called me *samseng*, which in the Malay language refers to a person who is naughty and mischievous. I believe their repeated name-calling aggravated my already vulnerable childhood.

At the lower secondary school level, I was repeatedly involved in fights with pupils from a nearby Chinese medium school. They branded me *ang mo kau*, which in the Chinese Hokkien dialect literally means a 'red haired dog'. They were biased against those who attended English medium schools. I was always on my own in any fights. At times, I fought several of them simultaneously.

GHOST STORIES

Listening to stories was a common pastime during my early childhood. I was exposed to ghost stories which caused me to develop a fear of darkness. One common assumption was that ghosts appear at midnight from behind banana trees.

When I was about thirteen, I worked in my home town as a labourer in a rubber factory to help pay the family household expenses. Usually, I worked a shift that started at six in the evening and ended at midnight. This was because I had to attend school during the day. On one of those nights, at the peak of the monsoon season, it was raining heavily as I rode my bicycle to the factory. I reluctantly decided to return home utilising a shorter alternative route. To do so, I had to lift my bicycle and carry it across several railway tracks. I struggled because the bicycle, made for adults, was too big and heavy for me. In the heavy rain, I was soon drenched and shivering with cold.

As if that was not enough, I started to tremble with extreme fear as I cycled past some banana plants, imagining ghosts would at any moment appear from behind them. It was exactly the same setting as the ghost stories that I had often heard. In the dark, I imagined that a ghost was sitting on the carriage of my bicycle, an idea which scared me to death. I cycled so fast that on crossing an undulating wooden bridge, I lost control and crashed. The next moment I was staring at the wide, swollen river below. Although I suffered serious injuries, I consoled myself that I was fortunate not to have fallen into the river and drowned.

Despite all these fears in my early teenage years, I was also showing some academic inclination. Delving into the rationale behind my father's behaviour, I do understand he considered me the only one among my siblings who showed academic promise. He therefore turned slave driver, pushing me to study hard through the use of corporal punishments and verbal abuses, as he thought that was the right approach to achieve his aim of educating me.

I was also influenced by the thought that money was more important than life. I clearly recall an incident where my father was cutting Chinese herbal roots into slices with a big chopper. The conversation turned ugly when he exclaimed that he was prepared to have his head chopped off in exchange for money. I was confused by his strong stance, when he raised the chopper and placed it on the nape of his neck, just to emphasise his point.

In my early adulthood, I was the first among my siblings to inherit a shop house from my father while he was still alive. I chose to transfer ownership to my younger brother. This action was probably due to my negative response towards anything that interested my father.

The harsh treatment I received throughout my childhood culminated into my developing a very defiant personality. Ironically, I became a chip off the old block, consumed with anger, hatred, vengeance and distrust. The late American actor, Charles Bronson, was one of my favourite actors. I admired the aggressive approach he adopted to resolve difficult situations.

Chapter Three

MY WORKING LIFE

"HOORAY!" I CHEERED SILENTLY when I turned nineteen and my life as a student came to an end. I felt relieved I would not experience any more stress associated with studies. I would also not need to show any respect to teachers or other students.

"You are free now!" I told myself.

"From now on, you can do whatever you want."

"You don't need to kowtow to anyone any longer!"

"Should anyone impose on you or throw their weight around, you can retaliate even harder!"

These were some of the things I reminded myself as I waltzed into adulthood. It was not long before reality set in. I needed money to support myself. What should I do? I had to find myself a job. It was entirely due to a need for money that I looked for work.

My first job was as a temporary schoolteacher in a government secondary school. I enjoyed it. I thought it was better to be approachable with my students to gain their confidence. I also hoped that would get them interested in their studies. Another of my aims was to avoid repeating the mistakes that some of my teachers made when I was a student, such as indulging in unnecessary punishments, excessive shows of authority, and projecting the attitude that the teacher is always right.

The school where I taught was not short of notorious students. The headmaster, well-known as a disciplinarian, made several rounds daily, during the morning session for the Upper Secondary classes, and in the afternoon for the Lower Secondary. The cracking sound of his caning could be heard from one end of the school compound to the other.

That headmaster was tough. I naturally associated him with my father. I found myself deliberately behaving in a crude way towards him, even though he never directly antagonised me. I realised I tended to be sympathetic to the oppressed, to victims and underdogs, whatever the situation.

I recall an incident where I had annoyed the headmaster on purpose by being confrontational, even though he was merely having a casual chat with me. It was clearly uncalled-for behaviour. When the time came to review my status as a temporary teacher, I did not wait for its outcome, as I assumed I would not be reappointed. I was pleasantly surprised when I later received a new letter of appointment, although I had already moved to Kuala Lumpur, where I had taken up a job as a salesman with a starting salary of RM 150 per month.

I ENTER THE BUSINESS WORLD

The company was a one-man firm, dealing with furnishing and upholstery fabrics. Customers who made purchases were required to issue a confirmed and irrevocable Letter of Credit in favour of the manufacturer. In return, the firm would earn a commission of 3% to 5% for services rendered.

This firm was located in the owner's residence. I understood that was not only for convenience, but also to reduce costs. It was agony working in this firm, as the owner had a very foul temper, which he never failed to lose. He was in his early forties, very knowledgeable, and was endowed with a powerful physique. One day, in the middle of our work, the owner scolded his wife, who was on the upper floor. His stinging rebuke to his much older wife still rings clearly in my ears: "Either you live in peace or in pieces!"

At that moment, I knew my time working with him would be short. I decided to stay as long as I could, as I was becoming interested in indenting business. Personally, I was also struggling to understand why I so frequently became involved with people who had tangled webs of flawed relationships. I myself was rapidly maturing into a fully-grown monster, the result of my difficult and damaging upbringing. My experience working with the owner of this firm only reinforced my own belief system, which was that I needed to be hard and aggressive if I wished to survive and succeed in life.

Like a twin to my foul temper, I had a very severe and troubling health problem. It had been with me since early childhood. I suffered from an eating disorder that caused poor digestion and resulted in severe hemorrhoids. From an early age, I often suffered pangs of hunger, experienced as a growling in my stomach. I had a voracious appetite that led me to consume one or more breakfasts, more than one lunch, a heavy dinner, followed by a late supper. Sometimes I continued eating until two or three in the morning. Each day I also consumed many soft drinks. Simultaneously, a serious sleep disorder set in. I struggled, often with great difficulty, to avoid falling asleep during the day. Nonetheless, and despite these disorders, I still handled my work quite satisfactorily. I remained active in sports, which probably helped me avoid even worse symptoms. My emotional imbalances and poor health continued to affect me throughout the prime of my life.

Meanwhile, I learned fast in my job as a salesman. I found the work very interesting, as I learned about market demand for a product, networking, currency exchange rates, and how to communicate and correspond with principals and customers. My most memorable achievement was my initiative to visit an up-market furniture retailer, then located at Shenton Way in Singapore. This was in 1974. I closed an order for upholstery fabrics worth a total sales value of USD 70,000.

When I called the firm owner to inform him of the successful deal, he asked in an overbearing tone if the customer had stamped their company seal on the purchase order. Of course that had been done, but I could not understand why he spoke to me so crudely. He was unable to express his happiness even over a very successful sales order!

On another occasion I witnessed him spewing his temper on a road-user during a minor traffic jam. He reversed his car, a Volvo, and drew level with another car on his right. That car had an open roof-top and was driven by a man wearing a Red Cross uniform and beret. My boss wound down his window and shouted at the man in an intimidating manner: "What the hell are you scolding me for!" The man, who was completely stunned, replied sheepishly, "Erh. No. No. I was only singing." As my boss continued our journey, he remarked snidely, "Luckily, he said he was singing. Otherwise, I would have clobbered him!"

A short stint in this firm was enough for me to understand the erratic behaviour of my boss. Being self-employed, he was also a loner, had an unhappy marriage with a woman who was much older than him and who he complained was not responsive, and had to single-handedly raise three sons who were then still attending school.

As would be expected, my last day with this firm soon arrived. My boss and I had a very heated exchange while we were travelling in his car. I cannot now recall why, but it was probably due to poor sales, which triggered a mood swing in him. On the other hand, I cannot remember a day when he did not lose his temper. I left that firm without any regrets. In fact, I was quite surprised I lasted there almost six months!

BECOMING A TRAINED TEACHER

In 1975, I decided to again take up a post as a temporary secondary school teacher, this time in my alma mater. The headmaster, Mr. Tahir, was a very pleasant man. I enjoyed teaching and had a good working relationship with the students and my fellow teachers. A year later, I was selected to attend a newly set-up Teacher Training College in Kuala Lumpur. I believe a supportive letter of recommendation from Mr. Tahir helped me gain a place as a trainee teacher.

Looking back at my college life, I spent most of my time in sports and social activities. My lifestyle was disoriented. I was habitually late for lectures. I remember a lecturer of TESL (Teaching English as a Second Language) caught me arriving late on several occasions. Once he greeted me with "Good afternoon", even though it was still morning.

Towards the end of the two-year teacher training course, I became preoccupied with the problem of my youngest brother, who was an addict. A school dropout, he was involved with drugs and triad activities. I tried to help him kick his habit by getting him a place in a government drug rehabilitation center. Despite all my efforts, he returned to drugs. He remained deeply involved with triad society throughout his life. At the time of writing, my brother is suffering from a terminal illness. I could not do anything except let destiny take its course. Today, I include him in my prayers. However, I wish I had kept in touch more often, especially in his final years.

I consider myself fortunate to have passed the teacher training course because I was more involved with social activities. Teaching is a noble profession, and was then viewed as an ironclad livelihood, since one is virtually assured of a stable income till old age, assuming one remains a teacher until retirement. My future appeared secure when I was posted to a secondary school as a qualified teacher. As fate had it, the school I was posted to was only about fifteen kilometers from the small rural home town of my wife-to-be.

I found teaching interesting. Once, while I was teaching history, I noticed a male student was inattentive. He was engrossed with drawing. I quietly took the paper from him and saw he had drawn a picture of a naked woman. I kept my cool and continued teaching. The boy was nervous. He wore a guilty look as I counselled him after the lesson. I told him that while it was natural for him to be curious at his age, he should pay attention when the class was in session. That friendly talk did help. He went on to become one of the better-behaved students.

The school regularly checked students' hair length. During the once-weekly school assembly, senior teachers weeded out students who kept their hair long. These teachers deliberately called out, asking me to cut their hair. This was because my hair was usually quite long, too. To maneuver myself out of that situation, I quickly asked the students several questions, such as:

"Students have to wear uniforms when in school. Do teachers have to wear any uniforms?" The students typically replied, "No."

"Teachers can smoke in school. Can students smoke in school?" Again, the students replied, "No."

"Teachers can keep their hair long. Can students keep their hair long?!" Except this time, I asked the question with a stern expression on my face. Again, the students answered, "No!"

The next day those students were back in school with their hair cut short. I continued to enjoy a good rapport with them.

While working as a schoolteacher, I stayed with the family of my wife-to-be in their rubber and oil palm estate of more than 160 acres. My mother-in-law to be, Kathleen, a Eurasian, inherited the estate from her British father, James, who had bought the land at five Malayan dollars per acre in the 1930s from an Indian man. This was just before the outbreak of the Second World War. A large part of the land had been swampy. The water was drained and refilled with fresh earth, and the land cultivated with rubber trees.

The late James had a distinguished career. In addition to owning several other plots of land, he had interests in tin mining and bus transportation. With a group of his countrymen, including a certain Mr. Cameron, he opened a route that led to a mountain top in the state of Pahang. The place was named Cameron Highlands, after the late Mr. Cameron. Cameron Highlands has remained a popular holiday resort, being famous for tea plantations, flower gardens and vegetable farming.

James later left for England, where he had planned to spend his old age with his children from his first wife. Instead, they put him in an old folks' home. He quickly returned to Malaya where my mother-in-law took care of him till his last breath, at the age of 96. I was told that the government of then Malaya acquired a strategic plot of land in Tanah Rata, that belonged to the late James. He was compensated with a sum of RM 350,000 (Malaysian ringgit) in 1959. That piece of land is where the present hydro-electric-power station was built. I found it rather unusual that all these lands were subsequently acquired by the Malaysian government, even though they were at different locations.

My mother-in-law, who passed away in her early eighties, is worthy of mention here. She was a very refined and soft-spoken lady. I learned that she had endured many difficulties in her early life, such as miscarriages, the death of one of her twin sons, the deaths of two daughters in their teens, and of another son in a traffic accident. Her husband died of a heart attack in his early fifties while watching a wrestling match on television. I observed that despite those challenges, my mother-in-law had always maintained a calm composure. Just before she passed away, I asked her a question: "Mother, what do you think is the most important quality one should have in life?"

"Kindness," was her immediate reply. Her answer was like a beacon of warmth and sincerity, a true reflection of her character.

I have also observed the kindness of my late mother-in-law in action. An Indian man, who had been sacked from the estate for a serious offence, came back to ask for a place to stay, as he was at an advanced age. He seemed to have been disowned by his own family members. He was probably already in his late seventies then. I observed that my mother-in-law personally served him food and provided other basic necessities with patience and love.

My late mother-in-law also shared how she had met her husband-to-be in a *wat* (Siamese temple). Her British father, a devout Christian, asked her future husband about Buddhism. The latter highlighted the Eightfold Noble Path. Her British father was open-minded enough to accept him as his son-in-law. My mother-in-law also told me that her husband was a very compassionate man who had made regular contributions to wats.

My father-in-law had a dream just before he passed on. He dreamed he was living in a place where all his neighbours were Chinese. It was actually a premonition, for after his death he was buried in a Chinese cemetery. It was also strange that just before his death he took his second son, George, on a tour of the family estate and asked him to take care of it. George took on great responsibility after his father's demise. I will write more about him in Chapter 8.

Since I appeared to be enjoying a laid-back lifestyle as a teacher, everyone was surprised when I made a drastic move away from teaching to rejoin the world of business.

BACK TO THE BUSINESS WORLD

I had two reasons for returning to business. Life as a teacher had become too monotonous. When I observed the older teachers, who were nearing retirement age, I told myself that I would end up like them if I remained a teacher. My life would be so uninteresting if it continued being that predictable! Around this time a good friend was trying to persuade me to join him in business. He was then involved, with several of his brothers, in the wholesaling and retailing of haberdashery products in the capital city.

During several visits to my friend's office, I was struck not only by his repeated enticements regarding the big money that could be made from business, I was also awed by the bustling business activities in his workplace. My imagination ran wild. I thought business would bring wealth to me and my family. This friend was warm and helpful prior to me joining him in business. However, inexplicable changes in his behaviour began to surface several years later, when a communication problem developed between us. Our relationship subsequently went into a tailspin with the onset of an economic recession.

I was inexperienced and probably too trusting of close friends. I came to realise the firm had no business plan, nor the necessary basic resources. Having to make bricks without straw, I struggled for several years. I also had to engage in some disagreeable practices. Businessmen commonly avoided paying high import duties. I found it stressful to do so, but it was simply unavoidable, as any honest declaration would result in a higher cost of goods, which would increase the selling price compared to those of one's fellow competitors who had avoided the duties.

Nonetheless, joy in our branded apparel business was short-lived due to the onslaught of the mid-1980s economic recession. Our partnership went bust, and so did my partner's family wholesaling business. It was compounded with both our private lives being shambolic. A lack of discipline all round seems to have been the major cause of our business failure, rather than external factors.

Desperation followed not long after the recession. I urgently needed a new source of income to make ends meet. Somehow, and again with the same friend, we opened a karaoke pub on the outskirts of Kuala Lumpur. Karaoke was then a fad. I had no job satisfaction, as I could neither drink nor was I able to deal with eccentric customers. The only consolation was the meager profits that helped support my family.

An incident that occurred after I had closed the pub late one night left an impact on me. I managed to save a lady in distress in the early morning hours while on my way home. She was driving her car dangerously, eventually careening to a stop in the middle of a road in a residential area. I found her motionless behind the wheel of her car. She was highly intoxicated. I decided it was safer to carry her home instead of handing her over to the authorities.

My wife was stunned to see me carrying a strange and beautiful female who was still unconsciousness. We put her in our daughters' room to give her a sense of security should she wake up. Questions ran through my mind. What would have happened to this lady if a different character had bumped into her? Why me? I then wondered what a human life was actually worth. Having concluded that any human life is priceless, I could not fathom the outcome if she had instead met with harm. The lady recovered and left, grateful.

After about a year or so, I foresaw that my karaoke business would not be self-sustaining, due to it being a fad. Besides, the income was not encouraging. I decided I should get a stable job before selling off my karaoke pub. Not long after that, I obtained a job as a manager for an apparel marketing firm. A good friend took care of the karaoke pub while I began looking for a buyer.

I found only one interested buyer. He made an appointment to view the premises. In order to impress on him that the pub was doing well, I invited more than twenty of my friends and colleagues on the appointed night. They all understood the purpose of the gathering. In return, their drinks and everything else were on the house.

I sold the pub for a tidy sum. I then re-invested the money in the share market, based on the recommendation of a childhood friend who was a regular share market player. Both the stocks I invested in went bust. (This childhood friend and his family have been, and still are, my residential neighbours. My friend died unexpectedly in 2013.)

MY FOLLY CONTINUES

I was fortunate to be employed as a manager in the apparel marketing firm by the time I reached my late thirties. The thought of a stable income brought me a sense of relief. However, today I find it unbelievable that I spent nearly two decades with this firm, until my retirement in late 2008. A deep-seated fear of having no income probably caused me to stay.

Meanwhile, I invested again in the share market, using money saved from my early working years. At that time there was renewed investor confidence in the stock market, and it went bullish. How could I not invest, especially when it was in the shares of the company I was working for? It had just gained a listing on the Stock Exchange and management, through the General Manager, reassured the employees of its profitability. This investment also turned out to be a disaster!

My woes were compounded by the morbid fear I would not be able to meet the financial needs of my family. Thoughts of my children, especially regarding their future educational expenses, troubled me constantly. I realised that time was not on my side, as I was in my early forties and still living from hand-to-mouth. The need to have enough savings grew more pressing. But the means remained elusive. Further testing my will to survive, at this time my life was turned topsy-turvy with the birth of my fourth child, who suffered from cerebral palsy caused by birth difficulties.

Outspokenness, anger and aggression ran riot in all my interactions with people during this period. I had no concern regarding how it would affect my reputation, as long as I believed that what I did was right and true. In the workplace, I had infuriated the firm's Growth Promoter just several months into the job. I was the manager of a brand which marketed foundation garments. One of the products was imported ladies' pantyhose. The main supplier was from Korea. This Korean supplier purposely conducted all correspondence through the Penang office, where the Growth Promoter was based. I was in the Kuala Lumpur office. The Korean supplier contended it was difficult to fax to the Kuala Lumpur office, which was clearly an excuse. I realised that the Korean supplier preferred to deal directly with the Growth Promoter rather than me, because he was exploiting the Growth Promoter's ego to make him commit to bigger purchases of goods and of a very wide choice of colours.

I took on the challenge of drastically reducing the number of colours. Later I went so far as to drop the Korean supplier in favour of a new supplier from Thailand. When the Korean supplier discovered I had done so, he paid a visit to the Kuala Lumpur office. In the middle of the meeting, the Growth Promoter joined us and started questioning me aggressively about the Thai supplier's cost price. This was in the presence of the Korean supplier. When his criticism turned to condemnation I lost control. The Growth Promoter apparently wanted to show favour to the Korean supplier. But my mind was telling me to clobber him. It must have been easy to read my intention from the look on my face, because the General Manager quickly led the Growth Promoter out of the meeting room.

That incident started a horrible decade of pressure, which included several attempts to sack me. I was aware of the General Manager's intention, and the only thing in my mind was to prepare retaliatory moves. I was dying to see him eat humble pie. On reflection, I cannot believe I was capable of such negative and harmful thoughts. Later, when I was involved in VCM, a haunting message came from The Infinite: "What is truth without wisdom? It is nothing!" This led me to appreciate the folly of my actions.

Chapter Four

RAISING A FAMILY

I LEFT MY SMALL TOWN TEACHING JOB and moved to the city to begin a new career in business. It was then that I got married and my family started to grow. I am still married to the same woman, who has been a wonderful wife, and a much-loved mother and grandmother to our children and grandchildren.

Being raised in a typically conservative Chinese family, it was expected my first child would be a boy. My wish was to have only two children, a girl and a boy. I consulted so-called Chinese experts on the almanac, Bai-Zi, astrology and fung shui to ensure that the years of my children's birth would be compatible with those of my wife and me. The whole purpose was to ensure success in life. I also wanted to quickly complete the task of raising two children. This was to gain more time and space for my wife and me later in life. Having thought that the groundwork was done after those consultations to help us have a boy, my wife and I started off with great confidence when trying for our first child.

On the day of my first child's delivery, I arrived at the hospital early in the morning. I was excited, and curious as to whether my first child would indeed be a boy. I waited over twelve hours for the birth. During those long hours, I remember reacting with a smirk to an incident in the hospital waiting area. A Chinese man and the elderly woman who had accompanied him had disappointment written all over their faces when they were shown their baby was a girl. Except for one or two boys, all the other babies delivered that day were girls. Based on the higher percentage of girls compared to boys born on that day, I reckoned my first child was also likely to be a girl. True enough, my first child was a girl.

Although my wife and I did not achieve my aim of having a boy as our first child, I was confident that our second would be a boy. Two years later, our second child was also a girl. I felt a little disappointed and wondered if we should try for a third child, in the hope it would be a boy. Because having a third child was never part of my plan, it took me some time to consider making another attempt. To help ensure the third would be a boy, I sought Divine intervention by consulting Chinese temples and mediums. I also sought advice from experienced couples. They suggested that consuming certain foods could increase the probability of having a baby boy.

After several years of preparation, we made our third attempt. The result was another girl! This time it was me who wore the look of disappointment, as I recalled the poignant scene of the frustrated Chinese man and the elderly woman six years earlier. We then impetuously decided on a fourth attempt to have a son. However rashly, I simply refused to believe it could be so difficult. I had always viewed it as being a 50:50 chance whether we would have either a boy or a girl. As I already had three daughters, I consoled myself that the odds of having a boy on this fourth attempt should be higher.

Not only was our fourth child a girl, but, to my horror, complications caused her to be born with cerebral palsy. Never in my wildest dreams did I imagine becoming father to a disabled child. Shattered, I adamantly refused to accept my bitter fate. I blamed God for my misery. The birth of this special child accelerated the intensity with which I sought an answer from the Supreme Creator to account for the myriad of woes I was facing.

This was not the only blow that arrived during this period. I also got into a fierce verbal exchange with the Growth Promoter of the firm I was then working for. Every now and then he would pick on me, with the aim of getting rid of me. This unhappy situation climaxed with the arrival of the Asian currency crisis. It almost put the firm under. Desperation led the Growth Promoter to make me his main punching bag at one of the meetings with all the managers present. Prior to that, a message from The Infinite had forewarned me: "Tough time ahead." At that time, I did not know what exactly the message meant. It was only when the currency crisis broke, and I had to endure the Growth Promoter's attacks, that I realised what the message was referring to.

My wife, a spiritually evolved person, frequently receives messages from Divine sources. At the outset of the crisis a message for me came through my wife: "I am come that you shall know Me, Athan. Watch your temper. Be patient. Be at ease. Heed Me". The message was signed off with the infinity symbol.

I did not appreciate the relevance of the message, especially as I was feeling fine within myself. However, several days later my superior, who was the son of the Growth Promoter, had a one-on-one meeting with me. It lasted late into the night. He was very concerned that we tackle the firm's adverse situation. I remember I lost control and scolded him in the middle of the meeting. Almost immediately, the advice I received through my wife came to mind. It then made sense. I had been forewarned, but did not take heed.

In hindsight, I see that I have always found it difficult to interact with people in authority who had bloated egos. Yet, I realise, I was no better. Ego was a serious issue for me. I began to understand it was a vice. Furthermore, just like anger, it was virtually impossible to expel.

I also realised, with great difficulty, another bitter lesson regarding speaking honestly. Honesty, in itself, does not promote sound interactions with our fellow human beings, especially with those in positions of power. To be effective, our honest sharing of truths has to be complemented with wisdom. Otherwise, it will never be received positively. This was a lesson I learned from The Infinite: "Truth without wisdom is nothing."

Throughout the journey of my life, I have struggled to eliminate my temper and other vices. I am aware there has long been messages, coming from deep within, reminding me to be gentle, kind and humble.

Chapter Five

PLUNGING INTO CULT PRACTICES

MY LATE PARENTS PRACTISED IDOLTARY. Both my grandmother's and mother's understanding of supreme power had a great influence on me. Due to their teachings, I grew up with the belief that different races have different supreme powers. They urged me to take particular pride in Chinese deities. Examples are the Goddess of Mercy, who oversees peace and harmony, the God of Wealth and Prosperity, whose title is self-explanatory, and various Earth deities, the caretakers of home security. There are many other Chinese deities of which I am not even aware.

My mother and grandmother prayed to numerous deities, offering food and burning incense paper, joss sticks and other paraphernalia. The purpose of these rituals was to appease the deities in order to seek refuge and blessings from them.

CHINESE IDOLATRY PRACTICES

A feature of Chinese idolatry is ancestral worship, where an ancestral tablet is placed before the altar, accompanied by other idols. Ancestral worship is undertaken in the belief that ancestors provide protections and blessings to their living descendants, and vice-versa. In addition, different Chinese temples house particular deities who are channelled by mediums. Worshippers seek help from these temple deities, depending on their needs and grievances, such as financial difficulties, to break or cast charms, or even to seek vengeance. For the Chinese, there seems to be a supreme power overseeing every possible human action.

In accordance with these customs and beliefs, I have consulted palmists, fortune tellers, feng shui masters, astrologers, tarot card readers, Malay shamans (known as bomoh), Indian and Chinese mediums, Hindu and Chinese temple priests, and monks of Buddhist Siamese, Sri Lankan and Chinese origin, including a Tibetan llama. I have also sought assistance in Chinese temples located across Malaysia. This was possible because my work involved travelling throughout the country. In addition, I have attended sermons preached in Christian churches of different denominations, and have also tried understanding Islam from Muslim friends. Furthermore, I have attended professional seminars and workshops on subjects like motivation, the power of excellent communication, effective high-performance leadership, developing positive mental attitude, neurolinguistic programming, and others. Finally, I bought and read books on all these subjects. Over the years, I spent a great deal of time and money in the hope they would be beneficial. Except for some fleeting moments of satisfaction, even bliss, disappointment remained overpowering.

The cost of engaging mediums was extremely high. I remember one medium who charged exorbitantly for a prayer offered for a customised talisman. Each cost hundreds of Malaysian ringgit (dollars). When more blessings and assistance were prescribed, and prayers subsequently performed, the cost always came to several thousand ringgit.

Other costs similarly depleted my earnings. On several occasions, I travelled a significant distance from Kuala Lumpur to Singapore just to seek one particular medium's help. He advised me to exhume the coffin of my late grandmother, concocting a tale that the coffin was not well-aligned to the surroundings of the graveyard. Adjustment of its position was required to prevent bleak futures for me, my siblings and my descendents over subsequent generations. It was from him I learned the term, *hei kum*, which in the Cantonese dialect refers to the exhumation of a corpse from a graveyard. That advice did it for me. I refused to pay for his high-priced services any more. I will always remember him for his trademark—an expensive gold watch with a thick gold chain.

Though frustrated by this experience, I continued exploring other means of salvation. Mao San Kung is one of the many Chinese sects who practise idolatry. I was once invited to their temple to witness a ceremony which invoked spirits. The chief medium and his group of followers performed rituals to enter a trance. Their cheeks, mouths and tongues were pierced with short, sharp instruments. Variously sized fishing hooks were also hooked on to the skin on their backs. Through the medium and his disciples, devotees then asked the spirits for help. I had supported this sect's fund-raising activities by buying one of the numerous idols used in daily worship that are put up for bidding. Barrels of beer were also supplied to support their religious festivities. Having received no sign of an improved situation, and due to my constantly asking him for a remedy, the chief medium suggested I try an alternative. This was to perform a night ritual in a Chinese graveyard, the purpose being to invoke the dead and seek their assistance.

It was around this time that my fourth and disabled daughter was born. I was too down-hearted to take up the medium's suggestion. In fact, I lost my belief in him. After a long lapse of time, the medium phoned to ask how I was. I burst out in frustration that not only was he unable to resolve my financial woes, but that I had had to take on the additional burden of having to raise a disabled child for life. His parting remark was that a master was, after all, also a mortal being, and so had many limitations.

OTHER SUPERNATURAL BELIEFS

While most of my experiences were with Chinese mediums, on one occasion I called on a Malay shaman. This was my first and only experience with Malay shamans. This particular shaman was highly recommended for his ability to achieve postive results. I needed help to sustain my karaoke pub business and improve my earnings to support my family. The shaman operated from a single-level terrace house. On entering, I discovered a Malay woman seated behind a glass showcase filled with packets of incense and other items. She was the shaman's assistant. I bought a packet of incense, a standard requirement, and took a queue number from her as I awaited my turn to meet the shaman. When my turn came, he began with a self-promotion exercise, claiming that a certain royal person was his patron and sought his service regularly. He supported this claim with photographs of himself with the royal person.

It is commonly believed that a shaman is capable of casting spells or charms on others. I therefore impressed on the shaman that his service would only be acceptable to me if no unethical means were used, and no harm befell anyone. He readily agreed, and proceeded with burning the incense I had bought from his assistant. This action was accompanied with a brief incoherent incantation. He then started to shout. A response erupted instantaneously from another spot inside the house. He explained that the booming echo was a stamp of approval from the Force that my karaoke pub business would be very successful.

Skepticism and curiosity led me to inspect the room from which the unusually loud blast had emanated. I found nothing in the room. That gave me confidence that this visit would provide the help I needed to improve my pub business. However, despite having carried out the shaman's instructions meticulously, there was no subsequent improvement. That was my last exploration of quick remedy measures.

On another occasion, a priest was brought to Malaysia from India by a local Indian politician, who was himself facing difficulties during the mid-eighties recession. I was introduced to the priest by a friend, a Malaysian Indian, with whom I had attended college. My inclusion in the group consulting the priest was to help defray the cost of bringing him from India. My Indian friend also acted as our interpreter, since the priest spoke only an Indian language.

After collecting my personal details, the priest chanted and performed certain rituals, ringing his tiny little bell and occasionally referring to a booklet that was tinged yellow from constant use. I asked the priest how much money I would have in the future. He wrote a figure of 15, 000, 000 on a piece of paper, with all the zeros written in a clockwise direction. I then asked him if the currency would be in Malaysia ringgit or Indian rupees. He replied that it would be in ringgit.

Involuntarily, I laughed out loud. My friend thought I was being rude and asked if I was expressing cynical disbelief. I explained to everyone present that I was dying to believe him, as I currently faced difficulties just to make ends meet. The session ended when the Indian priest gave me a pocket-sized piece of metallic sheet. It had nine equal squares, with a depiction of nine different Indian deities on each of the nine squares. Encouraged by his prediction, I placed this small metallic sheet on my home altar. As was the case with all my medium ventures, there were no encouraging results, despite my having carried out the required offerings faithfully.

I SEEK FURTHER AID FOR MY DAUGHTER

Meanwhile, my adamant refusal to come to terms with my fourth daughter's incurable disability led me to continue my search for heavenly intervention to cure her. During this period, even though I knew my attempts were futile, I maintained irregular visits to places of worship I had previously patronised. However, I now adopted a slightly different approach, patronising instead places of worship that offered different racial or religious practices.

Another Indian friend recommended that I consult a particular Indian medium who professed to be able to communicate with an Indian deity known as Kali. At the entrance of the shack from which the medium practised stood a statue of Kali. Respectfully addressed as Kaliamma, she had wide eyes and a very long protruding tongue that extended to below the level of her belly button. Both her hands held several bloodied human heads. She was reputed to remove all this planet's evils.

While sitting in the waiting room, I wondered if there were indeed different gods for different races. Why do some gods project violence? Was it was really possible for an Indian god to help me when I was of Chinese origin? My turn came after a long wait. I asked the medium if she could cure my daughter's disability, to which she replied in the affirmative. Consequently, I made regular visits, together with my disabled daughter, and accompanied by the rest of my family members, to seek treatment from this medium. With a large sum of money spent over a period of time, and with no improvement in sight, I eventually stopped consulting her and sought help elsewhere.

Having had unsuccessful trials with Indian mediums, I decided to bring my daughter to the Indian temples located at the famous Batu Caves in Kuala Lumpur. This is where the grand Thaipusam festival is celebrated every year, mostly by the Hindu Tamil community, on the full moon in the month of Thai, which occurs in January or February.

On arrival at the base of the cave, I found an Indian priest chanting and ringing a tiny bell. It is believed the sound of the bell wards off any negativity in the air. The priest held my daughter as he chanted a prayer. I then ventured further, carrying my daughter in my arms, and climbed the 272 steep concrete steps leading up into the cave above. Inside this extensive cave another Hindu religious ceremony was in progress. I made my way through a large crowd to yet another priest, who performed a prayer for my daughter. I continued to seek help from these Indian deities during the Thaipusam festivals.

On one occasion an evening procession was in progress. A brightly lit float ferrying an Indian deity, Lord Murugan, passed by my house. I rushed towards it and raised my disabled daughter with both my arms to the priest who was sitting atop the float. He conducted a prayer for her. My attempts to seek a cure for my daughter continued with visits to several other Indian temples. Sadly, none of my efforts alleviated my daughter's condition.

Another friend then introduced me to a travelling Chinese master. He had come to Kuala Lumpur from China to promote healing through the art of *qi gong* (literally, energy work). He was plying his trade from a rented house in a distant part of Kuala Lumpur. I made many tiresome journeys through the heavy city traffic almost every other evening, bringing my disabled child to him for healing. Treatment involved the use of special equipment he directed towards my daughter, who was laid in a supine position. The master's body pulsated vigorously throughout the treatment.

Despite further time and money wasted, and fruitless outcomes, I did not want to give up. I began to wonder if any other possible sources of help existed in other countries. In fact, I learned of a famous organisation in India, to which I contemplated taking my daughter for treatment. But it was wishful thinking. I was by then financially depleted. Yet I continued my search for a cure for my daughter. As I had by now exhausted almost all options, I reverted to seeking help from Chinese temples. These were temples I had never visited before.

I discovered one temple that I could only travel to on weekends. It was located far from where my family was living. Every visit began at dawn and ended at dusk, as the travel involved a total distance of over 500 kilometers. As expected, the temple housed a large statue. This one was of the Goddess of Mercy. Smaller sized idols of other deities were also present, even though the temple was named after the Goddess of Mercy.

Within the temple the male and female healers were all dressed in white. I was led to a spacious chamber where many people were already being treated. I was made to sit on a chair, my daughter lying in a restful position on my lap. A male healer sat opposite us. Without any ado, I posed my routine opening question.

"Can you cure my daughter's illness?" I asked.

"Yes, I can," the male healer replied confidently.

After several trips, I became increasingly frustrated due to not seeing any signs of improvement in my daughter's ailing condition.

I attended another temple that was a very popular temple among Chinese devotees. Inside was a miniature pagoda, which had lighted oil lamps spiralling all the way up from its base to the apex. Patrons had to arrive before dawn to have a chance of obtaining a queue number, due to the number of consultations being limited each day. This medium's favourable reputation had spread widely by word of mouth.

She was definitely different. It was the first time I had witnessed a Chinese medium conducting her channelling in English. The medium was seated facing an idol. Lighted joss sticks stuck in a pot had been placed on a pile of incense papers and offered to the idol. When my turn came, I asked my usual question, in the English language for the first time.

"Can you cure my daughter?" I asked.

"No!" came the answer.

"Are you not a god?" I was upset by her negative reply.

I flatly refused to accept the medium's reading, and insisted that she provide a cure for my daughter. She obliged reluctantly, writing down some herbal prescriptions, which included dried deer's tendon. I dutifully bought the prescribed herbs. The medium said it was not necessary to give my daughter more than three servings of the prescriptions, should there be no improvement. While it proved yet another futile attempt, this medium was unlike all the others I visited. She, at least, said that there was no cure for my daughter's ailment.

Nonetheless, I continued my pursuit of a cure for my daughter. My next attempt was with a medium devoted to the deity San Pau Kung. I learned that the deity was the famous Chinese Admiral Zheng Bo, who had visited Melaka, an historic state on the west coast of Peninsular Malaysia, at the turn of the fifteenth century. On arrival at the temple, which was also the medium's residence, I noticed the medium had a daughter who was also handicapped. That instantly deflated me. I realised it was another wasted effort.

THE SUPERNATURAL AND MONEY

Having made no progress in achieving a breakthrough in my daughter's condition, my focus shifted to improving my financial situation. A decade or so after the first occasion, I was re-introduced to San Pau Kung. It happened during one of my working trips to Kuala Trengganu, on the east coast of Peninsular Malaysia. The businessman who took my friend and me to ask this deity for gaming numbers had actually once had a big win. He was also doing very well in his retail business of selling infant's clothing and accessories. Several years later, I learned he had suffered heavy losses from his gambling misadventures, and that his business and marriage had also suffered. I guess neither of us had much luck with San Pau Kung.

I then heard rumours that people had obtained windfalls from another temple. I decided to pay a visit one Saturday afternoon, with several of my colleagues. Old and tattered photographs of those who had visited in chartered buses hung on the walls of the temple as proof of its glory.

Following the customary purchase of prayer paraphernalia, I burned incense paper and placed the lighted joss sticks in front of each idol. The medium put on his Taoist garb and immediately swung into action. Sitting on his grand chair, he began a rambling incantation before the main altar, which was populated with idols of different shapes, sizes and expressions. All were colourfully designed and costumed. They were also adorned with weapons and instruments of all kinds.

The medium slammed a sword onto a pile of incense paper, causing a thunderous sound, which cracked the otherwise quiet afternoon. Being caught unaware by the sound, the Chinese tea spilled from the tiny cup in my hand. This loud gesture marked the commencement of the medium's channelling. He spoke in the Cantonese dialect. The medium was channelling Nar Zar, a Chinese deity, who is typically depicted with one foot planted on the Sun and the other on the Moon.

Medium: "I am Nar Zar." This was uttered in a roaring voice.

Me: "Nar Zar, do I have any gaming luck?"

Medium: "Gaming luck? Hmm. Do you eat satay?" (Satay is a popular Malaysian barbecue delicacy of beef, mutton or chicken skewered on bamboo sticks.)

Me: "Yes, I do eat satay. Why do you ask?"

Medium: "You cannot eat satay." Raising his voice to emphasise his point: "You won't have gaming luck if you eat satay!"

Me: "Oh! I see. Okay, I won't eat satay again. Can you give me gaming numbers?"

Medium: "Alright, I will give you gaming numbers."

Following this consultation, I stopped eating satay and bet on the numbers given me by Nar Zar. A month or so later, after several failed betting attempts, I went back to consult the medium. He began with the familiar explosive opening ritual. Despite anticipating this, I was still shocked by the sound as he slammed his sword onto the pile of incense paper. The tea again spilled from the cup in my hand. The channelling session had begun.

Me: "Who are you?"

Medium: "I am Nar Zar." (Uttered with a roaring voice to make his presence felt).

Me: "Nar Zar, can you do a feng shui reading of my house?"

Medium: "Of course, I can. Where do you live?"

Me: "Puchong Jaya."

Medium: "Is your house an end unit?"

Me: "No, it's an intermediate unit."

Medium: "Hmmm. Is the road frontage level higher than the ground level of your house?'

Me: "No." I next spoke in a raised voice, as by then the medium had made two wrong readings. "Nar Zar, are you not a god? Can't you predict accurately? How is it you predict wrongly?"

In response, the medium stole a peep at me. I placed myself on alert. Appearing annoyed, the medium gripped the sword even more tightly. To diffuse the situation, I asked the next question gently.

Me: "Nar Zar, can you give me gaming numbers?"

Medium: "Yes, I can. Do you eat satay?"

I had not eaten any satay since he advised against it during my first visit. Having not entirely regained my composure after his erroneous answer to my first question, I snapped.

"Hey! I have consulted you before! I have not eaten satay since you told me not to. Why are you asking me the same question? Why are you giving me the same advice?"

After these inaccurate readings, I had no reason to patronise that temple again. It was clear to me why this temple only displayed old photos. Its glory had long gone—if it ever had any glory at all.

THE IMPORTANCE OF FAMILY

I had many similar experiences. When celebrating Chinese New Year, the first day of the Chinese lunar calendar, I religiously followed the advice of the so-called experts of geomancy regarding the right way to welcome the deities, specifically the God of Prosperity, facing the appropriate cardinal points, noting the correct time of the deity's arrival, and so on.

Through the years, the income I earned was barely sufficient to meet all household expenses. Much of my time was spent helping my wife and my mother-in-law to take care of my youngest daughter, who still required regular medical treatment due to her occasional seizures.

Meanwhile, an old classmate, a Chinese woman who was childless offdered to adopt my fourth daughter. She lapsed into silence when I told her my daughter was a special child. Another childhood friend, a Malay Muslim, also wanted to adopt my daughter. The manner in which this friend expressed his desire to do so stunned me. He stated that one is blessed to have such a child, and for that reason he wanted to adopt her, even though he already had children of his own.

Whether it is a blessing or not, I felt duty bound to raise this special child, although my efforts to find a permanent cure for her had all proved futile. Nonetheless, powerfully determined, I never gave up searching. I still harbour the hope that someday I will find a way to heal her so she may live normally.

My preoccupation with my fourth daughter consumed all my energy and finances. Yet deep within, I have always loved my wife and my other three daughters, for who they are and always will be to me. However, I was rarely able to express my love for them, which was a failure on my part, a weakness that has long limited me. I did realise that they needed my love and attention, but I was only able to give it to them sporadically, rather than always being there for them.

Chapter Six

EXPERIENTIAL COSMIC AWAKENING

ON THE EVE OF A PUBLIC HOLIDAY IN 1994, I spent the whole afternoon playing mahjong with a close friend and two acquaintances. In the evening, we went on a fishing trip to the Kelang estuary. My brother-in-law joined us later. Though moonless, the night was dimly lit by streetlights which stood in regular intervals. A long bridge overlooked the wide estuary. A huge water pipeline, easily a meter in diameter, ran parallel to it. Alongside the base of the pipeline was a two-foot-wide metal platform, built to carry maintenance workers.

Traffic was heavy, mainly consisting of trucks speeding dangerously across the bridge in both directions as they ran between the nearby sea port and their loading and unloading bases. Below the bridge, perched on the edge of the metal platform, the fishing group was silhouetted against the night sky. Feeling uncomfortable standing on the side of the bridge, I decided to join them. The precariousness of the surroundings gave me a sense of imminent danger. Instinctively, I became extra-cautious. My close friend had the same sense of danger. As he had his very young daughter with him, he decided to drive to a safer fishing spot further away. My brother-in-law, the two acquaintances and I remained.

With a hop, I crossed from the bridge to the top of the water pipe. The narrow metal platform below was barely visible in the dim light. I was followed by my brother-in-law, Henry, who landed on the narrow platform with a clangor. The other two, Victor and Alvin, followed suit.

I stretched out my arms and took a deep breath as I enjoyed the savoury fragrance carried by the cool sea breeze. That brief relaxing moment was rudely interrupted by a loud clank on the metal platform, followed by the splashing sound of a heavy object plunging into the river. Turning first to my left, then to my right, I could not see Alvin. Anxiously, I asked if Alvin had fallen into the river. The other two nodded with shell-shocked expressions. Looking down, I could barely make out Alvin, who was beginning to be carried by the current towards the open sea. I repeatedly shouted his name, but heard no reply.

The next moment, an overwhelming sense of silent calm descended on me, followed by a strange two-way communication in my head.

The Voice: "Athan, can you swim?"

Me: "Yes, I can."

The Voice: "A life is there. Jump and save."

I learned much later, after I had gone into VCM practice, that the aforementioned communication is a rudimentary example of receiving.

Calmly, I handed my spectacles and wallet to my brother-in-law. With outstretched arms, I plunged feet first into the river. It must have been quite deep, as I did not touch the bottom. I immediately found it difficult to keep afloat. The weight of my clothes bore me down. Despite that, I was unwilling to take off my clothes and lose them.

Without any experience or knowledge of rescuing a drowning person, I did what I could. I managed to grab hold of Alvin. I then struggled furiously, huffing and puffing as I tried to pull him towards the river bank. It became apparent I was fighting a losing battle against the strong current. I was fast losing strength, struggling to even keep myself afloat. Fearing I might lose Alvin, an outcome that was simply unacceptable, I spontaneously shouted aloud:

"GOOOOOOOD! (God.) This is life, you know! How can you let this happen! Tolong! Tolong!" (*Tolong* is a Malay word that, used in this context, means "help".)

In the next instant, a Malay man jumped into the river. However, after he had swum over to us, he remained a short distance away, eying us warily.

"Saya tak apa!! Tolong dia! ("I am alright! Help him!")" I burst out, reassuring him he should help the victim, and that I would not endanger his life. The Malay man saved Alvin with ease, taking him to the bank.

I was feeling intense anxiety, because I found I could not lift my arms to swim. By now it was darker at water level. For a moment I feared I faced death. Then, as I tried to keep myself afloat, an unusual calmness came over me. I found myself using doggy-style strokes, which helped propel me towards the river bank.

When I at last reached the shore, I crawled out of the water and reached for the nearest mangrove tree. Holding onto its roots, I pulled myself up to stand. But the moment I released my grip I fell flat on the ground. When I tried to stand a second time, I slumped down again. I had lost control of my body. My energy was gone. I felt extreme exhaustion, greater than I had ever experienced before in my life!

Crawling on all fours, I made my way through a patch of wet muddy ground, towards the slope of the embankment. I slowly crawled up the slope, finally reaching the side of the road above.

I was thankful to whatever Unseen Force that had put me and the Malay gentleman into action. It had saved Alvin. It must have also helped me. Do such accidents happen for a reason? The answer is beyond our reasoning capacity. All we can do is accept that there are apparently Unseen Forces in action.

It was only after I had taken up the practice of Vibrant Celestial Meditation that I learned the significance of this experience.

MY FIRST ENCOUNTER WITH VIBRANT CELESTIAL MEDITATION

One day at work I received a phone call from a good friend, Mark, who spoke to me about Vibrant Celestial Meditation (VCM). He coaxed me to attend an upcoming basic VCM seminar. He chanted a mantra, "Praise Divine, praise sublime," several times over the phone. My immediate response was to remove the phone receiver from my ear. I felt strange and uneasy.

Perhaps I reacted that way because I was so disappointed that all my previous searching for God had been to no avail. By then I had established a firm conviction that it was not possible to know God. In fact, I had concluded that God did not exist! I had almost completely shut my mind against anything even vaguely related to God.

However, my interest was stimulated when he mentioned that the meditation technique in question was derived from all the world's scriptures, and was practised by people of different faiths and races. My curiosity was aroused, as in those days I had no knowledge of any of the world's scriptures.

Furthermore, Mark made me a promise: should I leave the seminar unsatisfied, he would refund the cost of attending in full. I wanted to learn more about the meditation he was talking about. But without the promise of a refund, I would not have agreed to attend the seminar. I had told myself that, after my many years of fruitless searching, I would never again spend a single cent on any activities related to God or religion.

With a leaflet on VCM in hand, I made a phone call to the organiser. A voice message asked me to leave my phone contact. When the return call came, the caller introduced himself as Mr. Singh. He spoke with a very gentle and calm demeanour. I deduced he was an elderly man. He asked if I was interested in attending his basic VCM seminar. In my usual aggressive and brazen style, I began with my opening question.

"Mr. Singh, can I ask you a question?" I asked rather crudely.

"Yes, you may," he replied.

"I have four daughters," I continued. "Can you now check if all my four daughters are alright?"

He paused for a moment, then replied that my daughters were fine, but he felt a certain vibration regarding my fourth daughter. I had no idea what vibration he was referring to, and he did not say anything more about her. However, I decided it was worth my while to meet with him and understand more of what his meditation involved. He obligingly agreed to my request for an appointment, then asked me several questions in turn.

"Are you bringing your wife along?"

"Yes," I replied.

He again paused for a moment, then continued, "Bring along your eldest daughter, too."

"She is only twelve!" I reacted disagreeably. "I don't think she is ready to do meditation. And I don't have the money to pay for three persons!"

I was suspicious, wondering if he was more interested in profit, just like any commercial organisation. But he surprised me, maintaining the same gentle response with which he had begun our phone conversation.

"Never mind about the money," he said calmly. "Just bring her along."

I still would not agree to sign up for the seminar until I had met him, as I had some questions I wanted to ask in person. Mr. Singh agreed to meet me at his residence.

MY FIRST MEETING WITH BHAI SAHIB

One evening a colleague, the Finance and Administration Manager of my workplace, accompanied me to meet Bhai Sahib. Bhai Sahib's residence was nestled on a hill slope. We had to drive up a short and steep stretch of tarmac. A sharp right turn led to his mansion. Midway was a rooftop garden that allowed a panoramic view of Petaling Jaya city. A neat and well-placed swimming pool was on one side of this majestic mansion, with a lawn on the other. Its entire surrounding was made more magnificent with a backdrop of healthy and sprightly plants, while natural vegetation hugged the top of the gentle slope, which gave way to trees overlooking his home, lending it a lush and green landscape.

My colleague and I were shown into a side entrance that led to his library. I must confess During that first meeting, I was biased against Bhai Sahib due to his racial origin. He was a Punjabi. I went straight into my no-nonsense business mode. I recall questioning him explicitly about a meditation movement that originated from India.

"Mr. Singh, what do you think of the movement led by an Indian, that has about thirty million followers worldwide? Press reports note he was involved in sexual activities with under-aged girls." I later learned the leader of that movement had fallen from grace, an answer Bhai Sahib gave indirectly during the basic VCM seminar. I later regretted my unfounded inference, which I had made simply on the basis that both of them were Punjabis and talking about meditation.

Bhai Sahib just nodded and listened attentively as he stroked and, at times, twirled the end of his strikingly long beard, which was as white as snow. He displayed great humility and gentleness, which had a disarming effect on me. He was bare-chested and wore only traditional short pants, which I later learnt was called *kutch* in Punjabi. That was unusual. It was unlike any formal meeting, where one would dress in proper attire. Yet, I appreciated it, as he appeared sincere and displayed no air of superiority.

Several days later I again visited Mr. Singh. This time I went alone. I wanted to check if he had any access to a higher power that could help cure my daughter of her cerebral palsy, and resolve my financial woes.

Instead, he cleverly drew my attention to the effect of true and effective meditation. He explained it was akin to being in a state of sleep, but one would still have an awareness of oneself and one's surroundings. He stressed that if a subject is completely unaware of the surroundings while in meditation, and reacts in trance-like movement, then that subject is likely under the influence of lower forces. He quoted Edgar Cayce, an American psychic, who had already passed on, as an exception to those effects.

The term, *lower forces*, was jargon to me then. Over time, I came to understand its usage better, as it was often pointed out to me by Bhai Sahib in the many situations where we were both present, or whenever I asked his opinion on certain occurrences related to spirituality. He elaborated that the complete meditation course consisted of three levels, basic, intermediate and advanced. It was at this point that I posed more questions.

"Isn't a meditation just a meditation?"

"Are they all not the same?"

"Are there differential effects with the different levels in your meditation courses?"

Bhai Sahib just gave a simple affirmative, "Yes," in answer. He seemed more eager to carry out a meditation session on the spot with me than to entertain my barrage of questions. He gently asked me to stand relaxed with my hands held loosely by my side and with my eyes closed. I did so. What happened next was that I fell asleep in a standing posture.

Midway, I happened to open my eyes and was taken aback when I saw that Bhai Sahib was standing next to me with the palm of his hand held just above my head. I jumped involuntarily away from him. Months later, I realised Bhai Sahib was actually offering me his blessings and was initiating me into meditation.

ATTENDING THE VCM BASIC COURSE

It was easier for me to bring my eldest daughter, aged twelve, to the two day basic VCM course, than to persuade my wife to attend. I had to coax her into it. I felt it would be better for us to involve ourselves together as husband and wife. Because she bore the brunt of the stresses and strains bedeviling our family and marriage, she had thought that engaging in meditation was not suitable. Always the one to keep peace, she eventually agreed to attend the seminar.

The venue was Bhai Sahib's home library. The seminar was attended by more than twenty participants. The library was large enough to accommodate all of us. After sitting, my eyes began to explore the room. Displayed on top of a solid, long rectangular wooden table, with all its four legs specially fitted with movable wheels, were copies of articles written by Bhai Sahib that were offered for sale. They were priced from RM 1 to RM 1.50 per copy. It was the first time I had attended a seminar where the speaker's writings were sold at such low prices. That caused me to ask myself if his writings were worthy. Some of the articles were titled, *The Purpose of Life and the Role of Religion*, *The Similarity of Worship in All Religions*, *Why Spirituality? Which Method? What Benefits? With a Commentary on all Methods*, and *Vibrant Meditation and Charismatic Worship*.

As the seminar progressed, I was impressed by Bhai Sahib's simple style of presentation and the knowledge he was imparting. In particular, I recall the way he presented the Essence of God Almighty and meditation in a logical flow. He mentioned that it was through his arduous gleanings of all the world's scriptures that he had discovered and concluded that God Almighty had repeatedly stated the all-important need to surrender and submit to His Will within oneself.

He further emphasised that large portions of all scriptures are cryptic and couched in allegories. In other words, a believer has to practise patience in order to decipher the hidden meanings. Other topics covered in the seminar were on the importance of food intake, makings of the mind, dream interpretations, empowerment, trauma and discernment. I adopted an open-minded approach and listened intently to his explanations, since a large part of his presentations were new to me.

On the second day of the seminar, my wife told me that Bhai Sahib walked towards her after the end of a meditation session and asked if she had had any reactions. She told him it was strange that she was sweating despite the cool morning air, and with the air-conditioner working at full blast. She said a single stream of sweat was flowing profusely down the side of her body, from below her armpits to her waist, but it had not wet her blouse at all. Bhai Sahib had also said that if anyone received very strong reactions in their initial contact with this variety of meditation, that person would surely receive a strong response too. The response would be in the form of a vision or a message. I did not receive either.

Group meditations were held every Tuesday evening in a community hall. All the doors and the extra-large windows were left wide open to the full view of the public. All the lights were on and the ceiling fans were at full speed. About ten rolls of vinyl carpets had been laid across the hall. Participants were encouraged to move about freely on bare feet, or to simply relax and find their own comfortable position.

I stood at the back of the gathering, watching cautiously. My wife was at the extreme right, further to the front, where Bhai Sahib was standing and facing the participants. He commenced the meditation by asking everyone to stand relaxed and to close their eyes while he recited the opening invocation. I did not close my eyes as I felt I was in an unfamiliar situation. I therefore kept my eyes open to remain on guard—or so I thought.

Fifteen minutes into the meditation, humming and low groaning sounds emanated from several participants. After a while, I realised I had fallen asleep, even though I was in a standing position. At that moment, a participant suddenly began wailing loudly. I decided this meditation was weird, but tried not to be distracted by the sustained wailing. Finally, I opened my eyes, and was surprised that the wailing person was my wife! My next thought was: "Hey! My wife is possessed!! What should I do? How can I bring her back to her normal self!"

Just as I was becoming more concerned about her non-stop wailing, my wife spontaneously started laughing, loudly and apparently uncontrollably. This time I thought: "This meditation is really mad! I have lost my wife. But it's my fault, because I pestered her to attend this meditation!"

I was desperately trying to think of a way to stop the session when I realised I was the only one who was agitated. All the other participants seemed very relaxed and calm. The calm and relaxed atmosphere gave me second thoughts and held me back from interrupting the meditation.

At the end of the session Bhai Sahib called out to my wife, asking her to relate her experience. I noticed that my wife appeared radiant and had a refreshed complexion. She was smiling and appeared very happy. She told everyone that she felt very light and joyful. It was as though a burden had been lifted off her shoulders.

Bhai Sahib then asked my wife if she had received any vision or message. She replied in the affirmative, saying it was a message: "Do not consume pork!"

I was rather disappointed with this message, as *bak kut teh*, a Malaysian Chinese delicacy served with pork, along with many other Chinese pork dishes, were my favorite food. As far as I was concerned, I was only interested in whether the message, or vision, or whatever, would inspire me to win a lottery and gain a big windfall.

Several group meditations later, my wife received another message: "For whatever you are about to 'receive', always remember to help the poor and the needy."

She related that this message was accompanied by a vision of a magnificent crown decked with shimmering jewels, the beauty of which was beyond description, never being seen in our human world. She further related that the vision of the crown sped across her mind. Bhai Sahib, who was listening intently, verified the message and the vision, and remarked that she was going to receive a gift from God.

What did I learn from this experience? I learned that in a true meditation there must be reactions and responses, especially for those who are gifted to experience them. In all my years with VCM, I have seen only a few participants who were able to experience similar reactions of spontaneous laughter and crying. It is because of these, and many other reactions I subsequently witnessed, that I realised why many who have never been exposed to such a meditation may be put off by it.

VISITATION OF BABUJI

During this early period of practising VCM, I treated my wife like a medium from whom I could seek answers to my many queries. This was similar to the approach I had previously used with temple mediums.

One evening session took place in my bedroom. My eldest daughter was also present. Midway through the session I noticed tears streaming down my wife's cheeks. She bowed towards the bedroom window. My daughter gestured to me to sit further away from my wife. I obliged only after she gestured repeatedly for me to do so. When I sat next to her, she whispered that a being had just entered the room through the window.

"My goodness!" I thought. "Even my eldest daughter is able to see things when I can't see anything at all!"

The next instant, my wife bowed in the direction of the window and uttered a greeting: "Namaste!"

I later learned that *namaste* is an Indian word which means, "To the Divine in thee, I bow." I then understood why my daughter had whispered, and why my wife had bowed in the direction of the window.

I then began a conversation with this unseen being. "Who are you?"

"I am BabuJi," came the reply.

Thus began my wife's first channelling session. The channelled being spoke with a very strong Indian accent. I wondered if the nature of other cosmic dimensions was such that they were occupied by a variety of races, just like in our human world. If that were so, I wondered why the being, which seemed so Indian-like, had come to me, since I am Chinese by birth. Nevertheless, I proceeded to ask further questions.

"What are you? What do you do?"

"I am sent by God to help humans," BabuJi replied.

I then thought that the channelling was going to be interesting, since this was the first time God had been mentioned in all my years of searching for the Creator.

The next moment BabuJi had a question. "How shall I call you?"

There was a moment of silence.

"Alright," BabuJi continued, "I will call you Sahib. And your wife shall be Maam Sahib."

Since BabuJi claimed that God had sent him to help humans, I decided to ask about the prophets, as in the scriptures they are associated with God. I then rattled off the following questions:

"Where is Jesus Christ?"

"Where is Buddha?"

"Where is Prophet Muhammad?"

I asked about these three prophets since they were frequently mentioned by followers of my country's three main religions, Islam, Christianity and Buddhism. They were the prophets who immediately came to mind.

My wife, as the channeller, then bent her head to one side, as if waiting to receive an answer. The next moment, she turned to face me with her eyes still closed. She then uttered: "Not for you to know."

"Why?" I asked.

"Because you are not sufficiently spiritually ready to understand," came the reply.

I accepted the answer since I had no knowledge whether prophets did exist, or even, for that matter, whether God did, too. I then posed a question regarding my fourth daughter.

"Why do I have a daughter who is suffering from cerebral palsy?"

"She has nothing to do with you," BabuJi replied. "She is connected with Maam Sahib."

"Why should I then be involved in her life?" I shot back.

Again came the same reply: "You are not sufficiently spiritually ready to understand."

BabuJi revealed later during that session that my wife and I had been together as husband and wife for the past four lives. I was the wife in one of those lives. Several years later, it was revealed that our relationship as husband and wife, in this current lifetime, would be the final one. We would be walking different paths after this life.

With this revelation, I supposed that past lives exist. I also learned that it is not necessary to be born of the same sex in different lives. I was surprised I did not ask more questions, but was rather absorbing what had been revealed. I also seemed to have found some patience, being willing to wait for the time when more would be revealed.

Chapter Seven

THE CORE VALUES OF VCM

EMPOWERMENT IS A CORE VALUE IN VCM MEDITATION. At times, during a VCM group meditation, empowerment is introduced, where we direct the awakened holy Life Force to empower various parts of our body, as identified by a facilitator. Occasionally, towards the end of the empowerment mode, Bhai Sahib would ask: "How would an Englishman laugh?" This was to test for spontaneous reactions occurring among participants.

On one occasion, a new VCM participant attended. She was an elderly Chinese lady in her mid-seventies. I knew she did not understand English. Yet before Bhai Sahib could finish his usual question, asking, "How would an ...", the Chinese lady erupted into spontaneous laughter. This was despite the fact that she was new to VCM group meditation, and had never even attended any VCM seminar. I realised later that her laughter was a prompt for me to open my eyes to witness the incident. Usually my eyes were closed during meditation.

I learned from that incident that her higher self had anticipated and responded appropriately with spontaneous laughter, even though the question had not been completed. It showed that such an acuity can only take place when the higher mind is awakened and brought into action. I also realised that most people do not find it easy to develop such acuity, as they are limited by their deeply entrenched conscious thinking and habitual analyses. Just like Maam Sahib, this woman said she felt blissful, as if a heavy load had been lifted off her shoulders. Her late husband, a goldsmith, had been killed in a robbery, and she had single-handedly raised several children. VCM helped extricate her from that trauma. It taught her to cope with her present life situation calmly.

This meditation session additionally brought a realisation regarding the meaning of Lao Tzu's teachings. The prophet states that a worthless scholar, on hearing the Dao (Tao), is moved to laugh boisterously. Then comes the punch line: if he was not amused by it, the Dao would not be Dao. Dao is the creative Life Force always in ascendency throughout the universe. The Dao is also resident within every human being, but in a state of sleep.

Dao can be awakened during meditation like that of the VCM variety. Once awakened, one's reaction is the expression of spontaneous laughter, as shown by my wife and the Chinese lady. Unawakened observers may laugh scornfully at the awakened Dao, or may even associate the spontaneous laughter with that of patients in mental asylums.

GEOMANCY IN VCM: BABUJI'S GUIDANCE

Asians in general occasionally practise the art of cleansing their homes to ward off diseases and other negative elements. Feng shui masters and vasthu shastra masters are often engaged to do the cleansing. A feng shui master I had previously engaged had not cleansed the house to my satisfaction. I was curious whether BabuJi would be able to do a better job. Accordingly, I decided to call for BabuJi, who appeared instantly.

"BabuJi, could you please do an energy cleansing of my house?" I asked.

"Oh yes! I can cleanse your house for you." BabuJi replied. "I am now at the front porch of your house. You are to remove those plants." The plant BabuJi referred to is known as *koon yam chook* in the Cantonese dialect. Its scientific name is *dracaena surculosa*. Maam Sahib later told me that the plant had always succumbed to disease. She would replace it with a new plant without understanding why only this plant was disease-prone. I surmised it to be related to a lack of affinity or compatibility with the home or family. An analogy is human blood. One must receive the right blood group in a blood transfusion to live.

I realised that no mediums or shamans would, at an instant, be able to detect subtle weaknesses that affected the well-being and harmony of my family. Only a being of BabuJi's stature was able to do this. After that cleansing of the home, I observed one of the changes was that my children no longer required treatments for various ailments at a nearby private clinic. Their visits to the clinic had been so regular that, after BabuJi's house cleansing, I noticed a substantial saving in medical bills. I also noticed that the peeling skin on my palms, with which I had been afflicted for many years, had healed. At that point, I wondered if subtle energies in our environment affected our emotional states to the extent that diseases could subsequently manifest.

Next, BabuJi turned his attention to the inside of the house. "I am now inside your house," said BabuJi. "Remove the dark wooden picture frames of shells from the wall. Remove those characters (referring to Chinese written characters) hanging from the wall. Remove the big red coloured paper fan."

"I am now going upstairs," said BabuJi. "Remove the altar. Remove all the idols!" BabuJi exclaimed. "How many times must God tell you human beings there is no God in idols, only lower forces!"

I was left speechless, and began to wonder if it is indeed true that God forbids idol worshipping. Previously, I had believed that whoever tried to destroy my idols would only be able to do so over my dead body. I was dead wrong. I was so deeply committed to idol worshipping that I had spent thousands on an altar and various idols. I thought it was a right practice, as I had inherited the rituals from my mother and grandmother, and because the vast majority of Chinese are idol worshippers, and have been for thousands of years.

Much later, I came across the following text in *Hua Hu Ching: The Unknown Teachings of Lao Tzu* (Brian Walker's translation): "Do not go about worshipping deities and religious institutions as the source of the Subtle Truth. To do so is to place intermediaries between yourself and the Divine, and to make of yourself a beggar who looks outside for a treasure that is hidden inside his own breast. If you want to worship the Dao, first discover it in your own heart. Then your worship will be meaningful."

After understanding this verse, I realised that the Chinese religious following is far removed from the teachings of the great masters. I quote below a verse from the Sri Guru Granth Sahib, which I was encouraged to read in its translated version: "Kabir, someone sets up a stone idol and all the world worships it as the Lord. Those who hold to this belief will be drowned in the river of darkness." (SGGS, p. 1371)

I only acquired an appreciation of the above-quoted verses after I had been exposed to VCM practice, which was accompanied by an experiential nascent awakening.

With guidance from BabuJi, I decided to remove all the idols from the house and send them to their respective temples. I arrived at a Buddhist temple and left the idols in the temple compound with the consent of the Buddhist monks. Suddenly BabuJi uttered: "Oh! They are not happy, not happy. Never mind, never mind." BabuJi was referring to the monks not being happy that I had left the idols at their temple, which meant I had given up my practice. As for the Goddess of Mercy idol, it was returned to a Goddess of Mercy temple. The temple priest asked for a monetary contribution, a request I gladly obliged.

The newly-bought altar was the final item to be removed. The furniture dealer from whom I had bought the altar declined to buy it back, even with a substantial price reduction. Meanwhile, a two-and-a-half-day VCM advanced course was scheduled for that very evening, which Maam Sahib and I had planned to attend.

An unexpected channelling then took place. BabuJi said: "I asked both of you to remove the idols, but you merely talk, talk, talk. What about the altar? Remove! Remove the altar now!"

Maam Sahib and I were caught in a tight situation. We had only about three hours to heed the advice and then get ready to attend the VCM course at Bhai Sahib's residence. I wondered if I could leave the altar by the side of the road, in front of my house. But that would be an unpleasant sight for others in the neighbourhood.

In desperation, I drove around the neighbourhood. Eventually, I encountered a stranger driving a pick-up truck. I was able to convince him to collect the altar from my house for free. I even gave him a small token for his effort. The stranger appeared dumbfounded as he and his assistant carried the altar down the staircase.

"Mister," he asked, "can you tell why you don't want this altar?"

"Never mind, just take it," I replied. "Thank you for your help."

I was upset, as I thought that if I had disposed of it later I could at least have salvaged some money in return, but BabuJi was insistent that it be removed immediately. I assumed the urgency had to do with achieving a total and complete cleansing of the house.

In a related incident, a group meditation was held in the home of a couple who had just been initiated into VCM. This family was going through the tail end of their past idol worship observances. In the middle of the session, BabuJi spoke: "Verily, verily, verily. You never learn your lessons. How many times must I tell you, you still keep pictures and idols of deities you revered, which is not necessary when following VCM practice."

I was not only wrong in my belief of idol-worshipping, but also about ancestral worship. Ancestral worship, or ancestral veneration, is another long-standing practice among Chinese people. I realised that the right practice is not to pray *to* ancestors, but to pray to God Almighty *for* our ancestors.

While I was on the threshold of understanding the subtle energy forces emanating from our environment, I had another chance to closely observe BabuJi's influence in creating suitable homes for strengthening spiritual practices. A VCM practitioner who was living in a double-storey house was advised to shift out of that house because bad vibrations were radiating from deep below the ground. It had brought suffering to his family. I later learned that his immediate neighbours, a happy Indian family, also suffered from bad vibrations. That Indian man, a banker, revealed to the VCM practitioner that his marriage went on the rocks. He even lost his job as a banker and became a taxi driver. Realising all this, the practitioner shifted to a newly built house as a temporary measure. The house he chose was also subjected to VCM discernment. In a meditation session carried out in this newly rented house, BabuJi was present. He said:

"I am BabuJi. I will do a reading of geomancy for you now. You have not listened to Maam Sahib. You must not have those flowers in your house. They bring in spirits. They are favourites of female spirits. Keep them away. You also must not keep figurines of animals or humans, of any nature, in your house. If you want to live here in peace, in goodwill, you must not keep any thorny plants inside your compound. You must not keep any pets.

"You have done well to upgrade yourself. Goodness will come in installments. You must not keep any pictures that show dullness, negativity, darkness, or whatever. Only have happy pictures with happy, bright or neutral colours. No dark colours. You will do well to listen. Do not put your footwear at the doorway. We will ask that you be given another reading at another time for you have not brought in much of your furnishing yet.

"We bless this house with peace, harmony and love. We will protect this house. The soil that it is built on is sacred now. Woe be to all those who may harm this family. Woe be to them. This family has had enough. Always remember to keep God in your heart and soul. Do things with love. Farewell."

In yet another instance, BabuJi was solicited to assess a location. An MBA course mate, who was working as an in-house consultant for a conglomerate that had a big steel mill located on the west coast of Peninsular Malaysia, told me about strange accidents that were happening every now and then within the steel mill's compound. He mentioned an unusual fatal accident, in which a worker had slipped and fallen to the ground.

Bhai Sahib was in Canada. I contacted him by fax, asking him to check on the steel mill. Bhai Sahib was able to give a geomancy reading of the steel mill even from that distance. He told me he detected that the ground on which the steel mill was built was once an execution ground used by Japanese soldiers during the Second World War. Long before that war, inhabitants had also used the ground to carry out human sacrifices. Bhai Sahib also mentioned that those spirits still lurking in the vicinity were about to turn into poltergeists. Poltergeists are able to make loud disturbances and cause objects to move. They are able to bring misery to human lives.

This geomancy reading showed that ground condition is vital when one decides to carry out any activity. Many repercussions can be avoided if VCM technique is used to carry out feasibility studies of the ground and its surroundings.

Although the owners were reluctant to instil the advised good practice, one favourable outcome of this episode was that my friend surprised me when he attended a VCM seminar without any persuasion on my part. I was surprised because he is a very intelligent man who is sharp in his analysis. Normally, it would not be easy for one with such attributes to practise the VCM style of meditation, due to their over-reliance on critical thinking. He has remained a regular practitioner, which has since brought immense benefits to his family.

This led me to realise that The Infinite ultimately decides who are destined to practise VCM, and to sustain practice over an extended period.

VCM GEOMANCY AND CAPTIVITY

VCM practitioners learn that any form of captivity brings bad vibrations. This was reinforced to us during one of our meditation sessions. In a special six-hour akhand jaap (a continuous unbroken prayer) held in a fellow VCM practitioner's house, we were privileged to have a visitation from a spiritual elder from a far away galaxy, whose presence was sanctioned by The Infinite. This particular practitioner had decorated the front porch of his house with several empty bird cages, which he had inherited from his father. The extraterrestrial spiritual elder commented that bird cages, even if empty, resemble imprisonment, even if no birds are kept in them. It is also bad to keep birds, for they have to live naturally, too. We were told that this understanding and practice are more important for those who are on a spiritual path.

VCM GEOMANCY AND NEUTRALISING OPPOSING FORCES

We also learned how to overcome opposing forces in practitioners' homes. In this instance, the akhand jaap was held at the home of another fellow practitioner. The Infinite advised that at least fifteen senior practitioners were required to take part, together with support from unseen extraterrestrial spiritual elders who came from another part of the universe. I assumed there was a need for so many practitioners and elders due to the strength of the opposing forces that were present in that particular home.

On another occasion, during a normal group meditation, Maam Sahib manifested spontaneous utterances known as *akath kathaa* (speaking in tongues). She shared with me that during that moment of spontaneous utterances an extraterrestrial being of very high status visited. That being informed Maam Sahib of the work she would have to carry out in that part of the universe when her time here on Earth was over.

"How will I remember the work I have to do when my time here is over?" Maam Sahib asked the extraterrestrial being.

"Your soul will remember," the being replied.

From these incidents I realised there are beings living in other parts of the universe, just like on Earth, created and sustained by The Infinite.

VCM GEOMANCY AND THE DOS AND DON'TS

In another special six-hour akhand jaap held in yet another fellow VCM practitioner's house, a geomancy reading was given: "Green jade is okay. Dogs and fish are not allowed. Plants with thorns are not allowed. Test everything you want to keep first. You are VCMers. You must learn how to test yourself. Otherwise, learn the hard way."

This particular VCMer probably was skeptical of the above reading, as he had by then planned to keep a pet. Hence, the message: "Otherwise, learn the hard way."

It can be concluded that certain unfortunate incidents can be avoided if we practise some dos and don'ts in creating our home. It would, at least, lessen any undesirable impact on our lives.

DISCERNMENT AND TESTING IN VCM

Discernment is a VCM modality, in which a practitioner begins by learning to 'receive' intuitively. Either a Yes, No, or Neutral, is given as an answer to a question. Any question that is posed must be specific and sensible.

Different practitioners may have different manner of communicating the received Yes, No, or Neutral responses. As an example, a practitioner may spontaneously move his hand in an upward motion if the answer to a question is Yes. His hand could drop in a downward motion if the answer is a No, and move in a horizontal, side-to-side motion if the answer is Neutral.

A response can also be received as a percentage or any other unit of measurement, predetermined before any question is put. This is to facilitate an appropriate response according to the preset unit of measurement.

In a group meditation, Bhai Sahib introduced discernment using percentage as a unit of measurement. The topic was testing the degree of a practitioner's surrender during a just-concluded meditation. After that, participants gathered around Bhai Sahib to check their degree of surrender. When he was alive, Bhai Sahib would say 50%, and even up to 80%, to those participants who had consulted him. Out of curiosity, I also asked Bhai Sahib what my degree of surrender was. In a very soft and gentle voice, Bhai Sahib responded: "10%."

I recalled that earlier Bhai Sahib uttered, "Super ego," as he passed me towards the end of that meditation session. It was a gentle prompting that made me realise my ego was a stumbling block to achieving a greater degree of surrender during meditation. I had assumed that only I would know that I was pretending to be in deep meditation. I was therefore surprised that the lowest percentage of 10% given by Bhai Sahib was right. It showed that the VCM discernment is accurate. And that my surrendering to God was minimal. I made a mental note of that discernment.

DISCERNMENT OF BOOKS

During one home meditation session, BabuJi said: "Test all the books on the right side of the bookcase. Sahib, you help Maam Sahib bring the books and the other items to be tested."

As advised by BabuJi, I took out all the books and items for testing. I then decided to segregate them into piles of accepted or rejected. Maam Sahib was the adjudicator. Where an item or book was accepted, Maam Sahib would utter *jee*; when rejected, *nei*. Jee and nei were foreign words to me then. I later learnt that jee means yes and nei means no. The following books and items were among those that were immediately rejected:

∞ All reading materials and booklets associated with a certain Chinese spiritual movement were nei. Any materials associated with worshipping idols were also rejected. Among these are the Goddess of Mercy, and another deity known as Chi Kung, recognisable for his beggar's attire and a hand-held fan made of bamboo.

∞ Books written by a certain author on Buddhism were rejected, while other books on Buddhism were deemed neutral, neither good nor bad. That meant they were acceptable for reading pleasure, or that there was a small degree of truth in those materials.

∞ Also rejected was the pocket-size piece of metallic sheet depicting nine different Indian deities, given to me by a priest from India.

∞ Items that had been placed on the altar were all rejected. One rejected item was a set of prayer beads. Another similar set of prayer beads was accepted. The reason for these actions were not clear to me. The set of prayer beads that hung on the rearview mirror of my car was acceptable, whereas the set permanently kept on the altar was rejected.

∞ Other items placed on the altar with the idols were also rejected.

In the middle of the testing session, I questioned myself as to the accuracy of the discernment. I decided to retest several books and items, which had already been either accepted or rejected. The outcome of those repeated tests showed the same results. The acceptance and rejection were not random. There seemed to be a purpose, a focus. It dawned on me that those which were irrelevant, or a source of distraction, were counterproductive in my practice of true spirituality, and that they should therefore be removed.

DISCERNMENT ON CHOICE

Once, an elderly VCMer, a divorcee, wished to get married again. He was required to choose one of two lovely women to be his wife. He consulted Maam Sahib for advice. I will identify the two lovely women as Lady A and Lady B. Lady A was a good friend of ours. Lady B was a stranger. Logically, we would have recommended Lady A, since we knew her well. To Maam Sahib's surprise, discernment carried out during meditation was in favour of Lady B. My human mind could not understand the choice made through discernment. I could only surmise it was due to affinity.

One is required to go into a surrendered state within in order to receive an accurate response regarding any issue one has in mind. The Infinite's advice on making choices was as follows:

"When testing, you must not scold. You must not be angry if testing is wrong. You are all learning. Everyone is learning. Sometimes, it is better if you are allowed to be wrong. Arrogance is bad. I purposely make you fail once in a while to protect you from becoming arrogant. Someday, you will understand. It is a journey of discipline. Do not think of what your body needs. Think of your souls."

DISCERNMENT OF WORLD'S SCRIPTURES: BHAGAVAD GITA

While Maam Sahib was still in the channeling mode, with her eyes closed, I took the hard-covered Bhagavad Gita to be tested by BabuJi. The book was held in an inverted position within both her outstretched hands. In a single motion, from the mid-section of the book, the pages on both halves were riffled through outwardly from each other with both her hands. Almost immediately, she then clasped the book with both her hands. She bowed her head in reverence before it. In a soft measured tone, she uttered: "Krishna, Arjuna. Not below my realm, not in my realm. I must also learn."

I realised that the utterance was for me to appreciate that the Bhagavad Gita is a holy scripture. I later learned that Krishna and Arjuna are in the heavenly realm. (In the VCM advanced course a chart entitled *Condition/Location of the Spirit/Soul* teaches practitioners to discern where a spirit or soul dwells.)

Maam Sahib has always respected my private belongings. She would never touch any of my books without asking for my permission. She also did not know that I had passed her the Bhagavad Gita to be tested, as her eyes were closed. She later told me she had heard of Krishna, but not Arjuna. That book, Bhagavad Gita, had been given to me by a Hare Krishna follower in 1985, after he had approached me for a donation. I did not believe in it then, and had just left it on my bookshelf. I began to appreciate the Bhagavad Gita a little better after that vibrant receiving.

THE HOLY QUR'AN

BabuJi later asked Maam Sahib and me to purchase a copy of the Qur'an. He indicated the Qur'an is Divinely inspired. Prior to this prompting from BabuJi, I was not sure about the Qur'an. I was more familiar with the Bible, since I have friends who are Christians. I have never been able to seriously bring myself to embrace any of mainstream religion, for I have nagging questions that none addressed to my satisfaction. My only interest had been to seek a guide who could show me how to connect to the Creator.

Maam Sahib and I made a trip to Kuala Lumpur to buy a copy of the Qur'an, as advised. We drove to a Malay Muslim residential area known as Kampung Baru, as I thought it would be easier to find a bookshop there that sells Qur'anic items.

Inside the shop, I began browsing through several books written by local and foreign authors. My wife was moving slowly from one end of the bookshelf to the other end. I noticed she was using the palm of her hand to graze over all the neatly arranged books. By then, I had decided on a copy of the Qur'an that we should buy. The copy also contained an English version that had been translated by a foreign author. The price was RM 50.

"Let's buy this copy," I told Maam Sahib.

"We should buy this copy instead," she replied, showing me the copy she had selected.

"What is the basis of your choice?" I asked.

"It has the strongest vibration," Maam Sahib replied. Furthermore, the copy she had chosen was only priced at RM 20.

Riffling through the pages of the Qur'an chosen by Maam Sahib showed that it was in the Arabic language. It did not have an English translation. I asked myself why should we buy this copy of the Qur'an, as I could only read if it was in either English or Malay.

I then realised a lesson was to be learned from this incident. It dawned on me that once the Qur'an is translated into other languages, its essence was compromised. It was important that I accept the Qur'an without the English translation.

Thereafter I had another realisation. If translation can cause a difference to its essence, so too will interpretations of the Qur'an's verses. I recall a VCM seminar I attended where Bhai Sahib observed that gross misinterpretations of all the world's scriptures had given rise to wrong understanding, and wrong understanding consequently brought about wrong practice.

Bhai Sahib emphasised that most verses in all scriptures cannot be understood in an academic fashion, for they are cryptic and couched in allegories. Bhai Sahib also wrote articles in which he pointed out the gross misinterpretation of the Sri Guru Granth Sahib written by prominent Sikh scholars. From this, and later revelations by The Infinite, I understood why religious differences have afflicted humanity for so long.

Once, unintentionally, I came across a verse in the Qur'an which I felt referred to reincarnation. I went straight to Bhai Sahib's residence to check with him if my interpretation of that verse was correct. Bhai Sahib was then engrossed with his writing. He kept on writing without lifting his head even to glance at me as I repeated the verse to him. He remained silent throughout my questions.

Once my interrogation was over, the very next moment, he quietly walked away to his room upstairs. I was left wondering what was happening. He returned holding an old volume of the Qur'an that was yellow-tinged. On the inside of the first page was written a list of indices, among which was the word, "reincarnation." He wrote down the verse number mentioned by me together with several other verse numbers, which I believed were the outcome of his own research. By including the verse number I had mentioned earlier, and without asking me to repeat it, he proved that he had been listening to me very intently.

Bhai Sahib next closed the Qur'an and took it back to his room upstairs. When he returned, he continued to remain silent and resumed writing. I found the way Bhai Sahib had conducted himself in that situation rather unusual. He had not uttered a single word.

On reflection, I appreciated that it had been an experiential learning situation. It was an acknowledgment that my interpretation of that particular verse was correct. I realised I should keep that understanding to myself because Muslims in my country disregard reincarnation. Therefore, it would not be wise of me to share my thoughts openly. Doing so would give rise to misunderstanding. I learned that I have to respect the law of the land that I reside in. After all, these spiritual lessons are meant more for my personal growth.

And what did I learn of Bhai Sahib, who was in silent mode throughout that episode? An extract of Lao Tzu's teachings from the Dao De Jing (Tao Te Ching) would best describe Bhai Sahib for who he was then: "They are nourished by virtue ... developed, cared for, sheltered, comforted, grown, and protected, creating without claiming, doing without taking credit, guiding without interfering, this is primal virtue." (Translated by Gia Fu Feng and Jane English, Chapter 51.)

Another verse confirms my initial observation: "Not bragging, they never falter, they do not quarrel, so no one quarrels with them, therefore the ancients say, yield and overcome." (Feng and English, Chapter 22)

During a group meditation, Maam Sahib received this message: "You don't fully understand all the scriptures I have sent down to mankind. Your present messenger, Bhai Sahib, can tell you what they truly mean. This one sleeps and surrenders deeply so that I can speak clearly to you all. I am God. I love you all very much. I will not come down very often. Learn from your present messenger. God loves everyone. Yes, everyone, no matter what. Do not doubt My words."

In another situation, when a jaap was in session, a VCMer asked The Infinite why religions have caused so much negativity among the different faiths. The reply was: "Learn My law. Learn My words. It has been passed down through the ages, unchanging. Only Man has twisted My words. Count yourselves lucky that you are being enlightened by Bhai Sahib. Count yourselves lucky among humanity that you understand all humans are brothers. Your souls belong to Me. Colours, languages, should not be a barrier. You are all one. Do you think you are born of this colour, live, speak this language every incarnation? You are wrong. You were of many colours, of many languages before. You are all one. You will never understand this because you are not spiritually high enough. Therefore, I will not dwell on that. Remember this, you are My children. I love you all."

Bhai Sahib once asked a practitioner who was proficient in both the English and Chinese languages to get copies of the Dao De Jing, with translations into English by various authors. Later, Bhai Sahib, through his power of discernment, picked one of the copies, which when tested revealed the highest accuracy. Practitioners were then advised to buy the selected copy for their own reading. On another occasion Bhai Sahib validated that Lao Tzu was a prophet.

THE SIGNIFICANCE OF THE SRI GURU GRANTH SAHIB

Bhai Sahib encouraged Maam Sahib and I to keep a copy of the Sri Guru Granth Sahib (SGGS) at home. I learned that the SGGS is ordained as the Silent Guru. Bhai Sahib told me that one still needs a living guru to learn true spirituality, even though one has a copy of the SGGS.

The SGGS cannot be left unattended, and must be placed in a special and high location in one's dwelling. The SGGS has to be opened every morning and closed every evening. In doing so, one must ensure that one is clean before coming into contact with the holy book. Additionally, the SGGS has to be held on top of one's head if one moves it from one location to another.

Bhai Sahib also reminded me to bow and pay reverence whenever I am near the SGGS at home. Bhai Sahib mentioned that among all the world's scriptures, SGGS is the most vibrant. This is probably because it is the most current of all the world's scriptures, and is replete with more spiritual truths. Meanwhile, The Infinite revealed that the SGGS still needs human effort for the power of the SGGS to manifest and aid those who pray. On a VCM chart entitled *Superior Divine Development and Potency*, developed by Bhai Sahib, the power of the SGGS is listed at 1340. The highest is 1350.

Bhai Sahib once shared a story about a Punjabi man from Japan. They met sightseeing at the Dead Sea in Jordan. The Punjabi man told Bhai Sahib that a fire broke out in his house in Japan while a jaap was being recited. The man's father was seated behind the SGGS, engrossed in his chanting. He continued to chant even as the fire spread towards him. He refused to budge, using only his hand to wave away the raging flames as he continued chanting. To everyone's surprise, the fire stopped just before the SGGS. The firefighters who arrived promptly at the scene were completely stunned, as they also witnessed what had occurred. This incident could explain the meaning of The Infinite's revelation regarding the relationship between human effort and the power of the SGGS. Effort, as shown by the sincerity and faith of the father, who was waving away the raging fire even as he continued his chanting, had enabled the manifestation of the power of the SGGS to stop the raging fire.

Although the SGGS is a very vibrant scripture, I was also made to realise that because our planet is currently going through a dark age, satanic forces have the capacity to neutralise the SGGS's power. I reproduce below what a veteran VCM practitioner, a Punjabi lady, wrote to me regarding the SGGS and satanic forces:

"About the SGGS being neutralised, yes, Bhai Sahib told me the same thing. I witnessed it with my own eyes during a jaap. One lady became totally possessed! She sat behind the SGGS, recited the Mool Mantar, and then glared at everyone, screaming that the SGGS has no power, that it could not scare her. She then got up and kicked the SGGS. The holy book flew to the ceiling, and the table it was resting on broke, but one of our members managed to reach out and grab the SGGS before it hit the floor."

This stunned and shocked me! I called Bhai Sahib to ask him how it was possible this could happen during a jaap, which is supposed to be very spiritually powerful. Bhai Sahib told me: "Sometimes the negative forces are so powerful that the SGGS can be neutralised."

Chapter Eight

CAREERS, MARRIAGE, CHILDREN, TRAUMA

ON ONE OCCASION, MAAM SAHIB WENT INTO MEDITATION and called for BabuJi, who appeared instantly. I began by asking what had caused me to jump into the river to save my colleague's life. The incident had been bothering me. I felt that things do not happen without a reason, especially in life-threatening circumstances.

Me: "Why was I made to jump into the river to save Alvin?"

BabuJi: "Because you owe him from your past life."

This answer suggests past lives are real. And that we are here to fulfil our past karma. With that, the session shifted onto career advice.

CAREER GUIDANCE

BabuJi: "Sahib, you should resign and go into business."

This statement was followed by a long pause on my part. I knew the Growth Promoter of the firm I was working for wanted to sack me because I had rubbed him the wrong way.

Me: "Will I be sacked?"

BabuJi: "Yes."

Me: "I will not resign. I will face it!" Then another thought came to me. "By the way, will I become rich if I go into business?"

BabuJi: "Yes, you will."

BabuJi also warned me my family would suffer if I went into business. Although BabuJi did not say why, I realised it would likely be due to my personal weaknesses and attitudes.

Me: "Is M.H. a suitable partner for me?"

BabuJi: "Neutral. Not bad, not good."

Me: "What about E.K.?"

BabuJi: "Not bad, not good."

Me: "What about Marcus?"

BabuJi: "Yes! Marcus is good!"

Looking back, I realise that all my past business dealings with Marcus had been successful, although they were on an ad hoc basis.

Me: "What about Raghbir?"

BabuJi: "Raghbir and Marcus are the same person."

That is true. I had purposely posed the question to test BabuJi.

Despite the good advice BabuJi gave me, I was stubborn. So in the face of workplace difficulties, I decided to stay with the company. I wanted to fight for my position there, even if the outcome was disastrous. I now admit I was not wise enough to walk away from the situation. I would likely have achieved better results working elsewhere. Only Divine intervention ensured I was able to remain working in that organisation till my retirement. Having made my choice, I had to bear the consequences.

During another meditation session held at home, The Infinite spoke to me through Maam Sahib:

"You should not worry about your career. It is the way it is destined. There is nothing you can do to change it, unless you change yourself. You have to make yourself happy wherever you go. You have to get involved. Be happy and and be grateful. Many do not have jobs, do not have careers. Where you are is where you should be. Until you have paid your penance to these people, you cannot leave. When you leave is when you have paid your penance, just like your wife. She could not leave her old school when the new school opened nearby." (Maam Sahib was a school teacher.) "She had not paid her penance at that time. That is why I sent BabuJi to tell her she had to wait. Be kind. You must know."

My brother-in-law, George, once sought advice from BabuJi. The session went as follows:

George: "I have aches and pains from working in the field."

BabuJi: "Pound some black pepper and mix with coconut oil over a slow fire. Apply it to the painful area."

George: "I thought of planting vegetables."

BabuJi: "Don't plant vegetables. Hmmn. Plant papaya. Yes, papaya!"

Weeks later, I visited George in his home village. He told me of amazing events that followed that particular channelling session. Notably, he had had offers to plant papayas!

Much later again, George told me he had asked BabuJi if he had a future in their family's rubber and palm oil estate. BabuJi replied in the negative. George then asked if the estate itself had any future, to which the answer was also in the negative. George soon understood why the answers to both his questions were in the negative. The Government informed his family of its intention to acquire their family's estate via the Land Acquisition Act. The future of the estate was indeed in question, as BabuJi had revealed.

In another instance, a member of the VCM group was preparing to resign from his job to join a company as a business partner. The company was dealing with food flavours. During a group meditation in my house, discernment was carried out to determine if it was a right move. The answer was: "Not bad, not good, neutral." This was understood to mean that the outcome would only be ordinary. The next moment, The Infinite spoke: "I shall make it better for you!" In other words, The Infinite would see to it that the business venture succeeded. This receiving motivated him to resign and plunge into the food flavour business. Despite his lack of experience, he was soon answering calls from established branded drinks manufacturers who were interested in his product. This situation leads us to the realisation that The Infinite also works through the minds of humans to get things done.

Once, when I was on a short holiday in Kota Baru, Kelantan, on the east coast of Peninsular Malaysia, I met an old friend I had not seen for a long time. He introduced me to a businesswoman, a Malaysian Chinese hardware trader. I was encouraged to interview her on how she successfully developed her business. To my surprise, she agreed to the interview.

It started with the businesswoman asking me a question: "How many lorries do you think I own?"

"I don't know," I replied.

"Make a guess."

"Ten units?" It was a figure I plucked from the air.

"Not so many," she answered.

"How many lorries *do* you own?" I asked.

"Only nine," she said.

"Wow! Then the tenth unit is on the way."

She related that her husband had left her and married a Siamese woman. She felt helpless and alone, having to raise their two children, a boy and a girl, by herself. At that time she was renting a room for RM 300 per month. Although she had a sister living in the same town, her sister despised her for not having a proper livelihood. Fortunately, she also had a brother, working in Singapore, who was willing to loan her RM 30,000 to start a small business. Prior to that, she had been holding down two jobs to make ends meet. During the day she was a runner for an illegal gambling syndicate, while at night she sold sliced fruits outside a cinema. She later stopped being a runner, after she was arrested by the police.

With the RM 30,000 loan from her brother, she decided to open a hardware shop. She reasoned that hardware is more durable than groceries, which would make it easier to clear the goods should her business venture fail. She contacted an established hardware dealer in Kota Baru to supply her with goods. She told the dealer to recommend the most common and marketable items for her to start off her business. She also told him that should he mislead her, she would never make any future purchases from him.

Her business expanded rapidly. Some people were of the opinion that she had actually overtaken the more established hardware supplier. Subsequently, she also ventured into swiftlet bird nest farming. (Swiftlet nests, which the birds construct using their hardened saliva, are an Asian delicacy.) A businessman was in the midst of setting-up swiftlet farming in a row of double-story shops. She owned an intermediate unit. The businessman persuaded her to join in the venture, sealing the deal by agreeing to buy from her whatever hardware items were needed for the project. Her investment in swiftlet farming proved a second success. It was a low risk venture, being financed from the profits she made selling hardware items to the businessman for reconstructing the row of shops.

She ended the interview by walking away to continue her work. She appeared uncomfortable, and was probably wondering why she had shared so much information with me. After all, I was a stranger she had just met.

However, I knew it was providence that had caused the businesswoman to agree to the interview, for my benefit.

What did I learn from this episode? It led me to recall a question Bhai Sahib once asked me: "Why are there people who don't pray, yet are successful in their chosen careers?" I pondered long and hard. Matthew 5:45 states: "For He maketh His sun to rise on the evil and on the good, and sendeth rain on the just and on the unjust." Therefore, as far as livelihood is concerned, it does not matter if one believes in God or not. Even if one is an idol worshipper, as was the case with the businesswoman, providence does not forsake anyone. Every human being who has the courage to face challenges in life, working hard as they strive to earn an honest livelihood, despite being alone, helpless or even without any business acumen, will still be able to derive a good source of income.

Such an attitude corroborates a Divine message given to a group of regular VCM practitioners: "No effort, no gain. I have given you everything you deserve. You wholeheartedly say to those who work below you, 'I will give you what you deserve.' Similarly, I will give you what you deserve! There is no difference. Do you deserve what you have? My son, you must earn, all of you must earn. If you do not earn, then you do not know how to value. You will go astray. You will be lost. You will forget Me. You will even forget your family. If I were to pour abundance down onto you, you would all go berserk. You must earn it. No matter how hard it is, stay with the advice given to you. Abundance easily earned will easily slip away."

RENEWAL OF MARRIAGE VOW

One evening, Maam Sahib received a message about our marriage renewal. "Good to renew the vow of marriage. Bless you both, My children."

For the several days following that message I dwelt on the purpose of a marriage vow renewal. I had not previously heard of it. I asked myself what was there to renew. After all, I acknowledged I was married to my wife. The importance of marriage was not a subject to which I had ever given a second thought. I wondered how and where the renewal of our marriage vows would take place. With only questions and no answers, I dropped the issue and went about my daily life.

Just when I had forgotten about it, I was surprised to learn that my wife had bought a pair of silver rings at a cost of RM 7 apiece. I understood the rings were to be worn by each of us to symbolise the renewal of our marriage vow. I still did not pay much attention, until I received a phone call from Bhai Sahib. He told me of a gathering in town where couples would gather to renew their marriage vows. He advised me that my wife and I should attend the gathering. I agreed to oblige Bhai Sahib, but more to acknowledge his effort than to please Maam Sahib, or to adhere to the received message.

The ceremony was held in a rented shop building. It was conducted by a spiritual organisation. Over twenty couples were present. I sat in the third row and waited rather indifferently. This was evident because even when Bhai Sahib was giving a speech, I did not listen. I became lost in my own thoughts.

What happened next was simply a bolt out of the blue. The moment the pianist struck the first key on the piano, a strong vibration shook my entire being. I felt my mind descending into a relaxed state of calmness. The next moment, a brilliant and seemingly powerful Living Force appeared to have awakened from within me. Its sublime Presence was simply overwhelming. It seemed to have a mind of its own. It was an invisible Awakened Self within me. The myself of me was aware of that independent Awakened Self. That Awakened Self seemed to be all-knowing. It remained in a silent mode throughout.

I felt a knowing in me that the independent Awakened Self was waiting for the myself of me to do a self-assessment of my past commitment and contribution towards my marriage. The very next instant, tears began to flow down my cheeks. "How can this be happening?" I silently asked myself. When I tried to stop tearing up, the flow of tears became even more intense. All my attempts were in vain. I had completely lost control of myself. It was like the embankment of a dam had collapsed. And it was all happening in a silent mode. It was simply unstoppable. Thick streams of tears flowed profusely down my cheeks. I was amazed that my tear glands could be triggered to produce so many tear drops at an instant.

A sense of guilt and regret enveloped me. I realised I had failed to live up to the sanctity of my marriage. The manifestation of the Awakened Self played the role of a witness. It took a long, silent moment for the myself of me to perform a self-assessment and to acknowledge the wrongs I had done during my marriage.

When the myself of me had understood the purpose of the renewal of my marriage vow, the tears ceased. The experience ended with an instantaneous disappearance of that brilliant Awakened Self, like a switch had been turned off within. That was when I regained my conscious self.

On reflection, I realised there was absolutely no chance for the myself of me to argue, to question, or do anything to defend my past actions. The process had happened in a smooth, silent and effortless manner. I realised that while one can escape human law, one can never escape The Infinite's law. I also learned that when one decides to marry someone, one has to accept whatever karma manifests for that person, which they are required to deal with throughout the course of their marital relationship.

While thinking about this, I recalled that BabuJi had said my fourth daughter had nothing to do with me, that she was connected to my wife's karma. I was then not sufficiently spiritually awake to understand why. I realised that once I had willingly committed to a married life with my wife, I was obliged to shoulder with her the challenges she has had to bear with our daughter. Our daughter was apparently the mother of Maam Sahib in one of their former lives. I was not involved in that life. Presumably, Maam Sahib had agreed to help resolve her past karma, accrued when they were mother and daughter, in this current life.

While on the subject of marriage, I would like to share the experience of an ex-colleague in finding a life partner. He was a decent, pleasant and responsible man, yet had failed in his previous two serious relationship attempts. This ex-colleague had a dream not long after he joined VCM. He dreamed he was holding a red ribbon with an unknown woman. I interpreted the dream as indicating that he would be getting married soon. He asked how that could be when he was not seeing anyone. Soon after, he met a lady of the Catholic faith. He wondered if it was going to be a challenge due to the differences in faith. He mentioned it to Maam Sahib who advised him to be patient.

He is currently happily married to this lady. They are blessed with two lovely daughters. He adjusted himself well when he took the initiative and attended marriage courses. Some VCM practitioners made fun of him over his participation in the marriage vow. In a group meditation session, a Divine message was received: "Many laughed at those who go for marriage courses. Do not laugh. There is goodness in it. You do not do your duty and forsake your children for your work. Those concerned know it."

LIVING BY THE COMMANDMENTS

During a meditation session, The Infinite Spoke about the Ten Commandments. I realised that the Ten Commandments are still valid, even today. By then, I had learned that regardless of one's religious denomination, the essence of all the world's scriptures affect every human being.

In 2008, just before the start of our first group meditation for the year, several VCM practitioners were chatting about a sex scandal involving a politician. We immediately received a message that the politician in question had infringed several of the Ten Commandments. VCM practitioners were also reminded not to talk about such topics during a holy gathering. Subsequently, another message was received from a Divine source:

"We caution you to live by the Ten Commandments. By every commandment of God. We caution you to live in peace, in love. Do not be so cruel to those who are not of your colour or language. They are all God's children. They are your brothers and sisters. You have failed God in so many ways, yet God does not give up on you. God sent us to pass you this message. It is our service to the Almighty One whom we love. Obey God. Be good. Live long and be happy. He loves all of you. You are the chosen ones. Much more is expected of you than what you have shown. So be it." (Note: *Chosen ones* refers to a particular group of regular practitioners. They are not otherwise special or unique.)

KARMA AND ACCEPTANCE

I was getting increasingly concerned with the challenges of raising my daughters, especially my fourth, S.Y.. I still wanted to find a permanent cure for the cerebral palsy that had afflicted her from birth. In an evening drive with Bhai Sahib, I asked him if he could ask God to grant recovery to my daughter. When Bhai Sahib gently responded, "No," I reacted impulsively, shouting at the top of my voice: "If God can part the Red Sea, why is it so difficult for Him to give my daughter a normal life!"

I was surprised at my desperation and my raised voice. My outburst was followed by a long moment of silence. Bhai Sahib remained as cool and calm as ever. For a time he twisted the end of his shimmering white beard. He then gently said it is her karma, which she must go through. Several days later the following Divine message was received: "Everything is predestined. All karma must come to pass. I am always with you in everything you do. What you do is predestined."

Bhai Sahib subsequently confided to me that S.Y. was Maam Sahib's mother in a previous life. S.Y. did something that was not right in that life. Maam Sahib is currently S.Y.'s mother to provide support and to help S.Y. resolve that past karma in this lifetime.

During an earlier meditation session, we received a message that concerned my eldest daughter, with additional advice for me: "Love your children. This you must do, especially the eldest. She is a confused child. Forgive her her past trespasses. This lifetime you both must overcome past karma to be free of hate. Love must prevail. This one chooses to be born to help you love children, even in the the most difficult situation. You, Athan, must overcome the weaknesses that prevent you from doing this. This one cannot help what she does. She is also learning to correct her past karma. Help her. Do not forsake her. Listen to Bhai Sahib. He tells you what you should do to protect you from evil. You must not get angry. You must always love one another."

Years later, in an unrelated situation, The Infinite declared: "When I give dreams, who follows what they say? Who takes their dreams seriously? You expect Me to pour money down to you from heaven. You expect Me to give you messages directly. What contribution comes from you? The brain that I have given you, the arms, hands, feet, legs, your body, your eyes, your senses, you are not using! Do you know how many of these people who cannot use all these senses are lying around on Earth, praying to Me for those senses I have given you? You are abusing My gift!

"S.Y. cannot talk. So many cannot talk, cannot hear, cannot see. They are praying every moment of their lives: 'Oh, God, give me sight!' I cannot give them that. They have to pay their penances on Earth. You who do not have to pay this kind of penance, what are you doing with your perfect body? You know the dictionary meaning of *humble*, but you are not practising it!"

ON RAISING CHILDREN

After the message on penance, The Infinite continued His advice for parents and their relationship with their children.

"Family is very important. It is not enough to say your spouses and children know that you love them. It is also important to express that love in the things that you do for them. When there is a crisis, you have to be patient, especially if your spouse is not a VCMer, especially if your spouse does not understand. It is very difficult.

"You must exercise patience. Your children must be given attention. They too need your attention, your expressions of love. Human beings take each other for granted. Just knowing is not enough. You must show love. When you stop showing love, you take each other for granted. That is when you deviate, when you will walk off the path.

"We tell you to be patient with your children. God has provided them with the best to meet their abilities. They will grow in time. You must be thankful for what is only temporary. You will receive a much better future for them. Parents' wishes and mental opinions of their children matter. If you think negatively of them, you block the good energy that comes to them. Mothers must be careful. They must protect their children. Always think well of your children. You are their protector.

"Children need attention from both mother and father. You must all remember that I give both parents children. Both must contribute. Did not Bhai Sahib teach you that previously? You forget. It is very important for your next generation. No effort, no gain. Never think badly of your children or they will never succeed in life. Contribute to their success. Teach them. If you do not know (their merits and desires), how can they improve and achieve what you wish them to become? If you teach your children good things, they will become good. If you merely criticise, compare and scold, they will learn bad things and feel very low in spirit.

"In anything that you do, you must be patient. More so in taking care of your children. This future generation must be different. They must be better. You must change the future generation. Lead them back to God's path. That is your duty as parents. If you fail, woe be to you. That will be a weight on you. Do you understand? Pass on this legacy of love, of peace, of joy, and your future generation will benefit. They will walk on God's path.

"When you plant a seed, you have to water it, you have to fertilise it, you have to give it love. Only then the tree grows and bears healthy and good fruit. You are a gardener to human beings. Even such a simple, lawful process you do not understand. It is so strange to hear men say they work to feed and maintain their wives and children, yet they spend most of their time working. Maintenance is not restricted to money alone! We say maintenance covers all aspects of a child's upbringing. The children are the future. Take care of them.

"I have told you, Athan! Repeatedly you asked, repeatedly I have told you. The answers remain the same. Be obedient, son! Children learn through example. You must be a good example. Children learn habits from their fathers and mothers. You cannot expect one to do something and not the other. The child will not learn if you do things in contradiction! You must, for your future generation's sake, show a good example before it is too late. Children need guidance. You who are older, and have gone through so much, must teach them the right values.

"Bhai Sahib has taught you enough. I repeat: you must obey. You must heed the messages. Time and again you have asked the same questions. The answers will not change unless you change. When you do change it is for a time only. You then revert and fail yourself. I have not failed you.

"And the rest of you, do good deeds, be good examples to your children. Otherwise your future generations will fall into woe. Children are surrounded by so many bad influences. You as parents should be good examples. Preserve the goodness of your family. The children will remember you forever. I will bless your home and your descendants, not only yourself.

"Listen! Bhai Sahib has taught you enough. Recall. Learn again, and practice. Without enough practice, and without enough consistent practice, you forget yourself. You cannot speak to your family the way you speak to others. Woe upon your future generations if you do so. When you are old, the children will speak the same. Then you will know what I mean. I have forever to wait. Why do you want to repeat? You who are now open to VCM should know. End your cycle, come home.

"I am Infinity. I know all things past, present and future. You must trust Me more, and humble yourself before all My children (humanity). Show that you are true followers of Bhai Sahib. Do not fail your master! Do not fail Me! So be it."

KNOWING YOUR WORDS HAVE POWER

During one meditation session, The Infinite spoke of the importance of thoughts and words.

"From this day, speak well. You are responsible for what you speak. Whatever you say will come true for others. You have to be responsible for the consequences of what you say to others. *Think of me before you speak.* Your words have power. I have said it before, and I say it again: speak well. Bad karma will befall you if you say things that hurt others. Good karma will befall you if you say good things about others. Simple words from this woman (the channeller, Maam Sahib) are not so easy to follow, are they?

"Can you not do something right and earn yourself good karma? Can you not beat the clock and earn faster than you are earning now? There is not much time! Why do you want to be reborn? You must beat the clock like this one (Maam Sahib) is trying to do. You must not be reborn again. You must achieve that target. Cleanse your soul. It is tiresome. Do you not think of never learning the lessons that you are supposed to learn and so being reborn again and again? Truly, you are worse than little children. Even they learn more than their elders, for they are pure."

ON PAST LIFE TRAUMA

One interesting feature of VCM is its capacity to identify and remove trauma, not just from our present life, but from past lives. Trauma is described as a 'deeply distressing or disturbing experience', which can cause a person to behave in peculiar ways. Each person's behavioural patterns and attitudes are to a great extent shaped by previously experienced trauma.

A past life trauma described here found closure after a long period of time, fifteen years to be exact. This involved not just one, but three, VCM practitioners. These three joined VCM practice at different times. When all three were present during jaap sessions, the deep-seated trauma was disclosed. The first practitioner was Maam Sahib, who was the victim of this trauma. The second was Linda, who joined VCM several years later, and was Maam Sahib's mother in that particular past life. The third was Toh, the last to join VCM. In the lifetime in question, he was Linda's son and the elder brother to Maam Sahib.

The past life trauma unfolded during the jaap, when Maam Sahib clapped her hands. She then stretched out one hand and exclaimed: "Do you want one?" She had done this before, whenever a past life trauma was about to be revealed. Later she confided to me that she was a handicapped person in one of her past lives. She was left alone and confined in a dark room as a punishment. Linda, her mother, had lost a piece of jewelry. Toh, the older brother, had stolen the jewelry, then accused his younger sister of the theft. As a result, Linda punished her daughter by locking her in a dark room. This was traumatic for the child. Although Madam Sahib knew of this trauma, she did not reveal it to the other practitioners. It took another jaap session, when the trauma was further revealed.

This took place many years later, during a jaap in a fellow VCM practitioner's house. This time only Maam Sahib and Linda were present during the jaap's second station . Maam Sahib, in a meditative mode, again clapped her hands repeatedly. The next moment, she turned to face Linda. Her eyes were closed as she asked: "Do you want one?" Linda was quiet and also appeared to be in a contemplative mode. I alone witnessed the incident, but at that time did not understand the implications of this manifestation.

The karmic trauma was further clarified during a jaap held at Linda's residence. During this session, the karmic trauma finally found closure. After the jaap, Linda related what had happened to her in this current life.

"There was a big drawer in the shop in which a baby could be tucked comfortably when the drawer was left open. It formed a little bed for the infant. I was then less than a month old. My uncle said I was crying, so my father closed the drawer. My uncle opened it and picked me up, angry and concerned that I could have suffocated. Shortly after my mother left for Ipoh with me, having broken off with my Dad for the second time. That was what I was told when I was older. Of course, I had never been close to my father."

As for Toh, he related that when he was a young boy during this present lifetime, his sister had wrongly accused him of having stolen his mother's jewelry. This resulted in Toh being repeatedly caned by their mother, who wanted Toh to admit that he had stolen the jewelry. Toh stood his ground and vehemently denied he was the culprit. Toh's mother then concocted a tale, saying she had gone to a Chinese temple to seek the help of a deity to recover her jewelry. Spinning the tale, she proclaimed that by a certain time something terrible would befall the thief.

Before the hour was up, Toh's sister confessed to the theft. She did so out of fear, being a staunch believer in her mother's deities. But by then, it was too late. Toh had already been severely punished by their mother.

On reflection, it shows that karma is real and affects every human being. What goes around will eventually come around. It can be seen from this example that an act of karma that results in trauma in one life will boomerang on the perpetrator, even into the next life. It also means that whatever karma is accumulated in this present life will have its effects, if not in this present life, then in the next, or thereafter.

This incident made me realise VCM is a useful technique to help with trauma removal, no matter in which life it is accrued.

Chapter Nine

FOOD, DEATH, KARMA, SERVICE

AFTER MORE THAN TWO YEARS OF REGULAR VCM PRACTICE, I was prompted to sign up for a professional course. As I was involved in marketing, I opted for the Postgraduate Diploma in Marketing offered by The Chartered Institute of Marketing, U.K. My pursuit of tertiary education was undertaken more to satisfy the demands of the human world, for I have never placed much importance on paper qualifications. Yet after I had successfully completed my marketing course, I casually asked my wife to discern if I should undertake a Master in Business Administration (MBA). Soon after she told me she had received a strong prompt that I should.

ON PURSUING EDUCATION

I immediately backtracked. I told myself it was not possible for me to do an MBA, as I had neither the drive nor the money to pay for it. I was pessimistically and adamantly against the proposal. Eventually, I decided to seek the opinion of BabuJi to resolve the issue. The channelling session, held one evening, was attended by practitioners of different races and religious backgrounds. The session went as follows:

BabuJi: "Speak, Sahib, speak."

Me: "Must I do an MBA?"

BabuJi: "Why must you doubt God? God is preparing you to join the high status of the human world."

I did not ask the purpose of being in the company of those in high status, as at that time I was preoccupied with my financial plight and the health of my youngest daughter, S.Y..

Me: "Where am I going to get the money to pursue an MBA?"

BabuJi: "Waheguru (God) will provide."

Two days later, I received a call from an ex-DipMarketing course mate, who asked if I was interested in undertaking an MBA. A small discount would be given if we registered as a group. An installment payment plan was also available. I decided that all these occurrences, including the choice of the university (University of South Australia), were Divinely prompted, given I had not put in any effort to create the opportunity.

Meanwhile, I wondered how on earth Waheguru could sponsor me? I quietly hoped God would inspire me with numbers to bet on, so I could use the prize money to pay for the MBA course, with enough left over to add to my savings. I also wondered why God would want me to join the upper echelons of the human world. I told myself I was comfortable where I was, as long as I had money to sustain myself and my family. Soon after, my father passed on and left me money that was more than sufficient to pay for the course fee.

This incident made me realise that whatever we 'possess' belongs to God. It is only in our mind that we think that such possessions belong to us. In reality, we only hold it in trust. When we depart this human world we take no material possessions with us.

Pursuing the MBA proved stressful, as I had to struggle with my job as a manager while attending long hours of lectures, regular group studies, and completing assignments and exams, all while struggling with health problems.

One day, as I hurried home after work, with little time to rush to a distant town to attend a group study, the accumulated frustration got to me. Just before I left, I grudgingly asked my wife to seek God's approval to cancel my MBA program. When I reached home late that night, Maam Sahib was waiting for me. She had received a message from The Infinite, which she urged me to read. It stated:

"No, Athan must continue to do the MBA. My will must be done. It is for your own good, Athan. Have trust in yourself. And in Me. I have told you I will guide you, and I will. Fax your friend, Jerry. He must try to help you. He owes you this."

My immediate reaction to that message was to deny His will. I told myself that I am in charge of my own destiny. I decided I would purposely fail the MBA just to prove His will can be frustrated. This was an opportunity to prove that God is not almighty after all.

Yet months later, as I threw myself on a couch, having just learned I had successfully completed the final thesis paper, a group assignment, I spontaneously became alert. I recalled my intention to purposely fail my MBA, just to prove I could challenge God's will. At that moment I realised that if anything is truly the will of God, it will surely come to pass.

I later dreamed in colour of a gathering where I had to shake hands with a group of very tall dark-coloured men dressed in business suits. I was amazed by their height, even as they smiled at each other. Bhai Sahib said that the very tall men symbolised human beings of high standing, and that I would soon be joining their company.

(Just as I am about to finish writing this book, I recall God's plan to prepare me to join this group of individuals in the human world. I had a hunch I have more work to do to serve humanity, insofar as spiritual work is concerned, though I am not sure. I may be wrong.)

ON THE CONSUMPTION OF FOOD

The prophets have offered this message: "In the time of Kali Yuga (the current dark age), you who are the open ones, the chosen ones, are behaving like those who have not come into VCM. Sometimes you forget yourselves. Bhai Sahib taught you to eat correct food. You do not follow his teachings! And yet you want the best of everything. What are you contributing?"

Let me begin this topic on food intake with a confession. I am one of the practitioners who did not follow the advice to eat well. It is understandable why I suffered a heart attack in 2014, and needed a triple bypass operation to save my life. This was followed by cancer in 2018. The discomforts and side effects of treatment have taken away my craving for food. I have since resigned myself to lead a life where I eat just to sustain my body.

I recall a dinner gathering with fellow practitioners from Australia. I was seated next to Bhai Sahib. I had by then filled my plate to the brim with rice, meat and vegetables, and was about to eat when Bhai Sahib gave a gentle slap on my wrist and said, "Be careful of food forces!"

I retorted: "Why don't money forces come to me?"

I then wondered if there is truth in what Bhai Sahib had said about food forces. Awareness of bringing my appetite under control would be helpful. Otherwise life-threatening diseases could eventually result.

On another occasion I had ordered beef noodles and asked Bhai Sahib if he was interested in having the same meal. Bhai Sahib gently responded: "I would have to write my will first." Bhai Sahib was merely telling me it was unhealthy food. I realised that beef noodle had high content of monosodium glutamate. Bhai Sahib was not in favour of using it in food.

As mentioned earlier, the first message practitioners received during my first group meditation was: "Do not consume pork." I could not accept thst message. I met with Bhai Sahib several days later to get a clarification on what the message meant.

"Bhai Sahib, why should we not consume pork?" Without waiting for Bhai Sahib to respond, I continued to rant: "The Chinese race has been consuming pork for so long. They live long lives. They are healthy, intelligent and hardworking. The same with Europeans, and many others. What I know is that only the Muslims do not eat pork, and I am not a Muslim!"

Bhai Sahib listened intently, stroking his well-kept white beard, twirling and tapering it towards its end. I continued, rattling off my next point: "Look, Bhai Sahib! Chinese foods have so many different dishes that use pork, and they are delicious. I enjoy them all! Have you heard of bak kut teh? It's a Chinese herbal soup of pork eaten with rice. Do you know it? It's my favourite. I eat it several times a week! How can this message not to consume pork be true? Do I look sick because of pork consumption? I am healthy and strong. And I feel good!" I ended by stating: "Bhai Sahib, nutritionists, and food scientists say pork has nutrients which are good for our health. How can they be wrong?"

Bhai Sahib, who had been listening attentively, his head noticeably lowered, answered when I finally finished talking.

"Why do you like to eat pork?" He asked this in his usual voice, reflective of his mild-natured self. It was more like he was validating that the message was correct. "Try to eat less of it if you must. Better still don't eat it at all!" Bhai Sahib ended with a gentle smile.

"Well, is that all?" I asked myself. Bhai Sahib's response did not convince me. I needed proof, especially when nutritionists and scientists did not discourage pork consumption.

I was later prompted to read the Bible, particularly a chapter in Deuteronomy that states pork consumption is not permitted. That was probably a rare occasion when I glanced at the Bible. Several other types of living things not suitable for human consumption are also mentioned there. My Christian friends were not able to explain why consuming pork was discouraged. In fact, all the Christians I know eat pork, too. I observed that Muslims do not eat pork. I obtained no proper explanation for this from my Muslim friends, except that the pig is a 'dirty' animal.

Bhai Sahib once mentioned that a university in USA carried out a test in which a cow, a goat and a pig were slaughtered at the same time. Their meats were left in the open to study their rate of putrefaction. The results were examined under a microscope. It was found that pork putrefied rapidly, while beef and mutton remained fresh.

Many years later, after I had stopped eating pork, I happened to walk through a lane in a neighbourhood market. As I passed, I caught, for a split-second, the stench of rotting meat. I realised it emanated from the pork stalls located in the lane. That moment was an eye-opener. Exposed pork meat does indeed putrefy quite fast.

Bhai Sahib reiterated on numerous occasions that we should reduce, or altogether stop, our pork consumption. Through his discernment, he observed it exposes us to the risk of developing stomach and throat cancer. My walk through the market lane helped me realise the truth that pork is not healthy. I also realised that my senses experienced beneficial changes after only several years of VCM practice. The changes were significant, as I found I could not tolerate cigarette smoke, although I was a heavy smoker for more than twenty years prior to my involvement with VCM.

While undergoing treatment for cancer, I observed that a great majority of cancer patients were Chinese. I recalled Bhai Sahib had mentioned in a seminar that Malaysian Chinese top the list of cancer patients, even though the Chinese population constitutes only about one fifth of the total Malaysian population. Bhai Sahib said the Chinese should learn their lessons from the unfortunate incident of the new strand of nipah virus that wiped out the pig-rearing industry in the state of Negeri Sembilan. The virus also claimed quite a few pig farmers' lives. In an article in The Star newspaper dated 22 December, 2014, titled, *Singapore Malays the unhealthiest*, it was reported that, "The only major illness which the Malay population is not the most likely to get is cancer. This is most prominent among the Chinese." I recall another Singapore news report that stated one in every twenty-five Singaporeans suffer from cancer, whereas the ratio was one in seventeen for Chinese Singaporeans. If it is true for the Chinese in Singapore, it is most likely also true for the Chinese in Malaysia, because they have almost the same diet.

All this lent credence to what Bhai Sahib had mentioned, that Chinese topped the number of cancer patients in Malaysia every year. Diseases commonly suffered by the Malays in Singapore such as stroke, renal failure, diabetes, and heart attacks are probably similar to that of the Malays in Malaysia. Again, these point to the similarity of their diet. Perhaps the Malay community needs to review the culinary ingredients and the way their meals are prepared in order to reduce the impact of those diseases.

I once tried to share my experience regarding the dangers of pork consumption in a gathering of childhood friends. One, who was very successful in his career, retorted with his index finger poking his own hand: "What are you talking about?! It's in the blood of the Chinese to consume pork!" I am reporting this incident to indicate that it will be a huge challenge to pork eaters, especially the Chinese, to remove pork from their diet.

INCIDENTS CONCERNING DEATH

A friend's death startled me. She was Madam Kheng, wife of an ex-colleague, who suffered from breast cancer. The disease later spread to her lungs and bones. I brought this to the attention of Bhai Sahib, with the hope that he would plead with The Infinite to favour Madam Kheng with a recovery. To my utter surprise, Bhai Sahib calmly answered in a serious tone: "You know, I received she will be in the angelic realm."

"C'mon, Bhai Sahib," I said. "Can we do something now to save her life instead of knowing where she would be in the hereafter?"

Bhai Sahib remained silent, despite my appeals. I understood the silence would be broken on another day. For many months, prayer after prayer was repeated in the hope that Madam Kheng would be healed. Her husband, Vincent, resorted to the use of oxygen gas and oxygenated drinking water as part of the treatment.

One day, Bhai Sahib showed me several sheets of paper written by Madam Kheng listing the foods that she had been consuming. I took a casual glance at the papers, as in those days I was still indifferent to the importance of food intake. Every item of the foods listed by Madam Kheng Bhai Sahib had marked either, OK, Neutral or Bad.

"Look, this is a recipe for cancer!" Bhai Sahib uttered. A great amount of food consumed by Madam Kheng was discerned as bad.

Many months later, Madam Kheng passed away. I then understood what Bhai Sahib meant when he confided that Madam Kheng would be in the angelic realm. Madam Kheng had been destined to move on. The prayers spoken prior to her departure appeared to be a preparation for her soul to be in the angelic realm, as foretold by Bhai Sahib. I later learned that Madam Kheng had a twin sister who had died of cancer, too.

Another incident involving a death similarly rattled me. This involved a family. Patrick, the eldest of the siblings and a former colleague, told me that his hospitalised father was dying of prostate cancer. Patrick was uncertain which religious rites he should follow on his father's death.

I shared Patrick's concern with Maam Sahib, then asked Patrick if he and his father were agreeable to the idea of me guiding his father to read Psalm 23 from the Bible: "The Lord Is my shepherd." With their approval, I met Patrick and his father in the hospital. I placed a bowl of holy water under the bed. I then told Patrick's father: "Uncle, it doesn't matter what religion you follow. What is important is that you believe God exists."

I asked him if he was comfortable with that knowledge. Patrick's father nodded approvingly. I then placed his right hand on the Bible I had brought with me. I asked him to recite the verses of Psalm 23. When he had done so, Patrick asked me if he should opt for a Christian or a Buddhist burial for his father. I said a Christian burial would involve the use of the Bible, and there would be mention of God, whereas there is little mention of the Creator in Buddhism. I ended our brief conversation by saying it was his decision.

On my way home, I reflected on what had happened. I thought it strange that this colleague would seek me, of all people, to perform that task for his dying father. I had assumed it should be done by a priest. I was not even a Christian, let alone a follower of any organised religion. I was just a VCM practitioner.

I told Maam Sahib what Patrick had asked me regarding the choice of a Christian or a Buddhist burial. Maam Sahib, who seemed to be listening even though she was busy preparing dinner, spontaneously stated: "He will embrace Christianity!" I did not share with Patrick what Maam Sahib had said, as I was interested to see if the outcome would be as foretold. Before long, Patrick was telling me of unusual happenings, in which Christians had unexpectedly turned up at his house to offer their prayers and support for his dying father. Patrick's father embraced Christianity just before he passed away.

The second death in the same family involved Patrick's mother, who died of colon cancer. About the time of her death, Patrick began to practise VCM. One day, in the middle of a group meditation, an utterance arrived: "Cold, son, cold." The soul of Patrick's departed mother was groaning that she was trapped in a cold and unfavourable realm. Consequently, a jaap was held at Patrick's residence, which was directed to his mother's soul, for her elevation. Just before the jaap began I experienced chilling coldness, as did several other VCM practitioners. The sensation became uncomfortably intense. It was unlikely to be due to the weather, as I saw other participants appeared comfortable. Then, the moment the jaap began, I immediately experienced a sudden change of body temperature, from chilling cold to an agreeable warmth. I realised I had experienced the chilling coldness of the realm that the mother's soul was trapped in, and that she had escaped.

A message later came through from a Divine source. It was directed to Patrick's mother, but it was also meant for the living: "You must forgive those who have sinned against you. You must be pure. You eat unhealthy food. Next time do not eat unhealthy food. I cannot help you if your body is already rotting. Your children must not follow you. You must be wise."

The message clearly stated that one must be able to forgive and forget all hate and hurt feelings in order to rise to higher realms, and to eventually merge with the Creator. In the case of Patrick's mother's soul, it appears she will have to undergo further reincarnations. Hence, the advice not to eat any unhealthy food in the future. In a subsequent group meditation, a message from a Divine source reminded Patrick: "Eat wisely, Patrick, and your ills will ease and you will be well."

These experiential learning situations revealed to me that diseases typically viewed as heredity could also be due to family members consuming the same unhealthy foods.

ON WARNING DREAMS

So important is the need to consume healthy food that warnings appear in our dreams. In dream analysis, such dreams are categorised as warning dreams related to diet, exercise, assimilation and elimination.

A Punjabi lady who practises VCM had a dream after attending a basic course. She dreamed of a holy man with a long white beard. There was also a snake, white in colour, which slithered towards her and bit her. During a follow-up group meditation, it was revealed that the holy man symbolised that the lady had been exposed to true spiritual practice. The white snake symbolised one or more of the five killer whites: white rice, white refined salt, white refined flour, white refined sugar and white milk. Bhai Sahib repeatedly reminded us to reduce our intake of these highly processed foods. The dream revealed that this lady has been consuming too much white sugar and refined salt. It was intended to warn her that her health would be affected if she did not reduce her intake of them.

In another incident, I visited a Punjabi VCM practitioner in his house. He was then in his forties. He held a test tube, checking his sugar level. He later confided to me that several years before he had been confirmed as a diabetic, and that Bhai Sahib had reminded him not to consume white sugar. This advice had clearly gone unheeded. Like me, he had to bear the consequences of unhealthy eating.

Bhai Sahib once shared briefly with me about allergies. He raised the example of an Australian VCM practitioner who was discerned to be allergic to soy bean. Bhai Sahib confided that through his discernment he found that this practitioner was the only one among the Australians who was not into recreational drugs. I later cross-checked this information with the practitioner. He answered in the affirmative. I have observed myself that it is not uncommon for most people, especially the young, to be unaware of eating unhealthily. It is to be hoped that this will change as more people start realising the importance of right eating.

ON ANGER MANAGEMENT

Let me begin this topic with another confession. As I described earlier, I have had a bad temper since I was a child. Anger has affected many areas of my life, including my career, my relationships, and my health. Anger is one of the five vices mentioned in the Sri Guru Granth Sahib as affecting an individual's overall well-being.

One of the earliest lessons I received after I took up VCM meditation was regarding my bad temper. VCM made me realise I was trapped in a web of anger, and that it was an impediment to my personal growth. My anger showed up in my dreams. This temperament is often symbolised by a tiger or a lion. Once, I dreamed I was driving a car. The door on the driver's side tore off completely, and the car temperature touched boiling point. I was awakened by this dream.

In dream interpretation, the car is a symbol of one's body. The high temperature shows that anger is again about to rise in me, to the extent it would affect my health, as shown by the broken car door. I became increasingly aware of my temper over the years. On reflection, a number of incidents indicated my lack of growth in this area.

I had numerous confrontations with the proprietor of the company where I worked until my retirement. After learning of his desire to sack me, I took the challenge head-on. I thought that in the course of my work I only needed to offer truthful analysis, then deal with the challenges I provoked. In reality, it did not work out this way, because adopting this course of action demanded human skills that I lacked. At times, my anger reached such a boiling point that my animal instincts almost took over.

While this issue was ongoing, a Divine message arrived for me: "What is truth without wisdom? It is nothing!" A year later, the owner's son took over the management of the company. In the midst of the Malaysian currency crisis, Maam Sahib received a message intended for me: "I am come that you shall know Me and My advice to you, Athan. Watch your temper. Be patient. Be at ease. Heed Me."

I thought over the message, but did not understand why it had come through. Several days later, the owner's son had a late-night meeting with me at the office. He was very concerned with the challenges the company was facing as a result of the currency crisis. In the middle of the discussion, I lost my temper with him. I do not recall the reason why, but I do remember that I pointed a finger at him and shouted: "Don't you talk to me like that!" Just at that moment, I remembered the Divine message. I had been forewarned, but I appreciated what it meant too late. It was only due to His benevolence that I was not thrown out of my job.

This awareness of guidance from Providence had a telling effect on me when my friends and I were playing badminton. I once lost my temper with a fellow player over a line call. The game was immediately abandoned. All the players left the court. They were seated at one end of the hall, while I was seated at the other end, alone. The next instant, I received a silent message: "Athan, you are wrong. Go and apologise."

For a moment, I looked around wondering which direction the message had come from. While I stayed seated, the message came through again: "Athan, you are wrong. Go and apologise." When I didn't respond, the message came through for the third time, "Athan, you are wrong. Go and apologise!" I then realised that the message had come from inside me. Perhaps, it was from a higher consciousness within.

I then walked gingerly towards my fellow player and apologised to him in front of the other players. This was followed with a handshake. That handshake settled the situation amicably.

Yet another incident of anger, and my awareness of it, came during a road accident. A truck had grazed my car. I shouted angrily at the top of my voice, demanding the driver step out of his truck. I wanted to hit him. The next instant, a silent message arrived within: "Athan, you are a heart patient, you know!" Instantly, I became totally calm. I quietly drove off without asking for any compensation from the driver.

My growing awareness of the extent of my anger did not stop me reacting in another road rage incident. I was involved in a fight with a pedestrian who was not even half my age. He charged and attacked me with his helmet. I was calm and retreated as he kept swinging his helmet at me. Without thinking, I stepped forward and connected two punches to his nose and teeth. He fell flat onto the road, his nose bleeding. For the next several days I bragged to several of my fellow practitioners about how I was able to floor a guy half my age during a road rage incident. Following that incident, Maam Sahib received a message during a group meditation session: "Kill self now before self kills you!" I understood I had to tame my ego-self, otherwise it would bring me harm.

There were many situations when I repeatedly lost my temper with people I thought were acting defiantly. Of course, losing my temper was a weakness, about which I continued to receive advice: "Athan, when the sea is rough, you must remain calm, or else you will be consumed by anger. There is nothing to be angry about. It is that person's attitude and manner that need to be corrected. You must teach them. If they do not listen, then so be it. You have tried. Leave the rest to Me."

Another message was subsequently addressed to me: "You must learn to control your temper. It is not doing you any good. You must do more for others. Remember to control your reactions to people when you talk with them. It is vital. You have a good heart, but your reactions, your sudden outbursts, must be controlled. Be careful of your ego. Your character must change."

During another meditation session, I received a further message through Maam Sahib: "You must have trust in Me. When you have total trust in Me, that is when no words can affect you or your behaviour. Whatever word is put to you, whether against Me, against My work, about whatever, do not let it affect your mood. You must be gentle, humble and calm, like Bhai Sahib. I have told you to be like Bhai Sahib. It is simple, but is not so easy to follow. Simplicity is a hardship for human beings. Yea, through the ages it has been so. I have spoken."

Yet another message for me received through Maam Sahib stated: "We are very concerned about your behaviour. You are contradicting the teachings of Bhai Sahib. You cannot behave in contradiction to what Bhai Sahib has taught you, for what he has taught you is sent and commissioned by God. You must be like God. How can people look up to you if you are contradicting God's teachings? It is imperative you believe in divinity and holiness. You must control your temper. Has God not told you that even in sadness you must show happiness? Even in joy you must share with others? Even in hate you must love? For God is in all His creation.

"Do you not remember the last affirmation? God in His mysterious way dwells in every part and particle of His creation. How can you criticise His creation when He lives in all? You must learn this. You do not have much time. We are all very concerned what you do with VCM. VCM must live. VCM is God's teaching. You must understand this. VCM Is God's teaching. You must believe, even if you do not know there is a Creator above you. You must believe in VCM. It is the proper and true way of prayer. Give God, give Bhai Sahib, a good name. Be as mild as Bhai Sahib, for no benefit comes from temper or aggression. We have spoken. We rest. That is all we are allowed to reveal to you."

ON BEING CARING

Other received messages focused on wisdom and our need to adopt a caring attitude: "Intelligence is one attribute that human beings look up to. But wisdom is more practical. Wisdom will bring you benefits. Therefore, I come to you to tell you that you must all support each other, you must all listen to each other with open mind and heart. Use wisdom. Use C.A.T. (Compromise, Adjust, Tolerate). BabuJi does not think you practise C.A.T. well enough. It has been advised from the beginning of human existence. But it has never been fully used by all, only by a few."

"You acquire wisdom through the inner voice when I speak to you. You have your lessons in life to learn. You learn it bitterly, My children. It is My Will that you will prevail. You are My chosen ones. Who can others turn to for salvation if not to you? You must persevere to save My children. Always remember, I am with you, guiding you, protecting you. Always remember to help My children. You will not be given a task that you cannot take on. You are always guided by Me. My children, do not waste your time on unnecessary things. Acquire wisdom. Listen to Me. Listen to your inner voice. Have I not provided for you all this time? My love is always for you. You must acquire wisdom. Listen to your inner voice. Prevail."

"To be humble means to lower yourself in speech, thought and action in each moment of your life, just like Bhai Sahib. It is very difficult for human beings to be humble. That is why C.A.T. is so hard to practice. Treat everyone as you would like to be treated. So be it. I have spoken."

ON SERVICE TO OTHERS

"Charity is considered to involve tithing. Giving one-tenth of one's income. But charity is also about service. Service in the form of spiritual help. The acts of providing service must permeate every thought, word and deed. When a man helps or does a good deed, that man is helping God. That man will receive help equivalent in weight to the help he has given, and the good deeds that he has done, equivalent to his sincerity, equivalent to the act being unconditional."

"Some have eyes but do not see and cannot even see pass the end of their nose. Yea, I tell you that if you do charity that is not God-approved, it is not counted. When you do charity, you must do it sincerely with whatever you have, without touching another person's property. Think well on what I have said. Charity must be unconditional. Make others happy and happiness will come back to you. The law is very simple. But do it with wisdom."

"You do not listen to My messages. You do not do enough charity. Open your eyes. So many are crying for help. Charity begins at home. It means that you have to be of service to My children. Kind words, kind actions. If you do not have the time, then substitute with material service. How many kind words have you given to My children?"

"Practise charity. Give more to the needy. Be more sincere. Be kinder and more merciful to the poor and the needy. A time will come when you will be in their shoes. Who will help you? You need to balance your karma. This is My advice. Be more charitable to the poor, the unfortunate. It is important."

Once, just before the commencement of a group meditation, the following sermon was spoken in an effortless and spontaneous manner by Maam Sahib: "We have been told that we must give charity unconditionally. We have been told that charity does not mean giving money. We also have to give in service. And we have to be kind to one another. In being kind to one another, we speak well to each other. We comfort each other when it is needed. We also comfort our friends in our working place, at home, or whenever we meet them. We comfort strangers, anyone we come into contact with. Little do we know these people are actually sent by God.

And in serving unconditionally, we are polishing ourselves, our souls, to remove all our bad karma so we can 'go home.' Of course, we can choose not to do this, and so take a longer road 'home' by being reborn again and again, and relearning the same lessons over and over. But since we are all in VCM, we are very lucky. We have been given the opportunity to cleanse ourselves, and invaluable advice on how to do it. Therefore, we should accept the advice, and apply it. We are most blessed. That is why God said do not always question what happens to you in your life. You would not understand, even if He was to explain to you. Your mind would not be able to absorb the explanation. It would not sound logical to you. Therefore, we are all continually learning. Let us now stand up and take our place to carry out our meditation."

Subsequently, in another group meditation, a message on charity was received from the Almighty:

- ∞ Giving without feeling loss is charity.
- ∞ Giving without giving your name is charity.
- ∞ Giving with love is charity.
- ∞ Giving with happiness is charity.

I sometimes went to extremes to help others, especially with prayers. In relation to this, the following message was received: "When one does charity, one must not put oneself into trouble. Charity means what you can afford to do." I understood there is a limit to what you can do to help others. No extreme effort is required. Just do what you are able to, at that time. But whatever is done to help others has to be carried out with sincerity.

ON ACCEPTING HARDSHIPS

On occasions, messages were received about accepting life's hardships.

"Life should be simple, not difficult. But you all make it so difficult. For millions and millions of years, you have done this. Do not reject My teachings. Do not reject hardship. Lessons can only be learned through hardship. Go into alpha mode and you will know whether or not the teachings are correct. When I say be kind, be merciful, you only do so towards some. You must do so towards all."

"You are all old spirits. It is time for you all to come home. I want to share wonders with you. Come home to Me. Wash your karma. Service, service. How many reincarnations do you expect to go through? Come home. I will keep you informed. Meanwhile, listen! I speak through all My creation. You must listen. Do not close your mind. You ask Me for guidance, therefore I give you guidance. Do not alter what I give you. It will not work your way. If it would work your way, it would have worked years ago, my children, years ago! Enough. So be it."

"Excel in everything that you do. Treat it as spiritual training. Mundane life is nothing. Spirituality is everything. Life belongs to God. You must be like God. You have been told to be like Bhai Sahib. Remember how he is, how he responds, how he talks, how he reacts to situations. Be like Bhai Sahib. Verily, you have much to learn."

"Blessed are those obedient ones. Those who have great love in their hearts. For God watches over you. He knows everything and He gives you only the best, even though you do not feel it so. God will not give you 'abundance' and make you lose your spirituality. Therefore, you must show that you deserve it."

"The gifts God gives you, use them, practise! The guidance God gives you, follow! The lessons that Bhai Sahib has taught you, follow! Give God, give Bhai Sahib, a good name. Be as mild as Bhai Sahib."

ON MONEY

The message received regarding money and Earth-bound happiness is a clarion call.

"What we have learned through the ages is that money is the problem. Money is always the reason people fall. That is why we are tired of money issues. Widespread corruption is always due to money. Earth-bound happiness, so-called ... mmm ... Earth-bound comforts. When you die, all these become the weight of your sins. And they will pull you into hell. Do you understand?

"Yet people take this advice so lightly. It is best to leave your children, your brothers and sisters, your parents (if you leave early) with love. Leave them love and happiness. Leave them with good memories. That is good for you. Then your karma will be lightened. You will be blessed with a higher realm when you pass on. Teach your children this. You must change the future generation. Lead them back onto God's path. That is your duty as parents. If you fail, woe be to you. That will be a weight on you.

"Do you understand? We do not usually like to mention this. Try your very best. God understands your capacity. We take our leave. Bhai Sahib wants you to know that you are all better off if you eat well. Be more particular about what you eat. Otherwise, when you grow as old as him, your health will be affected. So be it."

Chapter Ten

ACCEPTING THE UNEXPECTED

ONE DAY, AFTER A LONG BREATHER FROM the successful completion of my MBA, I casually asked Bhai Sahib if my destiny or karma included having a son. Bhai Sahib responded in the affirmative. However, I was so little excited by his response that I soon forgot all about it. This was because I was already aged forty-six, while Maam Sahib was forty-two. I also had to be practical. Maam Sahib and I already had four daughters, with our fourth, S.Y., needing unflagging support.

Not long after that, Maam Sahib received a message via a dream: "My son, a singh is coming to stay with you." To Punjabis, *singh* refers to a male, whereas *kaur* refers to a female. It was obvious that this projected fifth child would be a boy. It was also likely an indication that the boy had been a Punjabi in his previous life.

Maam Sahib decided to seek the Almighty's advice. During a group meditation, to the question of whether He wanted us to have a son, the answer was affirmative. Maam Sahib later told me that even before she could pose her next question, she received a reassuring message: "Do not worry. He can manage."

We were naturally concerned about raising a fifth child. Maam Sahib was no longer young; another child was a risk. Furthermore, as I had only nine more years of employment before retirement, I was uncertain whether my savings would be sufficient to support a fifth child. Maam Sahib told me she had positively accepted The Infinite's answer, but she was hoping she would not have to suffer the severe pains caused by her varicose veins, which she had endured during her four previous pregnancies. The soundness of our decision to try for a fifth child was further verified by Bhai

Sahib and was confirmed by a series of supportive messages. During a meditation session at home, Maam Sahib, her eyes closed and both hands outstretched, experienced spiralling vibrations. They were followed by a spontaneous utterance: "When a child is born." I didn't understand then what this statement meant.

On another occasion, as Maam Sahib and I were driving to our usual group meditation, she saw a vision of Jesus Christ against a backdrop of brilliant purplish light. It was followed by a message: "Woman, receive the child of the Holy Spirit." Maam Sahib also said she felt a sensation of the child's soul entering the womb. This took place when Maam Sahib was at the end of the third month, beginning her fourth month of pregnancy.

Earlier, the subject of abortion had crossed my mind. I vaguely understood that the Catholic Church opposes abortion, on the grounds it destroys human life. From the experience disclosed by Maam Sahib, I surmised that a foetus could not be considered willfully aborted or killed if the soul had not yet entered the womb.

Maam Sahib further told me that during another group meditation the baby in her womb spoke, saying: "I am Joshua, alias Hu." This message was conveyed to Bhai Sahib, who confirmed that his name would be Joshua, but that in his future working life his colleagues and friends would sometimes call him by his Chinese name, Hu.

I recall a tense moment when Maam Sahib went for one of her early checkups. The doctor suggested that a special test be carried out to determine if the child would be born normal. Presumably, he was concerned, because Maam Sahib was in her forties. The traumatic event that occurred during the birth of our fourth child was another factor. When we subsequently sought Bhai Sahib's advice on whether to opt for the costly test, he gently said: "No need to carry out the test. God gives." We decided my wife would not undertake the recommended test.

On 28 April 2000, Joshua was born. Bhai Sahib suggested we hold a thanksgiving jaap to thank God for blessing my wife and I with a son. Held in my house, the jaap lasted twelve hours. Towards evening, Bhai Sahib took his place behind the holy Sri Guru Granth Sahib to perform the closing invocation, which he chanted in Gurmukhi. I, of course, could not understand what he was chanting. All of a sudden, he pointed a finger in my direction and stated: "He will be a guru!" Bhai Sahib later confirmed it was Joshua who would be a guru.

At the time of writing, Joshua has turned twenty. He is mildly autistic. He does not have any friends. When he was in secondary school, he was often bullied, and was also misunderstood by the school authorities. On one occasion, he was the only student still in class after a final examination. He spent his time cleaning the classroom, clearing the debris left behind by his classmates. A teacher who happened to pass by saw what was happening and quietly videoed what Joshua was doing. The principal saw the video, was impressed, and awarded Joshua a certificate of commendation.

The Divine messages we received assured us Joshua will be unlike other children. We were advised to provide Joshua with extra mental exercises to nourish his curiosity. The Infinite also told us he would be a great teacher one day. I suppose Joshua will be a spiritual teacher.

When Joshua was young, I felt it would be good for him to be circumcised. I thought scriptures advised that circumcision is mandatory. Friends recommended clinics managed by Malay Muslim doctors, but when I sought them out they were closed for holidays. Meanwhile, I informed Bhai Sahib that I intended to book Joshua for circumcision. Bhai Sahib told me I should not do so. I reasoned with him that it was hygienic, and that the practice is advocated in the Muslim and Jewish scriptures. Bhai Sahib very gently responded that the foreskin serves a purpose, and that believers have misinterpreted the scriptures. I realised then that the practice of circumcision and genital mutilation are not correct.

In an unrelated incident, one Christmas Day Joshua and I were lying on the floor watching a Christmas program. He was then about ten years old. A few coins rolled out from his trouser pocket. I collected the coins and put them back into his pocket. A while later, the coins again rolled out. I remarked: "Son, can you take care of your money?" He responded: "Money has no life, but it can be used." His eyes glued to the screen, he seemed oblivious to what he had said.

I realised it was a message from the Almighty, spoken through Joshua. Not long after, during a seminar, a message from a Divine source stated the following: "Your future generations, what will you leave them? Money? Money is filth if it is considered a luxury. Money is a necessity. Keep it as that. Do not revere money over God. We have seen so many human beings fall because of money and lose their spirituality. We are indeed tired of money. You do not see what We have seen, My son. The danger of money, how many people fall from grace because of it. Such a waste!

"Do you know what 'falling from grace' means? Once you drink of the cup of spirituality, there is no turning back. If you do not do what We tell you, you will indeed fall from grace. Woe be to your soul. You will be reborn over and over again. And your spirituality will start from the lowest. Do not fail God. Have no fear when you listen to what we say. Just know how serious this matter is."

On that Christmas Day Joshua had already alerted me to this issue, even before the great masters conveyed their message regarding the disquieting effect of money. In very simple terms, Joshua said there is no spirituality in materialistic effects. And I have been pursuing money and money-making for almost all my life!

Chapter Eleven

ON SPIRITUAL GROWTH

ON NUMEROUS OCCASIONS MAAM SAHIB received messages from a Divine source regarding our spiritual growth.

"You will all soon grow very fast spiritually. All of you possess a gift, yet you do not know what it is. It is forbidden for us to reveal. It is for you to discover. Do not look on God's gift as something which is to be kept, to be put aside, to belittle. God's gifts are more precious than any worldly goods. When you die, you return, but you cannot take worldly goods with you."

"Nobody is perfect. No human is perfect. Not one of you. Even Maam Sahib is not perfect. You are all human. Do not criticise people. You are no better. Always look at the goodness within everyone. All are God's creation. Be aware of their negativities, but always look at the goodness in people."

"What is going to happen will come to pass as God wills it. You must work at achieving what you want. You must obey the law. You must care and love. Show your love. Give advice to those you love when they are still alive. After they are gone, it is no use tearing your hair or clothes. You can cry, cry, cry, but they will not hear you. Only when they are alive will they hear you and appreciate what you do for them."

"Live like your life consists of only one day. What would you do if your life had only one day? Live every day like that. Be fruitful. Be productive. Be useful within the context of that day, the procedures of that day."

"Do not forget Me. Do not forget to chant. Do not forget to meditate. Do not overdo things. Such is your life as a human being. Beware of calamities to come."

"Pray for My children who pass on. Do not forget to perform another jaap for your ancestors before the end of the year. Do not forget to read My messages. There are still lessons to learn. I have provided clues. Read them. You will learn much from My messages. For today, you are much blessed. You will receive increased awareness. But your lessons will continue. For seniors, your lessons will be even more difficult. Do not fail to pray for strength and protection. So be it. I have spoken."

"You must have confidence. You must learn to forgive yourself. You must move ahead in life. There are many challenges coming, greater than what you have faced. As you progress through life, the challenges increase. You must meet all challenges. Face them bravely. Overcome and improve. Do not be ashamed of failure. Failure is a recognition of weakness, and the readiness to overcome and improve. Those who recognise weaknesses will improve. Those who admit their weaknesses will improve, must improve. Those who do not recognise their weaknesses and failures, who do not admit that they have failures or weaknesses, will never move ahead in life. They will remain static, causing harm and hurt to loved ones."

"My children, you are My warriors. Your journey is different. You are the chosen few of the chosen. Your duties are different. Do not compare yourself with My other children. They have their own duties, their own tasks to perform, just as you have your tasks and duties. Accept your duties. Perform them well. Do so in My name, with love, compassion and spiritual understanding. Live well in love, peace and happiness."

"My chosen ones must be strong. My chosen ones must have faith. My chosen ones must be tolerant. My chosen ones must have wisdom. My chosen ones must not give in to despair. You are My chosen ones. My chosen ones must prevail!"

"When you have done wrong, you must right the wrong. You must not do more wrongs. Act with love. Love is the most powerful weapon you have. Do everything sincerely."

"If you cannot see Me in My creation, how will you improve spiritually? How will you hear Me when I speak to you? Those who do not believe in Me, and instead fuss over petty things, will not grow. They will only face more spiritual challenges in their lives. They will wander here and there, in search of solutions for their problems, solutions for how to live their lives, thinking life is a sophisticated playground. The simpler your life, the more blessings you receive. The closer you are to Me, the safer you are. Again, I stress: love your children, treat them well, give them the best you can. And watch out for greed!"

"In the past all the prophets went through many difficulties. All those who learn spirituality must go through all you are going through. Your difficulties are very minor compared to theirs. I have spoken."

ON THE STRENGTH OF PRACTITIONERS

The following messages were conveyed to VCM practitioners:

"BabuJi has observed that C.A.T. (Compromise, Adjust, Tolerate) is not easy for human beings to learn. But you *must* learn. Much more is expected of you, who are the chosen ones, than of those who have not come to VCM. What do you think you are here to experience? Why do you think your life will not be as simple as for those others? That is why we have told you you are here to undertake stringent training, difficult tests. Practice! You don't listen to what you are told. And you forget when you are faced with difficulties like now, when you are faced with situations you say you cannot bear. *Cannot* is not acceptable from a chosen one. You must overcome. You are God's warriors. If you cannot even pass this little test, what about the greater tests still to come?"

"Live in peace, harmony and love and all will be well with you. Let others be. Leave everyone else to their own working, to be guided by God. Do not interfere where you are not allowed. So be it. We have spoken."

At other times, we received messages from the Almighty:

"My warriors must be brave. My warriors must be strong. My warriors must have patience. My warriors must prevail in all circumstances. Blessed are those who act in My name."

"You must learn love. To love is the greatest power on Earth and in Heaven. To love means to love unconditionally, to aid others unconditionally. I have spoken."

ON BLESSINGS

- ∞ Blessed are those who humble themselves before Me.
- ∞ Blessed are those who do My bidding without question.

- ∞ Blessed are those who know Me as their only Creator.
- ∞ Blessed are those who act in My name.
- ∞ Blessed are those who suffer in My name.
- ∞ Blessed are all children, for they are innocent.
- ∞ Blessed are those who seek salvation.
- ∞ Blessed are those who answer My chosen ones' call. (To be a chosen one is not for everybody.)
- ∞ Blessed are those who accept the life I have given them in this world. Even though others look down on them, they remember Me, they remain obedient.
- ∞ Blessed are they, for theirs will be the Kingdom of Heaven.
- ∞ Blessed are those who serve My children, who go through hardship to serve others. Yea, the Kingdom of Heaven will be yours too.
- ∞ Blessed are those who know one another, who know you are all My children, and you are all brothers and sisters. Blessed are you.
- ∞ Blessed are those who know My prophets and accept them.
- ∞ Blessed are those who know My scriptures. They are all Mine.

ON SPONTANEITY

Not long after beginning VCM practice, I was prompted to recall several true-life stories I had read during my younger days. There were no plausible explanations regarding what had actuated their positive outcomes, which were simply miraculous. As a result, I must have subconsciously mulled over these stories for many years.

VCM made me realise at least one similar but critical trait was present in the events described in each story. This realisation became even more acute when I was prompted to recall my own personal life-saving experience, when I helped save a colleague from drowning. I realised the trait present in all the real-life dramas I recalled was also present in my own life-saving experience. That trait is spontaneity.

Spontaneity refers to an act that is done naturally, without being forced or practised. I realised that spontaneous expression is a manifestation of the Divine. The following true-life stories have remained etched in my mind since my younger days. Information regarding where and how these events found their way into texts the world over is uncertain, but the life-saving drama at the core of each is remarkable. Such is the dramatic effect of these events that I consider they are worth reflecting over here.

∞ The first story took place in North America. A man fell off his bicycle while cycling in the woods, then was attacked by a bear that appeared from nowhere. He did all he could to fight off the bear. When he knew he was fighting a losing battle, and with the thought of death hanging over him, he spontaneously said aloud: "God! I don't want to die today!" What happened next was that the bear walked away and vanished back into the forest. The man was alive, amazed by what had just happened. Spontaneously calling out for God had saved his life.

∞ A similar event took place in Malaysia. This happened in 2004, in a place named Jeli, in the state of Kelantan. An elderly Malay woman was in the forest tapping rubber when she was attacked from behind by a tiger. In that terrifying moment, she spontaneously shouted: "Allah hu akbar!" (God is great!) The tiger, just like the bear, ceased attacking and went back into the jungle. The woman's spontaneous cry of "Allah hu akbar" saved her.

∞ Cat Stevens, an international artist who needs no introduction, once went for a swim in the sea, despite a signpost warning of the danger of doing so. The waves swept him far out into the open sea. He knew he would not be alive much longer. In that desperate moment, he spontaneously shouted: "God! If you spare me, I will dedicate my whole life to you!" The waves immediately changed direction. Instead of continuing their outward motion into the open sea, the waves reversed and trended towards the shore. The waves eventually brought him to safety. This occurred only after he had spontaneously begged God to spare him and promised he would dedicate his life to God. He was overwhelmed by that life-changing experience. It was reported that his brother was the first person he told about it. His brother later gave him a copy of the Qur'an. It was the first holy book he came into contact with following his phenomenal experience in the open sea. He probably took that as a sign for him to embrace the religion of Islam. He is now known as Yusuf Islam. That was the path he chose. He has shown, in his own way, a high level of commitment to fulfilling the promise he made to God, at least as observed from press reports.

∞ In 2008 or 2009 it was reported that a Malay woman, in her forties, sat on the third floor ledge of a building in a town in the state of Johor, on the southern tip of Peninsular Malaysia. She was about to commit suicide. Press reports stated she was heartbroken due to her husband's betrayal. Fire brigade rescuers arrived, but they could only observe from ground level. It was reported that just as she leapt off the building, she spontaneously shouted, "Allah hu akbar!" She survived the fall. A member of the rescue squad named Kesavan, a Malaysian Indian, managed to catch her with both his bare hands. It was amazing that the woman's weight, when falling from that height and with increasing velocity, did not cause harm to either her or her rescuer. She was saved, and her rescuer was not injured, due to her spontaneously shouting, "Allah hu akbar!"

∞ I vaguely recall an article I read in the *Reader's Digest* magazine many years ago about a private detective in USA. He was investigating a syndicate that targeted elderly people, cheating them of their life-savings. The detective needed a password to gain access to the syndicate's computer in order to gather evidence. Not having the password, the detective thought he had hit a dead end. However, just after he voiced his frustration aloud, a fellow worker, who was in another part of their office, suggested: "Try *hole in one!*" Taking a long shot, the detective keyed in 'hole in one'. Lo and behold, access to the syndicate's computer was obtained! They successfully arrested the criminals, preventing the further loss of life-savings and the ongoing infliction of misery on the victims. I recall that during their investigation the detectives had noted that the mastermind behind the crime was an avid golfer. That probably explains why the detective's colleague spontaneously chose that particular phrase. I wonder what the mathematical chance would be of obtaining the correct password? In this case, it was obtained through a spontaneous suggestion.

∞ Travelling back through history, it is interesting to note that the beautiful song, *Amazing Grace*, was penned by a slave trader, John Newton. It is said that many of his colleagues died on the high seas when a violent storm hit his ship packed with slaves. Overwhelmed, he spontaneously went down on his knees and begged God for mercy, pleading that he would dedicate his future life to God. The violent storm immediately dissipated and was replaced by complete calmness. John Newton supposedly gave up his profession of slave trader and became a church minister.

I end with my personal experience, recounted earlier, when I was made to jump into the estuary of the Kelang River. This was in an attempt to save a younger man who had accidentally fallen into the river from quite a height. As I described in Chapter Six, and will briefly repeat here, I first called out to the victim. He did not respond. While it was quite dark, I could vaguely see his body moving out to sea. The next instant, I experienced an unusual calmness. It was followed by a silent communication within my mind. The silent dialogue went as follows:

"Athan, can you swim?" asked the Voice within.

"Yes, I can," I said.

"Jump and save. There's a life there," said the Voice within.

I then calmly jumped into the river. Although I do know how to swim, I had no life-saving training, and had never attempted to save a drowning victim before. I was also fully clothed, and had difficulty staying afloat in the water. I reached the victim and tried with all my might to pull him to safety, but to no avail. I was fighting a losing battle as the current was too strong for me. By now I was completely drained, and sensed my own life was also in danger. At that moment I spontaneously shouted: "God! This is life, You know! How can You let this happen! Tolong! Tolong!"

The next instant a Malay man jumped into the river and helped bring the victim to safety. Despite being completely exhausted, I wondered why the bystander only responded when I spontaneously shouted out for help.

THE PROMPTING

VCM made me realise that in my personal life-saving experience, along with the just related real-life dramas, there exists a powerful Unseen Force whose imperceptible workings are indeed mighty and miraculous. This realisation has prompted me to draw a number of inferences regarding what the attributes of this powerful Unseen Force are. Specifically:

∞ This powerful Unseen Force is a Divine Force. An aspect of The Infinite is present in every human being, regardless of one's racial origin or one's professed religion. This can be seen from the people who participated in the previously related incidents, including my own, who have different racial and religious backgrounds.

∞ The Almighty is ever present, unchanging and impersonal. His love is unconditional. It swings into action when one calls out to Him for help, as long as one recognises Him as the Creator.

∞ The Infinite is the same yesterday, today and forever. This can be seen in the help rendered John Newton, in the miracle workings recounted during ancient biblical times, back into time immemorial, and into the present time. It shall be so forever.

∞ These incidents exhibit The Infinite's Omnipotent attribute. In each situation He was able to save people, even if called to do so at the penultimate moment. The oft-quoted saying, "With God all things are possible," makes sense. He is therefore most powerful.

∞ The incidents also exhibit The Infinite's Omnipresent attribute. This is revealed in the help that The Infinite rendered in Jeli, Kelantan, Malaysia and North America, and in my case, when I was in the water. He is therefore present everywhere.

∞ The incidents exhibit The Infinite's Omniscient attribute, as indicated by the occasion He inspired the detective with the correct password. He is therefore all-knowing.

∞ The Infinite permeates and pervades His entire creation, as shown by His help being rendered on land, at sea and in the air. The Infinite is, therefore, the Divine Director. Everything responds to His bidding.

Subsequently, I was amazed that my inferences regarding the exalted state of being spontaneous was further corroborated by the Sri Guru Granth Sahib (p. 1157), where it is noted that various benefits may be spontaneously obtained when one practises meditation regularly. Such practices must be profound in nature and be of the VCM type.

Chapter Twelve

ON THE DEPARTED SOULS OF DEAR ONES

IN 1995 MALAYSIA HELD A GENERAL ELECTION. My nephew, Keong, was driving back to his hometown to exercise his right to vote when his car skidded and crashed into the divider. The accident was fatal.

An unusual incident happened just before the fateful accident. I had rarely met with my nephew since moving to the city. Keong was a house painter. One day, I was surprised to see him in my neighbourhood. He said he had a house painting job near where I lived. He later came on his own accord to paint a section of my house. At that time, I was playing a game of mahjong in my neighbour's house. When he had finished, he bade me goodbye. I acknowledged his farewell without even looking at him, as I was engrossed in my game of mahjong. Little did I know I would never see him again.

This was also the start of my lessons regarding what happens when one dies. I learned it is important for a departed soul to cross over to the spirit realms. Otherwise, it will end up in a miserable state, either as a wandering spirit or by being earth-bound. The soul may even end up in terrifying realms.

Keong was able to cross over to the spirit realm through VCM prayers. My eldest daughter has the gift of being able to communicate with Keong. I learned that this too needed the permission of The Infinite. My daughter described to me how Keong's spirit would greet her by flashing his wide smile. His spirit visited my eldest daughter whenever he had a break. This means there is a time for work and time for a break in the realm where he dwelt. During one of Keong's visits, he presented my daughter with a bangle that radiated white lights. Keong told her that if she needed his help she only needed to shake the bangle. Keong would then know she wished to connect with him, and he would turn up in an instant. My daughter also told me that whenever the bangle of lights turned dark, it meant something unfavourable was affecting her.

Many years later, on my way back to Kuala Lumpur from Singapore, I made a stopover to visit my younger brother, Chong. Chong's second daughter was there, too, with her baby boy. It was the first time I had seen the baby, who flashed a wide smile at me. That instant, it struck me that my nephew, Keong, had been reborn as Chong's daughter's son.

Back home in Kuala Lumpur, I decided to test my eldest daughter. I asked her to shake the bangle of lights to call for Keong's spirit. She did as I suggested, but Keong's spirit did not appear. I suggested to her that Keong had probably been reborn as the son of Chong's second daughter. My daughter immediately checked with Bhai Sahib, who confirmed that was the case.

In an unrelated incident, I accompanied Bhai Sahib to an out-of-town gathering. That evening, an elderly man told Bhai Sahib he had dreamed of one of his loved ones, who had been reborn as a human being. Through his power of discernment, Bhai Sahib confirmed the elderly man's dream. Bhai Sahib further revealed the man's loved one was reborn in Egypt, and worked as a tailor.

These incidents signalled the beginning of my learning of the existence of various realms where a departed soul resides, it being subjected to repeated cycles of births and deaths, and how it works its way towards its ultimate salvation.

MY FATHER'S PASSING

In 1997 my father passed away. One evening, as I was driving home with Maam Sahib after an outing, I received a phone call from my brother, Chong. He had captured live via hand phone our father's dying moments. I informed Bhai Sahib of my father's death and that I was about to go with my family on a long trip for the funeral. He advised me to take a copy of the Sri Guru Granth Sahib (SGGS). Bhai Sahib also advised that Maam Sahib and I, on arriving that evening, should chant the Mool Mantra continuously for three hours in front of the SGGS. We should then repeat the three-hour prayer the next morning.

At the end of the prayer that evening, Maam Sahib had a vision of the Chinese earth deity, Tuti Gong. The deity was wearing black head gear and a traditional Chinese costume, blue in colour. The deity walked arrogantly towards us, as if wanting to know who had encroached into his territory. The Tuti Gong then walked towards the SGGS. What happened next was that the Tuti Gong was flung backwards by white light that radiated magnificently from the SGGS. Just before the three-hour prayer came to an end, a majestic being appeared in vision. The being wore a traditional Chinese costume and was glowing with shimmering white lights. The being smiled, then disappeared into the background. I later realised it was a manifestation of prophet Lao Tzu.

The next morning, at the end of the second three-hour prayer, Tuti Gong again appeared. This time, however, Tuti Gong was humble, quietly observing the prayers in progress.

Two weeks later, I visited my mother. My two younger brothers were also present. They were arguing over inheritance. Maam Sahib, who was washing dishes after dinner, caught sight of the Tuti Gong out of the corner of her eye. Tuti Gong was carrying a piece of luggage. He communicated that he wanted to leave, as there was no love in that house. Maam Sahib told Tuti Gong that approval from God was required before he could leave. Maam Sahib then asked me to go to the car and bring the SGGS, which we had brought with us. Maam Sahib later confided to me that The Infinite had said the Tuti Gong had been praying very hard for salvation. We then performed a meditation to seek Divine approval. Maam Sahib told me that at the end of the prayer the costume of Tuti Gong changed from blue to white. It signified that the Tuti Gong's earnest prayer had earned him elevation. As he waved goodbye to Maam Sahib, he expressed his gratitude for the prayers performed on his behalf.

A month or so later, Bhai Sahib called me over the phone. "Athan, I received that your late father is not in a good realm."

"Just leave him there," I replied.

"He is your father, you know!" Bhai Sahib exclaimed.

In those days I still did not like my father. On Bhai Sahib's advice, I agreed to carry out a meditation with Bhai Sahib, three times on different days, dedicated and directed towards my father. The purpose was to elevate his departed soul to a better realm.

The chart Bhai Sahib used to discern the whereabouts of my father's departed soul is titled, *Condition / Location of the Spirit / Soul*. The chart broadly shows the various realms, and where a departed soul could dwell after death. On the extreme left of the chart is written, IN TOTAL HELL, while on the extreme right is MERGED WITH GOD."

Not long after that I dreamed of my late father. He was very happy, smiling while standing behind the counter in his Chinese herbal shop. The furniture and fixtures in the shop were refurbished and upgraded. I learned from this dream that my father's soul had been elevated to a better realm. I followed up my dream with Bhai Sahib, who confirmed this was so. I then asked, "Is that all?" Bhai Sahib replied, "You expect your father to be in heaven?" I realised that my late father would eventually be reborn as a human being, continuing his lessons in life until he earned ultimate salvation.

MY MOTHER'S PASSING

In 2003, six years after the death of my father, my mother passed away. Prior to her death, my mother was bedridden for more than a year. She also suffered from bedsores. I drove the long distance to visit my mother once every fortnight. She always remained quiet, as her memory was fading.

During each visit I coached my mother to keep uttering repeatedly: "God loves me. I love God." Both my older sisters, who are Singaporeans, regularly travelled by train to visit her. On one occasion I learned from my brother that my sisters had just visited. I tested my mother, asking if she knew my sisters had been with her earlier. She answered, "No." I realised her memory was indeed fading fast. However, and to my great surprise, she then uttered: "God loves me. I love God."

One day, Bhai Sahib advised me to meditate online with him to plead with God to let my mother pass on. Not long after that, my brother informed me that my mother's bedsores had healed. Just when I thought my mother might recover, I received a phone call that she had passed away.

My eldest daughter later confided that my mother's departed soul had visited her on the evening of her death. She told my daughter: "What your father told me is right." I had shared VCM, and other spiritual matters, with my mother, which she had then not accepted. She only realised the spiritual truth of what I had shared with her when she became a spirit.

That same evening, the souls of my father and nephew also appeared to my eldest daughter. My daughter told me they were happy. I learned that all that had occurred had the blessing of The Infinite.

I later organised a jaap dedicated to my mother's soul. Towards the end of the jaap, Maam Sahib told me her soul seemed to be heading to a distant place, as she could only hear her utter: "Poh chun." My wife asked me what it meant. I replied that in the Cantonese dialect it means, "Take care." I know that with all the blessings, my mother is in a safe place.

MY ELDEST BROTHER'S PASSING

My oldest brother passed away in 2010, at the age of sixty-nine. He was the father of my nephew who had died in a road accident. During a group meditation in my home, I uttered a silent invocation dedicated to my departed brother's soul. The next moment, his soul spoke to Maam Sahib. He asked her to chant the Mool Mantra twenty thousand times. This was followed by, "No! you must chant it yourself. An angel will come and inform Me. Even when you were a human—"

From these utterances, I understood that my brother's soul had asked to be elevated to the realm where his son (my nephew) was. Evidently, he had been asked to chant the Mool Mantra twenty thousand times so that he could then be elevated to that realm. But he had instead asked my wife to chant the mantra on his behalf. This explained the utterance, "No! you must chant it yourself."

My brother must also have asked how, after he had chanted the Mool Mantra, he would know he would be elevated to his son's realm. Thus, the response, "An angel will come and inform Me." At the time of writing, my departed brother's soul had still not chanted the Mool Mantra the required twenty thousand times. Meanwhile, his son had already been reborn, as reported earlier.

As for the incomplete utterance, "Even when you were a human—", only I among all the practitioners who took part in the meditation could understand what it meant. When my brother was in human form, he never believed in God. This seemed to be the same even as a spirit. I firmly believe that his experience in the new realm would raise the level of his consciousness.

MY YOUNGEST BROTHER'S PASSING

In 2014 my youngest brother, Tong, passed away. He died of liver cancer and related ailments. For several years he had suffered severe pains. They must have been unbearable, because he threatened to commit suicide when he was hospitalised. Doctors had to move him to a ward at ground level to prevent him from doing so. He took his last breath there. Although he had a notorious life, my brother displayed compassion towards his siblings and friends.

As usual, I carried out a group meditation dedicated to his departed soul. He spoke through Maam Sahib, uttering, "No, not for you!"

I deduced that my youngest brother's soul was willing to chant the Mool Mantra twenty thousand times. However, for some inexplicable reason he was not entitled to the possibility which had been offered to the soul of my eldest brother. Most probably, the acts one commits as a human being determine the realm one ends up in on death.

THE PASSING OF MY BROTHER-IN-LAW AND HIS SON

Tony, who was my second eldest sister's husband, had passed on earlier, having succumbed to cancer. I always admired this brother-in-law, for he was a loving and devoted family man. Yet, despite all his good deeds, Bhai Sahib told me (as received through my eldest daughter) that Tony had only fulfilled fifty percent of his karma. This meant he would have to be reborn as a human being to realise salvation.

Several years later Tony's son, Leong, passed away at the age of thirty-seven. He had been handicapped since birth. Again, through a receiving via my eldest daughter, we were informed that Leong was not able to join his father, who was in a higher realm. However, Leong was still happy with the realm where he was located. That realm is higher than that of my younger brother, Tong. All these realms are within heavenly territory.

Leong then asked Bhai Sahib if his mother (my second eldest sister), would be able to join them when her time was up. Bhai Sahib's answer was a definite, 'No!' Leong then asked what could be done to help his mother cross over when her time was up. Bhai Sahib replied, "Your mother must do more charity." Presently, she is trying her best to carry out this duty.

THE TRAGIC DEATH OF MAAM SAHIB'S NEPHEW

Hong, son of Maam Sahib's cousin, died in an accident. He was struck by a bus. On receiving the sad news, Maam Sahib went into meditation. As I was present, I heard the following:

"Takut! Takut!" (A Malay word that means scared). I understood this was uttered by the spirit of Hong.

Maam Sahib responded: "Jangan takut, ikut lampu!" (In Malay this means, "Don't be afraid, follow the light.")

This communication with Hong revealed he was very scared of the situation he was in. Maam Sahib was able to calm him sufficiently to persuade him to accept his fate. She instructed him to follow the light, which would take him to the spirit realm.

DISTRESSED CALLS FROM A DEPARTED SOUL

Not only did my departed parents and siblings contact us, but other recently departed relatives also made attempts to communicate with us.

On one occasion, my wife, son and I were visiting my sister-in-law and her family. Standing just outside the main entrance were my sister-in-law and her exuberant flock of grandchildren, jovially exchanging New Year greetings. It was the second day of the Chinese Lunar Year. Suddenly, I heard a distressed call from Ping, the youngest child of my eldest brother: "Fifth Uncle! Fifth Uncle!" She called out these words anxiously as she ran towards me. She had been in the kitchen at the back of their house, preparing lunch, when she heard her family members announcing my arrival. Ping barged through the flock to stand right in front of me. She wore a gravely anxious look as she unashamedly described her seemingly traumatic recurring dreams.

Ping had been widowed in her early thirties. Her late husband drowned during an excursion at Desaru Beach. Their only child, a daughter, was still in her infancy. Ping and her sisters had previously sought my help to claim her infant daughter back from her in-laws, as they had been reluctant to let Ping take custody of her own daughter. Ping's narration of her recurring dreams is as follows:

"My late husband hounds me in dreams almost every other night. He tells me he is trapped in a dark and hideous place that emits fearful vibrations. He has repeatedly begged me to rescue him. At first I ignored the dreams, as they made no sense. But they kept recurring with increasing intensity until I felt I was also a victim trapped in that horrifying location. I was stunned to the core. Each time a dream reached its extreme, I woke and found myself experiencing horripilation, fear, agitation and sweating.

"I then sought help from various mediums and shamans, who were recommended by either my relatives or friends. After each visit, my late husband would appear in a dream to tell me he was still trapped there. That was how I knew that each attempt I made had not been successful. He continued to appear in my dreams, desperately begging me again and again to help save him.

"Finally, I decided to consult another medium from a Chinese temple, who charged me RM 500 for a prayer service. That same night my late husband again appeared in my dream. This time it was even more intimidating than previously. He told me the ritualistic prayers had caused him to sink even deeper into a dreaded abyss of fear.

"I had done all I could to help save my husband's soul. I was desperate and totally lost. In my dream, I was crying uncontrollably, knowing that all my efforts to save him had failed. I blamed myself for him having become trapped in an even deeper part of that realm. It was when I was crying uncontrollably in my dream that a vision of you, Fifth Uncle (referring to me), appeared! It was followed immediately by the vision of Aunty (Maam Sahib). I then woke up in a state of shock."

Ping was totally distressed. I calmed her and told her we would try to save her departed husband's soul. Ping gradually regained her composure.

Later in the day, I was prompted to lead Ping aside and gently ask her a question. "Tell me truthfully," I began. "What exactly was your husband doing when he was alive?"

Ping answered honestly. She said he had been involved in an unwholesome activity in order to obtain a second source of income.

Back home, in an attempt to rescue this departed soul, Maam Sahib and I went into meditation. We were backed by Bhai Sahib, who went online. Maam Sahib later shared with me how she managed to make brief contact with the departed soul. She described the realm as being enveloped in pitch darkness. The environment was piercingly cold, and its vibrations extremely fearful. Its atmosphere, while similar to what air is on our planet Earth, was dense and consisted of a jelly-like substance.

As she advanced into that realm to locate Ping's husband's soul, she could feel many invisible hands reaching out to her for help. She described the experience as a telepathic-like knowing of what was happening. On making contact, my wife confirmed that the departed soul was indeed trapped in a deep part of that horrible realm, thus confirming Ping's dreams.

Despite the extremely adverse conditions, Maam Sahib said she was able to remain calm. She attributed this to her experience, and the support of Bhai Sahib. Most of all, she was fully aware that this rescue mission was actuated by The Infinite. The contact was brief and restrictive. She had only enough time to advise the spirit to chant "Waheguru" repeatedly.

Several days later, my wife and I again went into meditation. This time she succeeded in helping extricate Ping's husband's spirit from that fearful realm. Not long after, I received a phone call from Ping, who told me she had had another dream of her late husband. This time she sounded more relaxed and cheerful as she related what turned out to be her final dream. In that dream, her late husband produced a divorce paper and asked Ping to sign it. I did not share with Ping what had been done to save her late husband's soul, as I knew it was something she would not easily understand.

This experience led me to reflect on life and death. Some deep concerns regarding the nature of life were poured into me.

The first is that there is life after death. One should observe Divine law, especially the Ten Commandments, when one is in human form. It will determine where one will end up after death. There are many realms, ranging from Total Hell to the Heavenly Abode.

The second is that the VCM technique of meditation is indeed very vibrant and effective. It can be used by gifted practitioners for many useful purposes. In this case, it had saved a departed soul in distress.

The third is that dream interpretation is an important topic of spirituality. Bhai Sahib rightly pointed out that in any recurring dream an important message is being conveyed. In this case, the message was from my niece's late husband, who was desperately crying for help because he was trapped in an unfavourable realm. Ping's recurring dreams lend credence to a verse in the SGGS quoted by Bhai Sahib: "Sleep with Dreams appears to be more preferable to Wakefulness, because we then have the Creator resident and expressing close to us." (p. 815)

The Infinite actuated the rescue mission through Maam Sahib. It was a spiritual lesson given to her by The Infinite, which was supported by Bhai Sahib. Another thought that has occurred to me is that it is wrong practice to resort to mediums, shamans, bomoh or temples utilising idols and statues for whatever reason. They are of the lower forces, which are opposed to the power of The Infinite.

My niece's final dream also conveyed a message. In this dream she was asked to sign a divorce paper, symbolically meaning that their relationship as husband and wife had ended in their current lifetimes. Any attachment is discouraged. The departed soul has to cross over to the spirit realm to continue with its journey, until its ultimate salvation. My niece, Ping, on the other hand, has to continue with her life in this human world.

That incident led me to wonder how one can 'travel' to a dimension beyond the human realm. I recall the teaching of Bhai Sahib, who explained that the nuclei of an atom can be likened to our Sun, with the electrons representing the various planets of our solar system. He went on to say that the space between the nuclei of an atom and the rotating electrons is relatively identical to the distance between our Sun and the planets orbiting it. This explanation is a scientific validation of the famous phrase: Microcosm (atomic particles) = Macrocosm (the external universe). Bhai Sahib expanded by referencing a scriptural injunction: "Yatha pinde tatha brahmande, yatha brahmande tatha pinde." (A verse from the Yajurveda, which means, "As is the atom, so is the universe," but may also be read, "As is the individual, so is the universe, as is the universe, so is the individual.") The large amount of space inside every atom means that no substance is really impenetrable. This probably explains how one with a well-awakened Holy Life Force is able to 'travel' through that space to perform specific tasks, as directed by The Infinite.

Bhai Sahib pointed out that thought waves (vibrations) also lie in higher realms, as shown in his illustration of the *Electro-Magnetic Frequency Spectrum of Nature*. (See the diagram on page 215.) He said that since thoughts are also vibrations they have the ability to radiate in all directions, which lends credence to a saying: "Thoughts are material things, they have body, mind and wings." Bhai Sahib commented that the fastest speed known to man is not that of light but of thought. While we can see lights, we cannot see thoughts, but we can 'feel' or discern them. With this understanding, it is important for us to feel, speak, think and radiate goodness, so that goodness will come back to us.

DEATH OF A DEAR FRIEND

If a soul mate can be described as a person with whom one shares a deep and natural affinity, then my friend and neighbour, S.T., fell into this category. Our friendship was forged in the mid-sixties, when we were kids attending the same school, sharing pleasurable experiences. Our relationship flourished through the years, beyond school. It included dating girls, work, marriage, and almost everything life ushered in. S.T. felt it was only natural that he approach Maam Sahib to discuss buying homes next to each other, so we would have each other's support in times of need.

Over the years, living immediately next to each other further increased our closeness, as our lives intertwined during the births of our children and through all the trials and tribulations that accompanied our marriages, bringing up children, and our budding careers. Looking back on this kaleidoscope of my life, with S.T. adding colours in the background, made me appreciate that for any relationship to flourish, constant nurturing acts are important.

Since my retirement in 2008, S.T. made the effort to spend even more time with me. Every other day we went out for either lunch or dinner. We also made the most of any excuse for a tea break any time of the day. Some weekends we made trips back to our hometown, which was a three-hour journey by car from where we lived. One afternoon, S.T. invited me to join him for a luncheon with other mutual school friends. I was travelling back from a weekend holiday with my family so was unable to join them. He caught up with me as I arrived home later in the afternoon and suggested going out for a drink in the evening. By the time I was rested and ready to join him, it was already past nine in the evening. I gave him the option of retiring early if he preferred, as he had to go to work the next day. However, he was eager for company.

The pleasant evening found S.T. slightly chattier than usual, singing praises of our mutual friends as he recounted conversations from the afternoon's luncheon. He asked about the health of my youngest brother, who was then suffering from severe liver failure. I told him my brother was terminally ill, and that he was just waiting for his time to go. S.T. didn't seem fazed. He appeared cheerful throughout our conversation. He shared his concerns about his children, especially his youngest daughter, who was still in school. As usual, I assured him that his children would be fine and that they should do well in life. Unknown to either of us, this was to be our last meeting in this lifetime.

The very next day, on the morning of 17 September 2013, only several hours after our night out, I was informed that S.T. had died in his sleep. I remained rooted to the spot, numb with disbelief. In automatic mode, I mentally flipped through my Standard Operating Procedures, and immediately started off with a prayer seeking God to protect the departed soul of my dear friend. Second, I contacted my eldest daughter, who had an evolved psychic sense (and who also had the strongest communication link with Bhai Sahib, my deceased master), to ask Bhai Sahib for assistance to guide the departed soul so he could cross over to where he was supposed to go. Third, I contacted Maam Sahib, who was then at work, for further assistance, as she is blessed with a two-way communication link with The Infinite. Fourth, I requested my fellow VCMers to help by dedicating their group prayers during their regular group meditations to my late friend's departed soul. All these years, throughout my conversations about God with S.T., he was never ready to become involved in any of my spiritual work or regular meditations. If he had, it would have helped him understand spirituality, and he would have realised how futile it is for a soul to remain overly attached to family, earthly possessions, food, drink, and other human experiences, when there was a whole universe out there to experience. Those attachments would impede a departed soul's progress, preventing it from moving on to another level of presence, where the soul could evolve and learn what it was meant to for that period. It was this that propelled me to do all I could for S.T.'s soul.

While all these thoughts were circling in my head, I received two mobile text messages from my eldest daughter. The first message read: "Daddy, don't be sad. Uncle S.T. has a kind and good heart. Both of you last chatted just yesterday evening. He had always shared things with you, taken you everywhere he went. Bhai Sahib said he would be placed in heaven, but not so high." The second read: "Already ... Uncle S.T. smiled and talked to me just now. He asked Daddy for a big favour. He asked you to help him to keep an eye on his family, especially his three kids. He said he will miss a lot of things in life. He can't see his children's success, marriage, etc. Too sudden! Even now, my tears flowed as he and Bhai Sahib spoke to me while I was teaching." Later, my daughter gave me an account of the post-death events and the conversation she had with both Bhai Sahib and S.T..

BHAI SAHIB IN S.T.'S HOME

S.T.: "Who are you?"

Bhai Sahib: "I am the master of your best friend, Athan, who is a practitioner of VCM."

S.T.: "What are you doing here?"

Bhai Sahib: "I am here to bring you home."

S.T.: "Home? What home? This is my home! I have to go to work!"

Bhai Sahib: "You are dead already! How can you go to work? Look at your body on your bed!"

S.T. could not accept his own death, but at the same time he asked Bhai Sahib to convey messages to his family members.

Bhai Sahib: "How can I pass your messages to your family members?

Both of us are dead! I can bring you to one who is given a gift from God and can help you to pass your messages to your family members."

The next instant, both the spirits of Bhai Sahib and S.T. were standing at a corner of the classroom where my eldest daughter was, teaching in a day care tuition center.

S.T.: "Sheen." (Sheen is the Chinese name of my daughter, Rosemary).

Bhai Sahib: "Call her Rosemary!"

As S.T. still could not believe he was dead, and that my daughter had the gift from God to see them, S.T. decided to test Rosemary.

S.T.: "What am I doing?"

Rosemary: "You are smiling."

S.T.: "Is this man next to me Bhai Sahib? What's the colour of his clothing?"

Rosemary: "Of course he is Bhai Sahib. He is wearing all white."

Bhai Sahib: "I am the messiah of the millennium!"

S.T.: "Wow! I must be very lucky! Will I be in a higher realm than Peter Wong?" (Peter Wong is a mutual friend who had died several years earlier, in his forties).

Bhai Sahib: "No, you will be in a lower realm than Peter Wong."

S.T.: "Are you sure?" S.T. was worried. He wanted to know the reason he would be in a lower realm than Peter Wong.

Bhai Sahib: "I don't know what the reasons are. But I know I am just joking with you."

S.T. was relieved and wanted to know where his destination would be. Bhai Sahib told him that he would be placed in a higher realm than Peter Wong. Furthermore, Bhai Sahib would lead him to that realm.

The following evening, while S.T.'s funeral rites were in progress, my eldest daughter 'saw' the spirit of S.T. stroking the hair of his two daughters. Bhai Sahib had appealed for the spirit of S.T. to have a short extended period of time on Earth, and had received permission from God that S.T. would be allowed to visit his family for the last time before the cross over. If S.T. missed this cross over because of his attachment to his family, he would be earthbound, aimlessly roaming around, with no rhyme or reason to exist. The time given to a spirit to cross over is very precise. It was only through the appeal from Bhai Sahib to God that an extension of time was granted S.T.'s spirit. On their deaths, human beings may become earthbound spirits if they have not crossed over in time, for whatever reason. This was my great concern for S.T..

With Bhai Sahib's help, S.T. conveyed a message to his family through my daughter. Rosemary passed on S.T.'s apology to his wife, Madam Christine, as he thought he should have treated her better during the last few years of his life on Earth. S.T. attributed this to human miscommunication and misconception. He asked for her forgiveness. He said that at least he was faithful to his wife and was not involved in any affairs, nor had he had any children with another woman.

S.T. advised Madam Christine to take good care of their children, to keep a diary, and to record what their children should do in order to lead a happy life. He advised his family to eat healthy food to lead a long life. He hoped their children would refer to the diary when the time came for Madam Christine to leave the world, too. It would be good to leave good written records as guidance for the next generation of children. S.T. said he would be waiting for her when the time came.

In a later conversation Bhai Sahib revealed to my eldest daughter that God said the traditional Chinese funeral rites carried out for the late S.T. were not the right practice and therefore not favourable. It was unfortunate that S.T. did not make an effort to attend VCM seminars, even though I had approached him many times when he was in human form. God was also cognisant that I had approached many of my other friends and relatives regarding VCM.

Bhai Sahib told my eldest daughter that S.T. was feeling lonely, because he did not know any of the fellow spirits in the realm to which he had been taken. He was refusing to let go and become detached from everything he had possessed when alive on Earth. Bhai Sahib commented he had advised the spirit of S.T. to socialise with his fellow spirits, but S.T. kept mumbling to himself his concern for his wife, children and friends still on Earth. He wanted to remain in the company of Bhai Sahib, but Bhai Sahib said that was not possible because God had given him a lot of other work to do.

S.T. asked why his mother, who was then in her mid-nineties, was still on Earth, and why he should have died earlier than her. However, S.T. could not bring himself to ask when his children would join him, as he was excessively concerned for them and, therefore, did not want to know. He was only interested in knowing when his wife or his older friends could join him. Bhai Sahib explained that it was all about karma, and that all decisions were orchestrated by God.

Even before S.T. could ask the question, Bhai Sahib told him that when the time arrived, I (Athan) would not be in the same or a lower realm compared to him. That was all Bhai Sahib would reveal to S.T..

With permission from God, S.T. was allowed to visit Peter Wong, who was in a lower realm. When they met, S.T. greeted Peter Wong: "Hi, friend! Long time, no see. How are you doing?" Peter Wong was shocked to see S.T.. At first he thought that he was dreaming. S.T. told Peter Wong that he had died in his sleep. Peter Wong smiled and said that S.T. had had a good life. He asked S.T. if he had left a will for his family. S.T. replied in the negative, as he had not expected to die that early. Peter Wong said that he was sad to hear of that. Peter Wong tried to cheer S.T. up, saying he understood why S.T. could not let go of his attachment to his family.

The meeting ended with the arrival of Bhai Sahib, who had to guide S.T. back to his realm. Bhai Sahib asked S.T. if he was happy to have met his old friend, to which S.T. responded in the affirmative. S.T. thanked Bhai Sahib for his help and told Bhai Sahib he would try his best to socialise with the other spirits in the realm he had been allocated.

As I was putting the finishing touches to this episode, with Rosemary sitting next to me on my right, my left ear drummed strongly for a second or two, something I had never felt before. My daughter told me Bhai Sahib said that the spirit of my late friend, S.T., was trying to pass a message to me. It is not possible for spirits to communicate with humans in this manner, as the human and spirit realms are different dimensions. It is only possible when one has a gift given by God. This gift should only be used to serve as directed by God.

In retrospect, I could link my perceptions on S.T., and on spirituality in general, to the conversations that transpired between Bhai Sahib and my eldest daughter. I can vouch that my late friend, S.T., had a peculiar attitude of not interacting with people with whom he was not familiar, when he lived on Earth. All the years I knew him, he would only mix with me and his other childhood friends, and at times with only one or two of his relatives.

So it is not surprising that, as narrated by my eldest daughter, who did not know anything of my late friend's peculiarity, S.T. maintained that attitude even as a spirit in the spirit realm.

As S.T. was unable to see any familiar spirits, such as his ancestors or any of his friends and relatives, in that realm, it is very likely they had already been reborn as human beings. Otherwise, they were in other, perhaps lower realms. I am sure that being an active and devoted VCM practitioner, my appeal to Bhai Sahib and God, together with prayers from my fellow practitioners, helped to elevate S.T. to a better realm.

Human beings are able to travel quite freely from one place to another anywhere on Earth, whereas when one dies and becomes a spirit, permission from God is required before that spirit is allowed to travel between realms. In addition, the time given for transition is precise. This is especially true for spirits who are in higher realms. Therefore, it is important for human beings to appreciate and to enjoy their time while on Earth, especially with family members and relatives, and secondly, with friends and others.

One of the greatest regrets when humans become spirits is that they had not spent enough time with their dear and near ones. Charity begins at home. Charity is much more than money. It is very important for one to spend sufficient time to enjoy a healthy communication and a loving relationship with fellow members of one's family, where all have respect for one another. It is of the utmost importance that while one is still in the human frame one should have a good understanding of, and practise, true spirituality. This will help one to earn a place in a better realm, if not the highest, that being the ultimate merger with the Almighty.

Chapter Thirteen

CLEANSING VICTIMISED SOULS

ALTHOUGH I HAVE HEARD MANY STORIES about charms, spirits and curses, somehow the three incidents I am about to describe have remained etched in my memory since childhood.

SPIRIT, CHARM AND CURSE: A PRELUDE

My first story is about the chief tenant of the shop house with whom we shared premises. This tenant was my father's nemesis. Despite being a child, I can still recall the chief tenant's fiancée, who died of an illness. After many years of bachelorhood, the chief tenant, a school teacher, fell in love again. He intended to marry a hairdresser, who had by then relocated her business to our shop house. This is when the incident I wish to recount took place.

As related by my father, one evening, just as the hairdresser was about to close her business for the day, a client walked into her salon and asked for a hair perm. In the course of doing her job, the hairdresser accidentally touched the client and felt her body was very cold. The hairdresser asked her why that was so, to which the client replied she had travelled to the salon from quite a distance on a motorbike. She was having her hair done as she had to attend a friend's wedding ceremony the next day.

After the job was done, the client asked for permission to use the toilet. She paid and proceeded to the back of the shop house, where the toilet was located. When the hairdresser realised the client was taking a long time, she decided to check on her. She was shocked to discover that the client was nowhere to be seen. She hurried to check the money the lady had paid and was horrified to discover that the money was afterlife currency.

(Afterlife currency consists of fake notes used by the Chinese to burn as offerings to ancestors or loved ones who had passed away.)

When her husband-to-be returned home, the hairdresser related the whole story. Responding to the description of the client given by the hairdresser, he rummaged through his drawers and took out an old photo. The photo was of the chief tenant's departed fiancée. The hairdresser was shocked and shivered with fright when she realised she had encountered the spirit of her husband-to-be's fiancée. This spirit was also described as being pregnant.

The second story was related to me by a childhood friend. It involves a charm that affected a person from my hometown. This man worked as a lumberjack in the state of Sarawak. While he was working there he began a relationship with an indigenous woman. He later deserted her to return to his hometown for good. Not long after, and for no apparent reason, the man suffered from swollen legs and feet. He also experienced extreme pricking pains whenever his feet touched the ground. Eventually, he could only move around in a wheelchair.

He later consulted a bomoh (shaman), who recited some prayers. The bomoh then asked the lumberjack to stand up. He was able to comply with the request. It was the first time he had been capable of standing after enduring months of suffering. He went home happy. However, soon after he suffered a relapse. The pricking pains flared up again whenever he was standing. He returned to the bomoh for help, but was told the bomoh did not possess the power necessary to deal with the new charm affecting the lumberjack. The bomoh advised him to seek help from his master, who was located in a different town. He did not follow through on this advice, as it was said that he did not really believe in it. Not long after, he died in agony.

The third story is about the evil power of curses. A couple was planning to get married. The woman, an unsuspecting person, worked hard to financially support her partner during his higher studies. After graduating, the man dumped her and married another woman. The rejected woman, together with her mother, gate crashed her ex-partner's wedding ceremony. She cursed aloud, in front of all present, declaring that the newly-wed couple's offspring's lives would be filled with miseries.

Time passed, and the couple had three children. The eldest, a boy, was a brilliant student, but from a young age was always shirtless and barefooted. He was often seen talking to himself, or asking strangers for cigarettes. He ended up deranged. The second child, a girl, was also good in her studies, and was employed by a bank. She, too, ended up insane. The parents remembered the curse and decided to send their third and only remaining sane child, a boy, to Australia to avoid it. They also went to the jilted woman and begged her not to harm their children, asking that they be punished instead. By then, it was too late. The damage had taken place.

These three stories occurred in the town where I grew up. They resurfaced in my mind after I became involved in VCM. This was because one of Bhai Sahib's lessons was about charms, black magic, and possession by different categories of spirits, a subject I absorbed with great reluctance.

MY FIRST ENCOUNTER WITH A SPIRIT

My first encounter with spirit possession occurred when I had just begun studying VCM. My eldest daughter, who was then twelve years old, told her mother a spirit was with her. She described it as a male spirit which had followed her from school.

I was greatly affected by this development. However, it was a subject I was not interested in, so it took me a long period of time to understand what it involves. The practical lessons given by Bhai Sahib helped me realise that spirits and spirit possession are very much a reality of life. Gifted VCM practitioners are able to expose the presence of these entities. I realised that spirits and possession commonly affect human beings, but the possessed likely do not know that spirits may be the cause of their woes. As this is a subject that deals with invisible entities, it is hardly a topic of conversation in our daily lives. In addition, people's egos are a stumbling block, as many think they have the strength of character to withstand obnoxious spiritual lower forces.

My eldest daughter told me that while she was in the school canteen, the male spirit had advised her not to eat a certain food sold there. She ignored the advice. She later suffered from food poisoning. The presence of this male spirit got on my nerves the following day when my daughter kept talking about it. She said the earthbound spirit wanted to join his parents, who had passed on. But whenever the spirit tried to emerge from my daughter's aura, a strange creature-like being appeared to want to capture it. My understanding was the earthbound spirit felt it would be safe if it hid in a human being's aura.

I instructed my daughter to warn the spirit to go away or face the consequences. The spirit told her he was not afraid of her father. I was angry, but did not know how to fight or drive away this invisible entity. I told my daughter I would call Bhai Sahib for help. My daughter informed me that the spirit became afraid at the mere mention of Bhai Sahib's name.

In the end, an invocation to redeem the spirit was recited to me by Bhai Sahib over the phone. I can now only recall certain phrases: ""Oh disembodied spirit ... in the name of God Almighty, take this journey ... guided by the Holy Host ... never again occupy a human body or a human abode .... cross over to your rightful realm .... to continue with your lessons in life ... until your ultimate salvation." This spirit's redemption was carried out by Maam Sahib, using the invocation given by Bhai Sahib. She went into a meditative mode, tears streaming down her cheeks. My daughter told me that as the spirit appeared from her aura, so did the accompanying creature-like being. Each was led to it own other realm, as determined by The Infinite.

CASE 1: POSSESSION OF A YOUNG MAN

A fellow VCM practitioner, Sarab, was a healthy and sturdy young man in his thirties. Together with several other fellow practitioners, we had gathered for supper. Our table was located under a tree outside a restaurant. Minutes into our conversation, Sarab collapsed. Luckily, his head came to rest on the table.

I rushed him to a nearby private hospital. I then called Bhai Sahib, who told me Sarab had been affected by a spirit lurking under the tree where our table had been located. At the hospital, the doctor suspected Sarab's collapse might be due to a heart attack. But tests drew a blank. In fact, the doctor found Sarab to be very fit. He was kept under observation, and discharged the following morning.

From this incident I learned that spirits are mischievous and capable of causing harm to human beings. They are able to simulate apparent illnesses and generate other undesirable impacts that affect human life. The following incidents illustrate the nasty behaviours of spirits and related entities.

CASE 2: POSSESSION OF A YOUNG HEALTHY BOY

A friend, Peter Wong, called me one evening. He needed my help to take his son to the emergency ward of a nearby private hospital. I was asked to feel his son's pulse, and found it was beating extremely fast. His lips looked dry and pale. I called Bhai Sahib for help. At the hospital, the doctor could not establish any medical reason for the boy's state. I immediately placed my hand to again feel the boy's pulse. By now his heart was beating normally. I also noticed his lips were pinkish, looking healthy once again.

On investigation, it was found that earlier in the day Peter Wong's son had been playing at the neighbour's house, which was vacant. The building was unoccupied because the previous occupant had committed suicide. Bhai Sahib confirmed that Peter Wong's son had been possessed by that spirit. I learned that Bhai Sahib was able to remove a spirit from a distance, as he was at that time in his home.

CASE 3: POSSESSION OF A MARRIED WOMAN

Bhai Sahib once shared an incident that involved a Caucasian couple. The man told Bhai Sahib that his wife refused to consummate their marriage. Bhai Sahib discerned that his wife was affected by an *incubus*, a male spirit that has sexual intercourse with sleeping women. Bhai Sahib helped to remove the incubus, and the couple were again able to enjoy their marital relationship.

I once read of an incident reported in a local newspaper column where a woman sought advice because her husband had never consummated their relationship since their marriage. The columnist could only suggest that she and her husband seek professional counselling. I suspected that the husband in question was very likely affected by a *succubus*, a female spirit that has sexual intercourse with sleeping men. I wrote to the newspaper columnist, giving my diagnosis and offered my assistance to remove the offending succubus. I did not receive any reply, but I was not surprised, for reasons I can only classify as disbelief.

CASE 4: A SPIRIT LOOKING FOR HELP

While my fellow VCM practitioners have had more experiences with spirits than me, I will share an experience that took place when Bhai Sahib was still alive. On this occassion a spirit followed me home from my workplace. Maam Sahib was having her afternoon nap in our room, so I slept on the sofa on the ground floor.

When I woke, I caught a subtle whiff of a baby's feces. Maam Sahib, who woke up later, shared a dream with me. She had dreamed of a female spirit, who identified herself as Lai Yoke Moi. She had her baby with her. The spirit asked my wife to pray for her and her baby.

Later in the evening, Maam Sahib and I carried out a meditation supported by Bhai Sahib, who was online. This was to help the spirit and her baby cross over to the spirit realm. Bhai Sahib discerned that the female spirit and her baby had died in a fire.

ENABLING SUFFERERS

After several years of regular practical lessons with spirit removal and redemption, our group of practitioners received the following message from The Infinite: "Black magic! There will be retribution!"

I will now relate two incidents that enabled me to later realise The Infinite had involved me and my fellow practitioners in such experiences so we would be able to help others by removing their spirit-related ailments.

CASE 5: A CASE OF BLACK MAGIC

A fellow practitioner, a successful Punjabi businessman, called me one day seeking help to solve his personal woes. I did not ask what his problems were. I merely consulted Bhai Sahib. He gave me the green light to take along several other practitioners to carry out a special prayer at the business man's abode.

It was a very vibrant meditation session, concluding with a Divine message: "You must prevail. You must overcome this obstacle. You must go through this karma. You are the chosen one (referring to the affected practitioner). I know it is difficult in this form. You must rise. I will heal you. I will remove all negativities. But you must know that you have to go through this karma. Confess your sins. Show honesty and humility. If not to yourself, then to Me. Ask, I will give you."

My fellow practitioner later related to me that over an extended period he had consulted the best doctors in Singapore to diagnose the ailment that was troubling him. The doctors could not find anything wrong with his health, except that his blood pressure was slightly high. I noticed that he took a long time to walk a distance of about ten feet. He also mentioned that he was slightly relieved of his symptoms whenever he went for a Bali bath, where salt was used.

I realised that this practitioner was being affected by a charm. He found relief whenever he went for a Bali bath without knowing that the salt water was able to counter negative energies, albeit only temporarily. The meditation session was able to improve his life situation.

CASE 6: ENABLING AN AFFECTED PRACTITIONER

A fellow practitioner, also a Punjabi, and a medical doctor, confided in me that his one-month-old marriage was on the brink of breaking up. He accused his newly-wedded wife of not being friendly with his housemaid, who had worked for him for two years. He also accused her of not being friendly with an Indian national who was staying with them.

I gathered a group of practitioners to conduct a jaap in his house. A typical jaap consists of three stations. The Holy SGGS is placed only at the first and second stations. Practitioners chant while standing at the third station, normally for a duration of about an hour and forty-five minutes.

The following message was received by a gifted one: "Do not take My third station lightly. Do not ever take My third station lightly. You must remember this, I am everywhere. When you have three stations, I am in all three. Do not take My third station lightly. Focus on the jaap. More energy, more surrender is needed. There is not enough, especially at the third station. Hear Me. God has sent me to tell you this. I am Gabriel. You know me from the Bible. Hear me. Do not take lightly God's third station."

A while later, Archangel Gabriel conveyed a message for the affected practitioner: "You must listen. You must listen to me. You have been charmed. What have you eaten? Violation ... violation of God's Law. An outsider has done this. You must listen to me. I am God's angel. An outsider has done this. Violation, violation of God's Law. This one must return to its master or I shall condemn it to hell!"

It was later revealed that the Indian national had used a charm on the practitioner. He was scheming to defraud the practitioner of his wealth. With this knowledge, I decided to go all out to help him, even though The Infinite conveyed that we had done our part and to leave the rest to Him. The demon then turned on me. Its effect became apparent when I began losing my temper and for no apparent reason started scolding my children, Maam Sahib and a fellow practitioner.

Hence, a cleansing meditation was carried out, during which The Infinite spoke to the demon, and later to the practitioners who were present. "You violated God's law. You have even affected those who have come to help. You have harmed My warriors. You have not learnt. You do not deserve My mercy. I condemn you to hell. You are useless. My angel, Gabriel, showed you mercy. You did not heed him. You did not return to your master. There is no mercy. I condemn you to hell. That is final! The Holy Host will deal with you, demon! (This was followed by speaking in tongues.) I am God, your Creator. Listen to Me, My children. I have told you that as you improve, more difficult lessons will be given to you."

CASE 7: ENABLING A YOUNG ILL PERSON

A senior practitioner brought a case to the attention of our group. The son of his good friend had been hospitalised. Despite the huge medical bills, doctors were unable to identify the cause of the ailment.

A group meditation was carried out one evening, dedicated to this person's recovery. Several hours later, the senior practitioner shared an email from the affected young man's father. The content of the email is as follows: "John started to walk yesterday. Today he could walk to the toilet without assistance. Soon, he should be fully recovered. Once again, I thank everyone's kind gesture in praying for his speedy recovery, which appears to have been answered."

Not long after, a jaap was held in this senior practitioner's home. During the jaap the prophets spoke via a receiving. It was meant for the practitioners as well as for the spirit possessing the young man: "Heavy is this jaap. Focus! Let go! You cannot consume. It is against the Divine law. You will be condemned. You must understand, you cannot have this hate, you must release it and forgive all those who have sinned against you. They will be judged by God, not by you. (Speaking in tongues.) It is the law that you cannot, you cannot. Your soul is not worth losing because of this anger. Love yourself first. (Speaking in tongues.) Do not condemn yourself. (Speaking in tongues.) Please take this journey. I implore you in God's name. In the name of all the prophets and their accompanying scriptures, take this journey. (Speaking in tongues.)"

We learned that this particular spirit was the mother of the young man who was hospitalised. She had committed suicide in her husband's office wearing a red outfit. According to Chinese beliefs, wearing red means the deceased intended to seek vengeance. As an earthbound spirit, the negative energy she emitted had instead affected her son. The spirit left the family in peace following the session.

I have randomly selected two of the many cases which involved earthbound ancestral spirits. It must be noted that ancestral spirits who we thought would be helpful are in fact just as conniving and harmful as any other category of spirits. I wish to especially reiterate here that the traditional Chinese practice of praying to their ancestors may not be wholesome. They should instead pray to God for their ancestors to be elevated.

CASE 8: ENABLING SOULS TO MOVE OUT OF THE DARK REALM

The spirit of a fellow VCM practitioner's late grandfather was deemed to have possessed the practitioner's wife. BabuJi spoke to the spirit thus: "Why do you make it such a difficult task for us to be of service to God? There are many who want to make this journey. You cling too much to your past. You must learn detachment. Do you wish to meet your ancestors in the spirit realm? Let the young ones have their turn on Earth. They need to go through life themselves. You cannot interfere, just as your ancestors did not interfere in your life. It is due to their prayers that you have us here today to help you cross over. Your ancestors would want that. Do not cry. It is alright. Awareness is good. Will you now follow the Holy Host who is waiting? Peace be upon you. I am, and we are, in God's Service. You must thank God for this opportunity."

Earlier, the spirit had confided he had been trapped in a realm so dark he could not even see his fingers. I recalled a former colleague, who had once phoned seeking my opinion on his fellow churchgoer's dream. The churchgoer had dreamed his late brother told him he was trapped in a realm so dark he could not even see his hand. In an ancestral jaap session, a group of spirits shared their grievances, saying: "What is a six hour jaap to you when we have spent half a century hovering and suffering in darkness!"

These incidents point to the existence of a realm of total darkness. Much later, a fellow practitioner, a Punjabi, forwarded to me a page taken from the Sri Guru Granth Sahib at the Golden Temple, Amritsar, India, which stated: "In the city of death, there is pitch darkness, and huge clouds of dust, neither sister nor brother is there." (p. 584)

I realised that such a pitch-dark realm does indeed exist, Furthermore, our experiential learning corroborates the verse in the SGGS.

CASE 9: ENABLING A LONG-DEPARTED SOUL

One day, Bhai Sahib telephoned and told me that through his discernment he had learned that my maternal grandmother's spirit had possessed my fourth daughter since birth. My fourth daughter, as noted earlier, is handicapped. The possession was only discovered when my daughter was fourteen years old. This incident indicates that ancestral spirits can be as harmful as any other type of spirit. It was so conniving it had possessed my daughter undetected for fourteen years!

A special meditation was then carried out, dedicated to my maternal grandmother's spirit. She said: "My family is very proud. I have no choice. But I will now leave. I must learn to be humble."

I have to admit that egoistical and temperamental traits exist in me and my siblings. And, as pointed out by my maternal grandmother's spirit, these unwholesome traits have spread from one generation to the next, affecting all. The lesson is to acquire wisdom and humility. These are attributes every human being should acquire during their life journey.

After more than a decade of being exposed to lessons with spirits and possession, I decided to foster my personal understanding by conducting interviews with spirits that came into my life. The following interview was conducted through my eldest daughter, who was the channeller.

CASE 10: INTERVIEW: CHAN MEI MEI

BabuJi wanted my eldest daughter to attend a particular weekly meditation session. BabuJi told her he would obtain permission from God to allow her to regain her ability to 'see' spirits.

BabuJi revealed to her that there was an old female spirit hiding in our house. This old female spirit seemed to be creating health problems for several of my family members. That evening, my daughter confirmed that the spirit was hiding in the ground floor bathroom. The next day, I decided to find out more about this spirit via a channelling session through my eldest daughter. The outcome of the channeling was as follows:

Athan: "Who are you and where are you from? Please tell me more about yourself."

Spirit: "I am Chan Mei Mei. I was from China, southern China. When I was in human form I lived in a wooden house near a forest where there was a river and a lake. My age is now 118. Therefore, I must have been born in the year 1889. As the eldest in my family, I was about to be married off. At that time, I was aged 28. My parents wanted me to get married earlier, but I was more concerned with taking care of my parents and brothers. I was the only girl among my siblings.

"One day, I went to a nearby lake to wash my family's clothing. While washing, I slipped and fell into the lake. I screamed for help because I could not swim. No one was around. I died from drowning. I only became aware I was dead when I tried to talk to my parents. My parents did not respond, and in fact walked through me. That was when I realised I was already dead.

"As a spirit, I lingered in the vicinity of my parents' house. I couldn't do anything except watch my parents and brothers. Later, somebody found my body and informed my parents. My parents cried and cried. Not long after, I met a male spirit in the nearby forest. He was a young Chinese boy whose name is Liang. Together, we travelled to see planet Earth.

"Two years later, I went back to see my parents and family. My parents' house had disappeared. I heard human beings talking about the house, which had fallen victim to arson. I also heard them say that all my family had died in the fire.

"I asked Liang where his family members were. Liang replied that they had probably followed the light and gone to a better realm. He explained that I had not followed the light the moment I died. I told him I was not prepared to leave my parents and brothers, who I was very attached to. That is why I am now an earthbound spirit trapped in this human world.

"I have been travelling from one country to another seeking salvation, but to no avail, as they are all involved in black magic. Finally, I recently 'travelled' to Malaysia. I noticed they are idol worshippers and knew they would not be helpful. Just before Chinese New Year in 2007 I happened to pass by Puchong Town. I had a strong feeling for this house (referring to my house), and saw Bhai Sahib's photograph on the wall. A light shone from the photo towards me. Bhai Sahib invited me to come in. He said that all my questions will be answered and I shall receive salvation here. I was so happy to have found someone who could help me receive salvation.

"Prior to this, Liang had received salvation. Two guards came to collect him. I wanted to follow, but Liang said they were only taking him. I was left alone to continue wandering around. When I was in Thailand I found the spirits there fierce. Their black magic is very strong. They tried to catch me with their black magic, but I managed to escape. I then quickly 'travelled' to Indonesia. Black magic in Indonesia is not as strong as in Thailand.

"I have been in spirit form for 90 years already, and I am very tired. I am afraid I will not receive salvation. There are lots of other spirits around. Most of them are very young. Some are infants, but most are middle-aged. I am the oldest among all these spirits. These spirits refused to mix with me because I am old. I have seen babies die, but they follow the light to salvation. I have seen male guards accompanying young boys and girls as well as middle-aged spirits, whereas female angels with wings come to collect baby spirits. I never believed angels have wings until I saw them collect baby spirits. Whenever 'light' appears to collect a soul, it is always accompanied by a beautiful but sad melody.

"Life as an earthbound spirit is very tough. I am lonely and always being bullied by other spirits. Most of the spirits are bad. Those bad spirits have not learnt to be good. They disturb human beings and cause havoc to them. These spirits are far from receiving salvation."

Athan: "As you were once human, what is your advice to human beings?"

Spirit: "Human beings should do more charity. Help the orphanages. Help poor children. Spend your time with them, even if you don't have money. As a spirit, I visited orphanages and played with the children. They are pure and innocent, therefore they can see me.

"Charity does not mean only contributing money, but also your time, love and advice to the less fortunate. If you are an employer, and if you employ the less fortunate, that is also charity. The meaning of charity is very deep. I have seen human beings going to orphanages to donate money. They leave the orphanages as fast as they arrive. But doing charity at orphanages means communicating with the orphans, showing complete love for them, because they are lonely.

""Spirits and humans are almost the same. A human being has a body, whereas a spirit does not. In other respects they are the same. Please be respectful to spirits. They are already in difficult situations. Do not say things that can hurt them. They can worsen your lives. They are capable of controlling your minds and causing you to commit mistakes. Spirits can make you commit serious crimes, such as accidents on roads. I have seen spirits disturb human beings' houses. Spirits can be very nice or very bad towards human beings. I have seen an angry spirit who caused a whole family to die in a car accident. Do you know how they do it? The spirit 'entered' the aura of the driver to take control of the wheel and cause the car to crash. This spirit caused the accident because he was looking for companions. He failed because 'lights' received the accident victims. No victims were trapped on Earth as expected by the spirit who caused the accident.

"Just as humans can treat other human beings cruelly and dangerously, so can earthbound spirits. Bad spirits also harass good spirits. Spirits cannot do much for human beings, except, for example, they can help to check out what is happening to your friend in a different place on the same plane. I admire this family (referring to my family) because all the family members are still around and are with others. Your mother (referring to Maam Sahib) can also communicate with God. There is love in this family. You are learning and carrying out the right practice. I am lucky to be able to communicate with a prophet like Bhai Sahib.

"Keep on loving each other, no matter what happens. Do not say things that hurt each other. Be loving! That will strengthen your family bond. Every problem has a solution. Family is very important. I have 'travelled' to many countries. People quarrel with each other. They should be gentle. I truly admire Bhai Sahib. Please take care of your health. Goodbye."

This interview reaffirms that one should place importance on maintaining a loving family. One should always speak well, be compassionate and charitable to the less fortunate, and gentle in interactions with others. One should also learn of true spirituality and detachment. It will enable one to smoothly cross over to the spirit realm when one's time on Earth is up, instead of being trapped as a miserable earthbound spirit.

CASE 11: ENABLING A JUNGLE SPIRIT

One Sunday, I went trekking in a forest reserve with a fellow practitioner and a group of his friends. A forest spirit followed me home. Maam Sahib realised a spirit was attached to me the moment I stepped into our house. An online meditation was held that evening with several other fellow practitioners to help this native spirit cross over to the spirit realm.

However, the spirit was stubborn and refused to do so. As a result, another meditation session was held, this time at our center, with more regular practitioners present. During this group meditation the spirit was advised: "You must take this chance or you will be condemned. We are helping you. You must listen. We, in our hearts, do not want to see you condemned. You are like our relative. Please, we beg you, take this opportunity. Follow the Holy Hosts. You will be taught the lessons you need to receive salvation. Why do you not take this opportunity? This is the final offer from God.

"Do not harm us. Do not harm my son. (This was Maam Sahib

speaking.) He is so small and yet you come and try to harm us. Do not do this anymore. You know it is forbidden. Please take this opportunity."

A message was then sent by The Infinite, through BabuJi, to the spirit: "It is from God that I come. Will you leave with me or will you not? Then follow me. You have done much harm. Follow me and I shall lead you to the proper realm."

Prior to the above, I had encouraged my eldest daughter to find out more about this native spirit. The following is the story the spirit told through my daughter. The spirit related how he saw me trekking up the hill that Sunday morning. His intuition told him that I could help him shift to a better realm. The spirit then 'entered' my aura and followed me home.

The spirit said his human name was Moniang. He related that while he was in human form he was killed by a stranger who shot him in his face. The incident took place in either 1959 or 1960. He had died at the age of 34. After his sudden death, he saw white lights. He also saw two soul ushers, who came to take him. But he refused to follow them. Instead, he ran away. He was not ready to go as he missed his wife and four children. The children were still young, and he felt pain at the thought of leaving them behind.

Moniang also said his family had not known he had died. Fishing was the family's means of livelihood. Coming from an indigenous background, he was afraid to go into the town, as neither he nor his family had proper identification documents. Hence, they hid in the forest, not socialising. They did not know what God is, and so did not believe in God. I explained that God is love. God is Omnipresent, Omniscient and Omnipotent. I advised Moniang that one has to learn compassion and humility, learn to forgive and forget, and learn to overcome feelings of hurt and hate.

Moniang informed my daughter that he would follow Maam Sahib's advice and leave. He visited his wife and children, who were still in human form, for the last time. Now that he knew his family members were well, he was happy to move on. He thanked everyone who had prayed to help him cross over to a better realm. He also asked VCM practitioners to pray for his family members. Moniang is a happy soul now, as he has crossed over to the spirit realm.

Bhai Sahib explained how a human being is possessed by a spirit. Spirits do not physically enter a person's body. Rather, they are entangled in the human beings' aura, or etheric body. This is a shimmering sheath that covers the body, up to several centimeters' distance. This entanglement is enough to affect the possessed person's physical and psychological attributes.

I shall now share two dreams experienced by my fellow practitioners regarding the departed souls of their loved ones.

CASE 12: ANCESTRAL SPIRITS IN DREAMS

A fellow practitioner dreamed he piggybacked his late father up a flight of stairs. He reached the top. In a quick change of scene, he saw his father, mother and another family member in a room resting in cozy chairs. Suddenly, a speeding car carrying quite a number of passengers crashed through a window. The lower part of the window, part of the wall, appeared modified with a spring mechanism, which enabled the car to go through without any damage. The dream powerfully affected his usual calm self.

Interpreting dreams requires contextual information. Obviously, the late father, as a spirit, had difficulties from which he could not free himself. The VCM practitioner took part in an ancestral jaap to help extricate his father's spirit from the difficulties, and to enable him to shift to the highest permitted realm. The dream indicated that this practitioner's late parents, along with another family member, are together in the same realm. The speeding car containing several passengers that crashed through the window symbolised other spirits had also been directed to that realm.

The lower part of the window, that seems to have been modified with a spring mechanism that enabled the car to go through without causing any damage, probably refers to the portal into that realm. The timing of the opening and closing of a portal is precise. Hence, the timing for spirits who are entitled to enter a particular realm is crucial. Equally important are participants in an ancestral jaap. They have to focus on their prayers. There should be no distraction. This is because prayers are like fuel that is needed to assist spirits to cross over. Any distractions will affect the spirits' journey, as it is possible some spirits may be left stranded.

Several years later, this particular practitioner again dreamed of his late father, just before an ancestral jaap was to be held. This probably meant that the practitioner's father's spirit was qualified for an elevation to an even higher realm. During an ancestral jaap practitioners pray to The Infinite to help ancestral spirits cross over to the spirit realm, or, if those spirits are already in the spirit realm, to elevate them to higher realms.

CASE 13: THE PATRIARCH IN DREAMS

A nephew of Bhai Sahib became involved with VCM after spending a period of time with another spiritual organisation. One day he shared with me a dream he had of his late father, who had passed on more than 20 years before. His father died at a ripe old age of 104. In the dream, his father told him that he wanted to go to the Golden Temple in Amritsar, India. The son told his father that not only would he take him to the Golden Temple, he would also take him to his village.

This dream needs contextualising. To the Sikhs, going to the Golden Temple in Amritsar is akin to a pilgrimage. In other words, his late father was ready for elevation and was qualified to enter God's realm, which was symbolised by the Golden Temple. By telling his late father that he would bring him home to his village in India means his father was qualified to reach the innermost of God's source, symbolised by the village. Because it is a birth place, it symbolises the starting point of one's life journey.

This advanced VCM practitioner was able to help elevate his late father to the heart of God's source, via a scheduled ancestral jaap.

REFLECTIONS ON SPIRITS AND POSSESSIONS

VCM practitioners are involved in the redemption of spirits, as that is our duty to humanity and our Creator. We do not go out soliciting to help spirits. After all, there are plenty of spirits everywhere around us, whereas our ability to help them cross over to the spirit realm is limited by the small group of practitioners we have. We only act when the mission is directed by The Infinite, or when impacted spirits are sent to us.

These spirits were previously human beings. Our actions helping spirits cross over are acts of charity initiated by The Infinite. Spirits are afraid and do not know what lies ahead of them, or they do not understand, and so they suffer. Spirits easily lose trust in everything and everybody. Practitioners should not lie to them, use any harsh words, or direct any negative thoughts against them. They can read human minds. We need to earn their trust to help them cross over to the spirit realm.

Therefore, when exorcising spirits, we need to do so with love. We should not frighten or condemn them, as they have suffered enough. However, we also need to be wary of them. Any further condemnation might cause them to retaliate. Bhai Sahib told me of an incident involving a Christian priest who, when he was exorcising a spirit, uttered: "In the name of Christ, I condemn … " Bhai Sahib commented that that particular spirit retaliated during the exorcism process and killed the priest.

On learning that I had acted on my own to conduct interviews with spirits, we were reminded not to communicate with spirits because spirits are not honest. They lie and trick. I was fortunate that the spirits I had interviewed were friendly. Others could be hostile and take the opportunity to generate harm.

CROSSOVERS AND PRACTITIONERS' DILEMMA

Once during a jaap several elders from another part of the Universe participated. The elders came with the permission of The Infinite to help guide spirits who were lost so they could cross over to the spirit realm.

It was revealed to us that some of the spirits had repeatedly broken all the rules and had to be led away by the Holy Hosts to be isolated. One reason was that the spirits concerned had not responded to the help that had already been offered to them. This rule should not be broken. Most spirits were ready to cross over; just some were not. We need to understand why it is sometimes difficult to encourage spirits to cross over to the spirit realm. It is like asking a human being to trust that he will be saved when asked to jump off a cliff. Thus getting the spirits to trust helpers is a major problem.

I was very uncomfortable with the subject of spirits when I first started to practise VCM. I then cross-checked with a senior VCM elder in North America and found they were not involved in any lessons on spirits. I shared that senior elder's views with my fellow VCMers here. I was, in fact, seeking consensus from my fellow practitioners to do the same and to stop dealing with spirits. That was when The Infinite spoke on why spirit redemption is necessary for the group.

"My children, My children. What you are doing is necessary. What you are doing is in accord with your destiny. All those who visit you have My permission. Do not doubt that what you are doing is part of the lessons in your spiritual journey. Have I not mentioned this in My past messages? That is why I always remind you to read My messages. Otherwise, you will forget what you are doing. You will be confused whether what you are doing is right or wrong. There is no wrong in what Simran (the VCM practitioner from North America) said. You can say "No" to the spirits, but there will then be consequences you will have to face. You will be rewriting your karma in your next life. The choice is yours.

"You can choose not to attend this jaap or any other jaaps others organise for spirits' redemption. Everything is your choice. It is your karma. I have an eternity to wait for you. I am timeless. I have been waiting for you for so long. What is a little bit longer? It is your journey. You are responsible. Every child has a different duty, My children, have I not told you this?

"You are different, each and every one of you. That is why, when I chose you, I chose the correct people. You have worked so hard all your lifetimes to come to this point, to this spiritual level. If you wish to park yourself, and stagnate, it is your choice. I can wait for you. I have always waited for you.

"Everything you do, I give you a choice. I do not force you. You must do things willingly, unconditionally, happily. If you are unhappy, then you can rest. Rest assured you will come back. I am not worried. You should be worried. How many lifetimes do you want to live? You asked Me to shorten them. You want to come back to Me and I lead you to this journey. Whatever you ask, I allow it. You want to stop, you can stop. It is your choice.

"Do things unconditionally. Do not compare yourself with others. They are dealing with different situations. Simran is all alone. Therefore, she can say "No." For her, her lessons are different. I am most fair. Here you are many. Therefore, your lessons are different. When I ask you to love each other and live as a family, you do things as a family. Yea, when you are ready, you will separate. But you are not yet ready."

That message jolted us into being more receptive to the idea of helping redeem spirits.

THE EXISTENCE OF SPIRITS

Some readers might still harbour disbelief regarding the existence of the spirit world on Earth. But there is sufficient evidence in our scriptures that such a world exists.

Bhai Sahib quoted from scriptures to support the existence of spirits. For example, in the Holy Bible: "There met Him (Jesus) out of the cemetery a man much possessed by unclean spirits ... And He asked him, what is thy name? The man answered saying, my name is Legion, for we are many ... And forthwith Jesus commanded the spirits to leave the man and enter a large herd of swine, about two thousand in number ... Whereupon the spirits came out and entered into the swine, and the herd ran violently down a steep slope into the sea where they perished." (Mark 5:2-13)

Bhai Sahib also mentioned that there are innumerable references to demons in the Qur'an. Spirits, therefore, must exist somewhere, in some form. Another quote from the Sri Guru Granth Sahib helps clear any remaining doubts: "Many millions are the archangels, the celestial singers, the kinnaras (spirit beings) with the body of a man and head of a horse, and other satanic beings. Many millions are the evil spirits, the ghosts, swines and tigers. Thou are farthest of the far, nearest of the near and filling all, yet thou standest apart from all." (p. 276)

Bhai Sahib explained that through the above quotation God reveals the various types of entities that inhabit this world with us, including those with satanic leanings. These creatures can influence our lives in many different ways. In hindsight, I have come to the firm conviction that a major root cause of human woes may be attributed to the interference of the lower forces such as spirits and other satanic influences.

Chapter Fourteen

ON SALVATION

THE TERM SALVATION HAS BEEN FREQUENTLY mentioned here, both with respect to the souls of departed dear ones and when considering the subject of spirits. This chapter explains the what, why and how of salvation.

THE NATURE OF SALVATION

Complete salvation is realised via the arousal and euphoric experiencing of the superconsciousness, which leads to one's merger and ultimate communion with the Divine within. Hence, it is imperative that every human being strives to achieve salvation. To understand this need, an extract from an article written by Bhai Sahib, entitled *Why and How of Meditation*, provides an introduction:

"It may be of interest to know that in accordance with Sikh and Hindu scriptures, an entity has to pass through 8,400,000 lives (*chaurassi lakh joon*) in the Mineral, Vegetable and Animal Kingdoms, before it is given the great good fortune of coming into the Human Kingdom. It is the embodiment of successive lives in human form, termed reincarnation, that one can expect to rise, and finally transcend the human barrier, to achieve the final goal of man, which is ultimate merger with God."

Bhai Sahib's explanation is corroborated by this verse from the SGGS: "... without the Naam, no one is liberated. People wander lost, staggering and stumbling through 8,400,000 incarnations. Without knowing the Guru, they cannot escape the noose of death!" (p. 1344)

It is of interest to note that this verse finds a parallel with a quote attributed to Rumi, an enlightened thirteenth century Sufi and Islamic scholar: "The dust of many crumbled cities settles over us like a forgetful doze, but we are older than those cities. We began as a mineral. We emerged into plant life and into the animal state, and then into being human, and always we have forgotten our former states, except in early spring when we slightly recall being green again." (*Rumi: Selected Poems*, p. 155)

Once, Maam Sahib was frying Venus clams (*lala*, as they are commonly known in my country). As she was doing so, her higher consciousness reminded her not to consume Venus clams again. She was told that there are spirits who are condemned to Venus clams, too.

During a group meditation held at the home of a fellow practitioner, a lizard started shrieking rather nosily midway through the session. This was most unusual, especially as all had been calm and quiet prior to the meditation. While driving home, Maam Sahib told me that the lizard requested her to put in a good word for it to God. This leads to the understanding that even a lizard is seeking salvation, as it hopes to be elevated to the human kingdom.

You have probably read stories of human beings having the acumen to communicate with animals, plants and even minerals. Bhai Sahib once told me that when he was in Canada he had been put up in the home of a family of VCM practitioners. They had a pet cat which, according to Bhai Sahib's discernment, would be elevated to the human kingdom in its next life.

During one particular sitting, The Infinite spoke: "Home, home ... when are you coming home to Me? All My children must be saved, even the thieves and the beggars!"

During another ancestral jaap, an ancestral spirit related to one of the participating practitioners was given permission by The Infinite to speak to us. He also spoke on behalf of several other ancestral spirits also present. The following is what was said before they crossed over to the spirit realm: ""We are the failures. We have been following traditional beliefs and forgotten the Ten Commandments. When we were human, we only cared to build our names for self-glorification, without any thoughts of God. Many others have already gone far ahead."

Just before they bid farewell, the ancestral spirits offered advice to their descendants (those practitioners who were present) to improve the perception of their generation. It was a reminder that we should not be overtly obsessed with earthly comforts, to the extent that we ignore the importance of salvation.

THE NEED FOR SPIRITUAL CONSCIOUSNESS

The attitude of human beings who live without spiritual consciousness is admonished in several verses in the scriptures. Bhai Sahib provides this illustration: "Man striveth hard for his family all the time to gather worldly riches. Thus disregarding and forgetting God he is influenced by the satanic forces ... In forsaking God, thy body becometh defiled as dust, leading to possession by these devilish tendencies." (SGGS, p. 706)

Bhai Sahib also shared his knowledge of an Indian historic figure who was condemned to the rock kingdom for blasphemy. According to Bhai Sahib, he can only be released from the rock kingdom if and when a holy man happens to pass by and releases him. He also gave us glimpses into the lives of the terrorists who were involved in the September 11 attacks. They were also condemned to the rock kingdom. In both these examples, the entities will have to again go through 8,400,000 incarnations before being able to return to the human kingdom. Clearly, their journeys will be long and tough, for an entity has to strive and earn redeeming points in each and every incarnation to move ahead.

Bhai Sahib also mentioned that human beings would transform, at the point of death, to that which reflects their negative thoughts. He quoted: "He who while dying thinks of money and dieth worrying so, he is born and re-born as a serpent. Oh beloved man, let me not forsake the Holy Spirit of God that pervades the entire Universe. He who while dying thinks of a woman, and dieth worrying so, he is created again and again as a whore. He who, while dying, thinks of the sons, and dieth worrying so, he is born and re-born as a swine. He who while dying thinks of his mansions, and dieth worrying so, he taketh re-birth as a devil (ghost) who takes abode in haunted houses. He who dwelleth upon the Lord and dieth reflecting thus, says Tirlochan, that man is emancipated, within him abideth vibrant entity, the Lord of all Lords." (SGGS, p. 526, Raag Gujri: The Pathas of Sri Tirlochan Ji)

Due to the above scriptural injunctions and experiential lessons, I began to understand why salvation is of paramount importance in our journey of life. I quote another extract from the same article as above, written by Bhai Sahib, which is self-explanatory:

"It is said that if a soul is excessively consumed with physical, mental and materialistic values, it may regress to those lower kingdoms. This is why one should work towards salvation to avoid those trials and tribulations. It is also enjoined in the Eastern scriptures that if we do not avail ourselves of the precious opportunity bestowed on us while in the human kingdom, by diligently developing our spiritual nature, but in its place devote our entire attention towards the physical, mental and materialistic values of life, that we may regress once again to the thralls of the animal and other lower kingdoms of life aforementioned."

Salvation, therefore, is the way to free oneself from the enduring quagmire of the cycle of births and deaths. "To avoid any regression, human beings should make an all-out claim for our majestic heritage. That is the primary purpose of our human life. Hence, the singular and the greatest accomplishment is the realisation of one's primal Self; a fully awakened Mind that unites in Oneness with the Divine within, while one is still a mortal being. All other human activities are, therefore, of secondary importance." (Sri Bhai Sahib, 2002)

THE PATH TO SALVATION

The how, specifically what it will take for one to achieve salvation, is a fundamental human concern. The main activity to achieve salvation is to practise a type of meditation, like that of VCM, which includes the elements of complete surrender and submission to the Divine within. It involves an effortless act to completely subdue one's ego and personality. Consistent practice leads to a spontaneous and easy flowing of an involuntary worship, moment by moment, that is Divinely inspired.

For beginners, it is necessary that one or more regular practitioners are present to guide them for their first sessions. This type of meditation, the highest and most potent, is mentioned in all the world's scriptures. I share below three of the many verses that were pointed out by Bhai Sahib.

"Oh mind of man, perceive at all times the close proximity of the presence of God. The cycle of birth and death is obliterated when one is totally saturated with the vibrant awakening of the Holy Spirit (Naam-Soul) in egoless God-guided worship/meditation." (SGGS, p. 34, Sri Raag)

"He who worships God in a state of Divine ecstasy has achieved life's fulfillment on Earth. The carrying out of good deeds and making donations to charity cannot equal the worship of Him in complete effacement and surrender, accompanied by an awakening and a stirring of the Soul, wherefore one's cycle of birth and death is completely curtailed." (SGGS, p. 927, Ramkali)

"Oh friends and saintly folks, carry out deep worship of the Divine, which constitutes a praise unto Him, but always in a state of relaxed alertness." (SGGS, p. 295, Sukhmani)

During one of our group meditations, the following was received: "No craftsmen can produce such trophies as those scars we receive in our services to God." According to Bhai Sahib, the word *service* appears in the scriptures of nearly every religion. He explained that except for several particular instances, it does not mean service to humanity or the like, but service to God, *God service*. He further said of God service: "It simply means worship or meditation dedicated to God, because God is not a human being whom we can serve, as we do other creatures." 'Scars' refer to the challenges one undergoes when one embarks on the spiritual path. This corroborates the message given elsewhere by Bhai Sahib: "Pain is remedy and pleasure the malady; where all is seeming solace, there is no yearning for God and no reality of His Presence."

One should not, therefore, expect the journey of life to always be smooth and pleasant. There are assuredly many obstacles along the way, which need to be overcome with patience and perseverance.

Bhai Sahib commented on the poor attitude that prevails among human beings regarding God and His Reality. I quote what the Almighty once spoke regarding free will, which He gave to humankind: "Always remember, I give you freedom of choice because I love you unconditionally. You show your trust and faith and love in Me, your Creator, when you practise your freedom of choice. This is how I can know whether you choose Me."

In this regard, too, BabuJi once said to a group of practitioners: "Life is a journey with no end. You leave the world, and you return. Therefore, it is a journey. One should not fear. It is a journey where one cleanses oneself, where one polishes one's soul. Learn to be a better human being, a better child of the Lord, your Creator. Walk in His way and return to Him. That is your journey, for you are His Creation, as all there is is His. All must return to Him.

"You must all remember that spirituality at such a level as this needs to be earned, needs to be carried throughout all your past lives until this life. Therefore, learn to regard it as the most precious gift that you have brought with you from your past lives. Do not fall from grace. Build on it so you will be able to help others, for you are the chosen ones.

"You must always obey the Ten Commandments and God's words. And remember to put them into practice. Do not always just speak of what should be done, but do what should be done. Do it with love. Do it in good faith and with humility.

"Sometimes you get cases you label as a 'no hope' case. But consider this: you can save a soul. The soul is the most precious being within a human. If you cannot save the body, you can save the soul. Always remember that when you deal with such supposed 'no hope' cases, the best thing to tell them is not to lose hope, that God is always with them. That they need to forgive others and themselves, then move on, detach, and think only of the Lord. He will guide them home. So be it."

Chapter Fifteen

THE GURU

ONE EVENING IN 1994, A QUARREL BROKE OUT between my wife and I. It led her to storm out of the house. I did not know what to do next, and could not think of anyone I could call on for help. A moment later, I found myself calling Bhai Sahib, even though I had only very recently met him.

"Hello, Bhai Sahib," I said. "I just quarrelled with Caroline. She has left the house."

"Never mind. I will call her back," Bhai Sahib replied gently. Bhai Sahib continued, "Afterwards, if you are in contact with BabuJi, remember to ask him two questions. Ask him what his relationship with Bhai Sahib is. Also, ask him what Bhai Sahib's spiritual level is according to the spiritual chart."

My mind was so occupied with my wife's safety that I did not pay attention to what Bhai Sahib had said about him calling her back. It was only when the episode was over that I began to reflect on what had happened.

Meanwhile, together with my eldest daughter, who was twelve years of age at that time, I drove to my wife's cousin's house. On arrival, I asked my daughter to check if her mother was in her cousin's house, and if so to coax her to return home, while I waited behind the wheel.

My eldest daughter returned just as fast as she had entered the house. Standing a short distance away, she shouted loudly: "Daddy! BabuJi wants to talk to you." She told me BabuJi had said to her, "What is your father doing in the car? Ask him to come in."

I went inside as instructed. In one of the rooms I saw Maam Sahib sitting on a bed in a lotus position. Her eyes were teary and closed. I could see that she was already in a meditative mode. I then spoke to BabuJi through Maam Sahib.

After I had said my piece about our tiff, BabuJi reminded us of Bhai Sahib's advice, which is CAT, an acronym for Compromise, Adjust, Tolerate. Bhai Sahib had taught us to put that acronym into practice in order to maintain a harmonious marital relationship. Just before the end of the session, I recalled the questions that Bhai Sahib had said I should ask Babuji.

Athan: "BabuJi, what is your relationship with Bhai Sahib?"

BabuJi: "Oh, we are one and the same. We are like brothers."

Athan: "What is Bhai Sahib's spiritual status according to the chart entitled, *Superior Divine Development and Potency*?"

BabuJi: "Oh, xxxx. (We have been advised that the spiritual status of Bhai Sahib should not be revealed.) They call Him, 'God on Earth'."

Later, after our minor argument, when things were back to normal, Maam Sahib told me that just as she had boarded a taxi on the way to her cousin's house, BabuJi asked her: "Maam Sahib, what are you doing here?" This unusual telepathic communication continued to manifest from thereon. It was from this receiving that I learned BabuJi is the spirit form of Bhai Sahib; Bhai Sahib is his human form as a spiritual master.

I recall an incident in which I asked Maam Sahib to buy gaming tickets for me while I waited behind the wheel. I noticed that she turned back just before she stepped into the gaming outlet. She was smiling as she walked back. She told me that BabuJi discouraged her from patronising gaming outlets. She told BabuJi that she just wanted to humour me by helping to buy the gaming tickets, but this was not accepted. I paid no heed to the advice and went inside to buy the tickets myself.

Although this incident made me realise that gambling is not encouraged for one who is on a true spiritual path, I also learned that there is a direct communication link not only between my eldest daughter and BabuJi, but also between Maam Sahib and BabuJi. In 1997, during a meditation at home, Maam Sahib received a message from the Almighty via automatic writing: "Bhai Sahib is my Prophet. The next Christ."

The following evening, Bhai Sahib asked my wife and I to initiate a Caucasian woman from Australia, named Tanya. Her husband was a Malaysian Punjabi. In the middle of the initiation Maam Sahib received the following message from The Infinite: "Bhai Sahib is My Messenger, My Prophet."

When I heard this message, I reacted with a neutral stance, as I was unable to come up with any authentic justifications to convince myself it was the truth. This was during the early days of my spiritual growth. I stayed with Bhai Sahib, and continued with VCM practice, to ascertain the truth of those messages.

You will have noted the presence of Archangel Gabriel when my fellow practitioners and I went to help the Punjabi medical doctor whose marriage was on the rocks due to a charm. Who was this Archangel Gabriel? Later that night, I reported to Bhai Sahib, who was in his residence. Bhai Sahib was always an excellent listener. When I had finished describing what had happened, he calmly raised his head and gently uttered: "Archangel Gabriel is inside me."

I later realised that Bhai Sahib's statement corroborated the experience of a young European woman in Australia, to whom was revealed that Bhai Sahib was a prophet. On another occasion, when the same lady was driving through the streets of Sydney, she had a very unusual experience. A voice commanded her to stop by the side of the road, whereupon the following message was received: "Bhai Sahib has Archangel Gabriel dwelling inside him. This draws spiritual truths to his lips and affirms that Bhai Sahib is a true miracle worker." She conveyed this message to me soon after this incident.

I later learned from Bhai Sahib that this same Archangel Gabriel was responsible for dictating the entire Qur'an to Prophet Mohammad. Bhai Sahib further mentioned that, as a matter of record, Archangel Gabriel had appeared to the Jewish prophet, Daniel.

Bhai Sahib also related the story of Archangel Gabriel, who is known to have accompanied Bapak of Subud when he was taken through the Sun on his journey to face God. Bhai Sahib was involved with Subud for about a decade. He told me that after a meditation session, Bapak pulled him aside and told him that he had received a message that Bhai Sahib would one day leave Subud to form his own organisation. In fact, Bhai Sahib confided to me that Bapak was in part here to pave the way for him to further propagate work for God.

I had wondered if there was any way to prove that the spiritual status of Bhai Sahib was xxxx. When I was a younger practitioner, I did not know whether to believe the chart that Bhai Sahib's spiritual value was indeed as revealed by BabuJi. At that time I had no convincing justification to believe it was true. It was only eleven years later, in 2005, that an incident proved to me that Bhai Sahib's spiritual status was indeed xxxx. The incident was in relation to a female Punjabi practitioner who claimed she was receiving messages from higher sources through automatic writing. I was of the opinion that the messages she had received were from an earthbound spirit. This meant the Punjabi woman was possessed!

Maam Sahib and I had a meditation at home to seek Divine intervention. We received advice that should the Punjabi woman in question make any more similar claims, I was to question her about Bhai Sahib's spiritual status. The opportunity to ask that question arrived when an akhand jaap was in progress at our meditation center. The following is the dialogue between the female Punjabi practitioner and me:

Punjabi lady: "Cleanse yourself, my children. (Repeated twice.) Put your mind and soul into this jaap. That's why this jaap is held, to cleanse your soul. Do not waste this opportunity."

Athan: "Can I ask you a question?"

Punjabi lady: "Yes, my child. What is your question?"

Athan: "What is Bhai Sahib's spiritual status?"

Punjabi lady: "Oh, very high. Have no doubt about him, my child. Have no doubt."

Athan: "What is his spiritual value on the chart?"

Punjabi lady: "Hundred upon hundred. Have no doubt, my child."

Athan: "I repeat. What is Bhai Sahib's spiritual value on the chart as designed by Bhai Sahib?!"

Punjabi lady: "Why are you having doubts about Bhai Sahib?"

Athan: "I am asking you a question. Please answer!"

Punjabi lady: "A thousand and sixty."

Athan: "Wrong! Who are you? Identify yourself!"

Punjabi lady: "I ... I ... I am Eliza. I died of a deadly disease in 1526."

Athan: "Out! Out! Out!"

Punjabi lady: "I don't like your world. I want to leave now. Okay! Okay! I am leaving!"

Indeed, the Punjabi lady was possessed by an earthbound spirit. She could not even utter "Waheguru" when possessed by that spirit. In her normal state of mind, she could recite the Sri Guru Granth Sahib very well in Gurmukhi. The spirit was later guided towards the light and crossed over to the spirit realm.

This experiential lesson convinced me of the validity of the chart and that Bhai Sahib's spiritual value was indeed xxxx. My experiential spiritual lessons, received over more than two and half decades, and which continued after Bhai Sahib passed on in 2011, have led me to realise that indeed Bhai Sahib was the Messenger of the Almighty.

I shall end this topic with a message from the Almighty regarding Bhai Sahib's spiritual status stated in one of our later meditation sessions: "There is none like Bhai Sahib in this world. He is the only one. You are so fortunate to have such an example, yet you do not know how fortunate you are. You do not follow his way. You should. Many do not have access to him personally to learn what spirituality involves. We must send these souls away to their rightful realm now."

EARTH'S GOLDEN AGE AND MEDITATION

Bhai Sahib revealed that Earth will, in time, advance from the current Dark Age to the Golden Age. This will only happen when sufficient numbers of human beings experience a high level of Divine awareness. This is described by the Vedic scriptures as a progression from Kali Yuga to Satya (truth) Yuga.

So far I have emphasised the soul over other human aspects, such as the physical, mental and emotional. This is because knowledge regarding the three other aspects is readily available from various sources. Empowering our soul involves meditation. Accordingly, I now consider what meditation is, why we need to meditate, and what we can expect from meditation.

Since meditation is of the Divine, it follows that the Almighty is the perfect authority to speak on meditation. If that is so, how may we communicate with the Almighty to learn the right practice? And how would we know if it is actually the Almighty we are in communion with?

All these questions were answered when I came into contact with Vibrant Celestial Meditation. I quickly came to realise that this meditation, as taught by Bhai Sahib, is in a league of its own. VCM technique is extremely simple and effortless.

While we are hopeful regarding humankind's future, we must bear in mind that although we are progressing towards the Golden Age, it will be no walk in the park. We have been forewarned of what is likely to occur. The forewarning began with concern for children, because they are the future. The children referred to are not only of one's own family, and not only of this nation, Malaysia, but of Earth!

People are the ones who build up or destroy the Earth. Humanity needs builders. Humanity does not need destroyers. There is great concern regarding the future of planet Earth and therefore regarding the people who are going to build or kill it.

Human beings have a duty, a part to play. We have been asked to perform our duty well. We have been asked to consider whether, when we leave this world, that marks the end of our existence? We have been asked to consider that question many times. We will be reborn. We are the ones who will be re-sent to this planet. Hence, we will suffer the consequences if we do not build this planet well. That is why we have repeatedly been told to build up this planet instead of destroying everything God has put in it. *We were asked to start putting it back before it breaks up.*

We were also told not to moan and groan about our situation. We were asked to start thinking about how to build and save the planet, *beyond just recycling materials*. This involves changing the mindset of people. This change starts with the children. We were asked to get the next generation ready so that they, in turn, may have the groundwork to positively develop the mindset of their next generation.

As I understand it, the above warning was given because we human beings have been extracting oil, minerals and other natural resources from under the ground to such an extent that it will eventually cause disequilibrium to our planet. When these activities continue unabated, they create extensive voids in the ground. Earth will consequently undergo violent movements in order to regain her equilibrium. *That will result in land masses here and there breaking away, or collapsing into the oceans, as we have been forewarned.*

We have been asked to think long and hard over what we have been doing, and the likely catastrophic consequences if we do not heed the warning. We were reminded that we will be the ones who will face the catastrophe, because we will have to return to the Earth. We will reincarnate as human beings, or perhaps as other lower life forms. We therefore have to start now to right the wrong, which includes remediating the damage done to the ground. To achieve this, we have to educate the younger generations who will manage Earth in the future. They will, in turn, prepare their next generations to continue with the task of healing Mother Earth.

This is where meditation of the VCM variety is relevant. It helps to equally develop our souls, mind and physical aspects, so we will then be able to maximise the use of our creative power within.

Let us not think that wealth, particularly money, is everything. Money is man-made and is ultimately lifeless. Let us not consider this warning only when catastrophe begins to unfold before our eyes. Do we really need that to happen to make us realise that in the pursuit of money we have all been inflicting irreparable damage on this planet?

Human beings, along with all aspects of nature, are the essence of Reality. They are creations of The Infinite. They are of such paramount importance that we should be concerned for them. The Infinite once lamented: "What have you done to My beautiful Earth!" The Infinite declared that humanity is destroying Earth, but we will have to bear the consequences of our own actions.

Bhai Sahib added in his discourse *Our Earth*: "The severity ... can be much lessened if VCM spreads more widely around the world. Hence let us try and fulfill our responsibilities by making an honest attempt at spreading VCM system as widely as possible."

THE TRUE GURU / DISCIPLE RELATIONSHIP

Having been cynical throughout my early adult years, I had the uncompromising conviction that I would never again look up to any so-called masters associated with religion or the supernatural. That conviction was the outcome of my earlier experiences derived from my all-out efforts seeking God, which had ended in vain. My conviction intensified when my fourth child was born with severe cerebral palsy. Finding no answers regarding the purpose of my existence, I concluded there is neither a God nor are there any genuine spiritual masters.

Nevertheless, the subject of spirituality has always fascinated me and has always been close to my heart. Consequently, in my later years I reasoned that if I have to learn as much as possible about true spirituality, the same high standards should be held by a true Guru. I assumed that a true Guru should be of the highest caliber, being one who functions as an intermediary between human beings and the Creator. Ideally, a true Guru is an enlightened person who potentially engages with The Infinite. I reasoned that if this premise is right, then the outcome should also be right, that is, that a real possibility exists that one is able to communicate with the Creator.

Having clarified this to myself, I then attempted to create a basis for understanding the nature of a true Guru/disciple relationship. The following questions formed the criteria for my assessment:

- ∞ What are the attributes of a true Guru?
- ∞ How may we recognise a true Guru?
- ∞ What are the roles of a true Guru?
- ∞ Is there a need for a disciple to revere a true Guru?

In order to obtain sensible answers to these questions, I sought the help of Bhai Sahib. He furnished me with relevant quotations from the scriptures. Paramahansa Yogananda, author of *The Divine Romance*, describes a true guru as "... ordained by God to help sincere seekers in response to their deep soul craving, [a guru] is not an ordinary teacher: he is a human vehicle whose body, speech, mind, and spirituality God uses as a channel to attract and guide lost souls back to their home of immortality. A guru is a living embodiment of scriptural truth. He is an agent of salvation appointed by God in response to a devotee's demand for release from the bondage of matter." (Yogananda, p. 457)

He further described a real Guru as one who has a balanced mind, who is an ocean of mercy, and who is able to remove aspirants' doubts and obstacles. A true Guru is also a Satguru, who is absolutely free from passion, anger, selfishness, greed, hatred and egoism. A true Guru is beyond worldly temptations. A true Guru is a living Master who is able to guide disciples towards God realisation. The title does not refer to a Guru who is dead and gone. This is because only a true Guru in living form can explain the mystical and life-giving truths abundantly enshrined in religious scriptures and framed in mysterious and allegorical language. It is observed that since time immemorial there has always been a living Master on Earth during any era. Bhai Sahib said that one such Master, or sometimes more than one, has been strategically planted by The Infinite.

My VCM practice over the last two decades has shown me what a true Guru is. I realised that a true Guru refers to a soul who has achieved mastery over those aspects of his nature that would otherwise impede him from achieving total God realisation. Since knowledge of spirituality is of The Infinite, and that knowledge is God-directed and God-guided, being obtained through His grace and blessing, it is only logical that the true Guru must be one who is deliberately chosen and commissioned by The Infinite to guide his disciples towards the realisation of their Divine nature, that being the pristine primordial nature which is Oneness with God.

Bhai Sahib was, to me, a true Guru. It took me several years to come to that realisation, after a continuous self-evaluation of my involvement with VCM, by observing the changes in and around me as well as the mannerisms of Bhai Sahib.

I was rather surprised that my assumption turned out to be correct, that being a true Guru is chosen and commissioned by God. The need to revere a true Guru is beautifully expounded in the Sri Guru Granth Sahib: "Valid worship/meditation is imbibed only through the guidance of a true Guru." (p. 602) My understanding of the word *valid* is that it means the highest form of meditation. *Clearly, the highest form of meditation can only come from God.*

In addition, if a true Guru refers to one who is commissioned by God to guide disciples, it should follow that a true Guru is in many ways the perfect embodiment of God. The following SGGS verse is similar to what was pointed out by Paramahansa Yogananda: "In the Guru is enshrined the Lord Himself, and He unites us with God. Oh blessed, blessed be the Guru ... It is through the Perfect Guru that one tastes the Taste of God ... Only he who serveth the true Guru can experience the welling up of the Divine Presence within him." (p. 997)

A disciple who reveres the true Guru will experience immense benefits from the true Guru/disciple relationship. This is written in the SGGS: "By great good fortune does one meet with the Perfect Guru, the guide." (p. 864)

And: "God blesses the disciple through the Guru by enabling him to feel the awakened Divine Presence in deep meditation." (p. 945)

The need for a true Guru, and the requirement for discipleship to maximise progress on the path to ultimate God realisation, is declared not only in the SGGS but in the scriptures of all other faiths. In the Bible, Jesus Christ emphatically states: "I Am the Way, the Truth and the Life, no man cometh unto the Father, but by Me." (John 14:6) Christ, like all the world's other prophets and messiahs, was a true Guru when he was on Earth. The words *I Am the Way* explicitly expounds that only through a true Guru will disciples be able to realise God.

It appears that from time to time The Infinite has sent a prophet/messiah to Earth to guide disciples in their return to the God-Source. All prophets and messiahs have had the same mission: to guide their disciples to merge with God via a process of profound meditation, of deep surrender, and of submission to the Divine within.

In the Bhagavad Gita, Lord Krishna reiterates this promise from God in the following verse: "To deliver the pious and to annihilate the miscreants, as well as to reestablish the principles of religion, I myself appear, millennium after millennium." (*Transcendental Knowledge*, Text 8) Jesus Christ specifies that the stature of a true Guru must be one with God, "I and the Father are One." (John 10:30)

This also applies to Bhai Sahib, who was one with God when he was on Earth. What prompts me to make this assertion? In Singapore, towards the end of a spiritual session, The Infinite spoke through Maam Sahib: "Athan, can you be kind to your children? I am God." The next moment, it was followed by: "Sahib, I haven't talked to you for a long time. Can you be kind to your children? I Am BabuJi." I knew at once that BabuJi was one with God.

Later, while on the way home to Kuala Lumpur, Bhai Sahib phoned me and asked: "Athan, is there any message from God?"

"Bhai Sahib, why do you ask? You already know it." I replied.

Bhai Sahib was in stitches after hearing my reply. With that, he ended the phone call: "Alright, I will see you when you are back in K.L."

Insofar as Bhai Sahib was concerned, several other practitioners, including a psychic from Australia, have been enlightened with messages from very high sources regarding the elevated status of Bhai Sahib. Auother distinguished practitioner from Canada was shown that Bhai Sahib was a truly realised Master, known as a Satguru in Sikh/Hindu parlance. I learned from Bhai Sahib that there can be more than one Satguru in the world at any one time.

The technique of VCM introduced by Bhai Sahib involves a deep state of surrender to the Divine within, which then stimulates spontaneous, effortless, ecstatic and euphoric responses. Only a living Guru who has the experience, wisdom and insight can interpret and divulge the critical yet elusive meaning of the term *surrender* in VCM. Over time, I began to appreciate the loftiness of VCM. It is indeed an authentic technique of profound worship that is from the Highest Source. I realised that it can only be taught by an elevated Guru who must be the choice of our Creator. All these point to Bhai Sahib as a true Guru.

Given my life experiences, my critical, non-conformist attitude, and the awareness I had acquired from my VCM practice, as well as the years of protracted observation of Bhai Sahib at close quarters, I came to realise that Bhai Sahib was the Messiah of the Millennium. He came back to show us the way towards God realisation.

Let me briefly share a true story related to me by a woman whose name was Madam Jaswinderjit Kaur. She confided that one early morning she was at a gurdwara (Sikh temple) located at Titiwangsa, Kuala Lumpur. She was praying earnestly to Waheguru (God) to guide her to a living Guru who could teach her the right type of meditation. Not long after, Madam Jaswinderjit returned a phone call from Bhai Sahib, who had called her earlier but the call had been taken by Madam Jaswinderjit's mother. The following is her narration of her phone conversation with Bhai Sahib:

Madam Jaswinderjit: "Hello, Uncle. Did you call me earlier? What can I do for you?"

Bhai Sahib: "It is not what you can do for me but what I can do for you."

Madam Jaswinderjit: "Uncle, why do you say that?"

Bhai Sahib: "You were disturbing my sleep so early in the morning. You were praying hard, asking God to guide you to a Guru to teach you the right meditation. Didn't you?"

Madam Jaswinderjit was dumbstruck by that phone conversation. She said that nobody knew of the private supplication she made before God in that gurdwara. Although Madam Jaswinderjit and Bhai Sahib had previously met each other, it was just once at a business gathering held in Goa, India. She was utterly amazed by the phone conversation.

Not long after that episode, she was also awakened to Bhai Sahib's high spiritual status. She once said that if she found there actually existed someone who is looked on as a true Guru, she had two hundred questions for him to answer before she would ever consider him as one. This was her way of saying that without that experiential awakening it would be hard for her to believe something of this nature, merely on the basis of reasoning. (Madam Jaswinderjit Kaur has migrated to Canada with her family. She has been elevated to the status of a VCM elder. She has also been given the task of researching dream interpretations by The Infinite).

Bhai Sahib did not share his conversation with Madam Jaswinderjit with any of the practitioners. It was through her that I learned of this incident. Bhai Sahib was indeed a true Guru who carried out his God-given task without any air of superiority or for the sake of self-glory.

In another incident, my friend Peter Wong was accompanying me to Kuala Lumpur City. I told him I had to drop by a friend's house first. (I was referring to Bhai Sahib's house.) Peter Wong did not mind. But the moment Peter Wong saw Bhai Sahib, who was then busy cooking, I noticed he abruptly took a step backwards. With a stunned expression, Peter Wong whispered to me: "Last night, I dreamed exactly of this elderly Punjabi man with his head covered with an orange scarf, and he was busy cooking a meal for me! Peter Wong was so startled he remained silent throughout my casual chat with Bhai Sahib. It was unusual for him to remain quiet, as he was a very approachable person who could easily converse with anyone.

Peter Wong later learned meditation from Bhai Sahib, although his attendance was infrequent. He was a street-smart guy, an underworld bookie who dealt in various forms of gambling. With gambling as a source of livelihood, it was not surprising the word *trust* was never in his dictionary. He was not one to believe in spirituality, either. In fact, he once said he only prayed to money. Consequently, I was surprised he had such high respect for Bhai Sahib, and for VCM meditation. Perhaps, his dream of Bhai Sahib stimulated a nascent spiritual to awaken within him.

It is worthwhile putting on record what Bhai Sahib said about the role of the true Guru. He said that a true Guru would make every effort to ensure that every one of his disciples could stand solidly on their own two feet in spiritual and allied matters. This would enable every disciple to tap adequately into the Kingdom of God that is awakened within, and as a result they would not have to lean too heavily on an external Guru.

Bhai Sahib also said that any master who over-emphasised a total dependency on him may not be a true Guru. I agreed, as I have always thought it natural for one to strive for independence in whatever one is pursuing. I feel there should not be any exception, even with respect to the subject of spirituality. That understanding also led me to discern the difference between a true Guru and a professor. My understanding is that while a professor shares with students knowledge that emanates from about 10% or so of his mind's capacity, a true Guru guides his disciples to use a much greater proportion of their minds.

Bhai Sahib, like any realised Master, in his lighter mundane moments may have betrayed and lessened his nobility once in a while by committing small inadequacies. Bhai Sahib once said that no human is perfect. Only God Almighty is absolute and is beyond blemish.

I also observed that where a practitioner began to lose faith in Bhai Sahib without any apparent reason, or began to speak critically of Bhai Sahib, that practitioner would end up being disoriented in behavior. A senior practitioner from East Malaysia once shared an incident with me. He told me about a woman who criticised and condemned Bhai Sahib's teaching. He said that Bhai Sahib later told him that the woman in question would bring suffering upon herself through her lack of faith and by failing to develop herself. The senior practitioner was surprised to have seen for himself the suffering that the woman subsequently went through.

I once witnessed Bhai Sahib being bombarded in an emotionally-charged gathering. I was amazed not only by his calm and humble demeanour, but his sensible response, despite the brickbats being thrown at him. He put into practice what he preached. One piece of advice he imparted to his disciples was: "Accept pebbles thrown at you like flowers being strewn in your path."

Bhai Sahib also stressed that VCM has nothing at all to do with proselytisation. He advised that if one is a Christian, be a good Christian; if one is a Muslim, be a good Muslim; if one is a Buddhist, be a good Buddhist; and if one is a Hindu, be a good Hindu, etc. Bhai Sahib never harboured any resentment towards his critics, nor ever manifested any negativity for that matter. He spoke well of all people all the time. It was a rare privilege to be his regular companion, as I always enjoyed his loving aura, which radiated wisdom and humility. Clearly, he was a role model for all his disciples; although, admittedly, it has never been easy for me to emulate him.

Sri Bhai Sahib merged with The Infinite in 2011, at the age of ninety. I have mentioned in this chapter that the term *true Guru* refers to a living Master. Since Bhai Sahib is no more on this side, I am now better able to appreciate why Bhai Sahib said that a true Guru will guide his disciples to stand on their own two feet in spiritual matters.

Herewith, I would like to share a message from The Infinite received by Eileen Caddy, author of the book, *God Spoke To Me*. She returned to God-Source in 2006. "You can be gently led or guided up to a certain point in your life by a teacher, a Master, a Guru, but the time comes when all outer help has to be withdrawn and you stand completely alone. In that state of aloneness, you come to KNOW ME with that inner knowing which nothing can shake or disturb. Every soul on the spiritual path has to reach this point before he or she can go on to greater things, before they can learn to use MY POWERS OF CREATION which are theirs to use when they are ready to use them to MY HONOR AND GLORY and for the benefit of all humankind. All power, all wisdom is yours when you are ready." (Caddy, 2006)

A PROPHET AND RECOGNITION

I was into my seventh year of regular VCM practice when Bhai Sahib asked me to write on this topic. Since then I have witnessed many revelations about who Bhai Sahib really was. Many VCM practitioners are still unaware of Bhai Sahib's prophetic stature.

A prophet is seldom recognised by people, even though they may be very familiar with that person. In this case, it may be due to people's general perception of Bhai Sahib: he appeared rather simple and ordinary. Perception can become reality. Hence, most practitioners were unable to recognise Bhai Sahib's spiritual state. Among them was the early me. Bhai

Sahib never wore the garb of a holy man. He never allowed himself to be called a saint, let alone the higher designation of prophet. It was thus difficult for insensitive practitioners to see his true quality. I now openly share some revelations regarding him. In the last lap of my life, I am aware that I would be failing in my God-given duty if I did not divulge this Divine truth.

Among the many utterances regarding Bhai Sahib's spiritual loftiness, which ranged from Archangel Gabriel dwelling inside him to the manifestation of several different prophets of the old during meditations, I shall limit myself to just the following two: "Listen. I sent Bhai Sahib to you all. Stand by him. Follow him. Listen to him. I am God ... Bhai Sahib is the real Messiah in these modern times. They call Him God on Earth."

On one occasion, a small group of practitioners was inspired by the prophetic status of Bhai Sahib and asked him to explain the true meaning of the scriptures. This is a self-explanatory extract from a message received from The Infinite: "Believe in and revere only One Supreme God. Listen to Bhai Sahib. He is your present Messiah of the Millennium. You do not seem to understand the scriptures I sent down to Mankind. Your present Messiah, Bhai Sahib, can tell you what they truly mean. I am God."

Before venturing any further, it is necessary to share my understanding of spiritual beings, and for that matter God, which is said to be able to manifest in various forms. On the evening of 15 April 2012, my third daughter, Quin, received the following message, meant for me: "One may feel sorrow in one's soul because of a fear of his or her life that may not be known. Only God knows, for He watches all, in every form and in every way. God has the power to see within one's eyes and to know one's fate. He is watching all, for we are His creations, His children, and His care, each and every one. Never feel sorrow in one's soul, for He is watching all."

Quin explained that God can take any form. (Quin is mildly autistic. She is not going to excel in studies, but has a talent for drawing. On one occasion she received a letter of commendation from a local university regarding her artwork. She does not seem to have any friends, but appears comfortable enough being a loner. She was rather impersonal when she handed me this second message—her first is discussed on page 218.)

This second message triggered me to recall an evening drive with Bhai Sahib, during my early days with him. On that occasion he advised me to see God in everything, for example, in a spoon, in a cupboard, in a tree, or in a hill. He said that if I cannot see God in that way, I will not be able to see God at all. At that point, I thought Bhai Sahib's advice on how I should engage with God was rather profound, but it was beyond me.

Several years later, as I became familiar with the SGGS texts, I realised that some of the verses actually reveal the manifestation of God in various forms and ways: "The Lord Himself creates us, watches over us, and places us on the path. Oh siblings of Destiny, there is no other than Him." (p. 601) "The Lord took the form of a dwarf and asked for some land. If Bal the King had recognised Him, he would not have been deceived, and sent to the Underworld." (p. 1344) ""The One Lord, who takes hundreds of thousands of forms, cannot be seen. He can only be described as One." (p. 1394)

A book titled *The Source of All Our Strength*, validated by Bhai Sahib as being from the God-Source, also mentions this attribute: "Do not think of God as a universal power without intelligence, love or personality. Some people deny the existence of a personal, anthropomorphic God. God took form. God still takes form and comes amongst you and you must look for Him in every form everywhere in your life. Seek, and ye shall find." (White, 1999)

It was reported that during some of Bhai Sahib's earlier trips to USA in the 1960s, certain psychics sighted a thick radiant golden halo around Bhai Sahib's head from shoulder to shoulder, and at times a bright golden aura enveloping him from head to foot. During one of his many trips to India, people saw not only the same golden halo around his head, but also a red flame rising from his forehead. Incidentally, a verse in Sukhmani Sahib, in the SGGS, supports such a manifestation, particularly that of a flame from the forehead. It records: "Pragateh joth mahant ke maathei, Nanak uthrei tein ke saathei", which translates into "a beam of light that manifests in a guru's forehead is enough to transform those in his company."

The revered book, *Prem Somarag Granth* (*Absolute Love, The Highway To God*), reputed to have been written by Guru Gobind Singh Ji, predicted a noble personality would be born in a Sikh home, who would introduce a type of meditation likened to intoxicated dance (haal ki mustee). Dr. Kanwaljit, a VCM practitioner from New Zealand, recognised that the prediction referred to none other than Bhai Sahib. Dr. Kanwaljit also insightfully saw that this personality would not allow himself to be called a saint (sant in the Punjabi language) or a mahaguru. This uncanny prediction by Guru Gobind Singh Ji was made some 250 years before the actual coming of Bhai Sahib. Another astounding part of this prognosis is that Bhai Sahib himself read this writing, but long after he on his own accord had decided that he did not want to be called a saint or a guru!

In the previous section on the true Guru/disciple relationship, I mentioned that Bhai Sahib had told me that one or more such Masters may be strategically planted by The Infinite on Earth. I recall an article written by Bhai Sahib in which he mentioned his findings of the *Prem Samarag Granth*, among which was the coming of a Muslim mystic. Bhai Sahib suggested this mystic was Muhammad Subuh Sumohadjiwijojo, from Java, Indonesia. Bhai Sahib validated that he was indeed a prophet.

Bhai Sahib was also revealed to have been a superior spiritual being in his many previous lives. Despite his background, Bhai Sahib still had to go through very severe and, at times, harsh spiritual training schedules where he was made to start almost from scratch. This was probably intended to prepare Bhai Sahib, giving him the necessary experience and knowledge to become aware of the many alleyways and byways that exist along the path of realising the Creator in our current misguided world.

During Bhai Sahib's early years, he practised all forms of yoga. He had been a Theosophist teacher, a metaphysician, a healer, and led Maharishi Mahesh Yogi's Transcendental Meditation movement for ten years. He also acquired knowledge of Sufism, Subud, Ogamisama's "dancing religion", Mahikari, Vedanta, Zen, Eckankar, Radha Soami, Ruhani Satsang, gestalt therapy, Gurdjieff, naturopathy, Jungian psychology and philosophy, psychosynthesis, metamorphosis, rebirthing, Silva mind control, radionics, neuro-linguistic programming, Divine exorcism, Scientology, Alice Bailey, Swedenborg, the White Brotherhood, and a host of other New Age esoteric teachings.

This journey ultimately led Bhai Sahib to discover that the highest, purest, speediest and most effective technique of spiritual practice had already been spelt out in great detail as a single universal system enshrined in all the world's scriptures. He chose to call this technique of spiritual practice Vibrant Celestial Meditation.

His insights into even ordinary things revealed his intimate knowledge of Mother Earth. Bhai Sahib related an incident where a man told him that an oil exploration firm was about to search for oil in a particular location. That exploration involved a huge investment. Bhai Sahib told the man there was no oil in the location they had targeted for exploration. Bhai Sahib also provided him with the percentages of the various types of soil composition they would find in that location. The outcome of the exploratory work proved Bhai Sahib's discernments to be correct!

Later, the same man asked Bhai Sahib where they would find oil. With a map in hand, Bhai Sahib pointed to a spot in the open sea. Test results at that spot showed that indeed oil was there. Unfortunately, they later learned that the location was in Indonesian waters.

Bhai Sahib was subsequently offered the post of a consultant to this oil exploration firm. The calling card from the firm was in Bhai Sahib's private library. Bhai Sahib told me he had to give up the consultancy post as he received direction from The Infinite that he was not permitted to use his powers for such purposes.

A drilling firm commissioned by a beer company in Selangor was entrusted with the job of drilling for well water. Water is one of the main resources required to brew beer. After many failed attempts to locate the needed water, Bhai Sahib helped locate a place. Initial drilling was not successful. Bhai Sahib advised them to drill even deeper, to a given depth. The firm then found water at the spot, at that depth.

Bhai Sahib related an incident where he was directed by The Infinite to take a flight to a particular country for an unspecified purpose. He told me many people were at the airport when he arrived that evening. He then waited for The Infinite to instruct him regarding his next move. He waited late into the night, until the lounge was virtually empty of people. Finally, he noticed, at quite a distance, a stranger walking towards him. The stranger issued an invitation to Bhai Sahib: "Sir, would you like to spend a night in my house?" Bhai Sahib said that night he was given the best bed in the stranger's house. He commented that God had really tested him until the eleventh hour!

A Punjabi lady once sought Bhai Sahib's help. Her son had been admitted into a mental asylum, with symptoms of mental illness, according to the doctors. Bhai Sahib related that the woman took quite some time to get in touch with him, because he was busy at work. Bhai Sahib said that through his discernment, he found that the cause of the boy's seeming madness was an excessive intake of white sugar. At Bhai Sahib's advice, white sugar was removed from the boy's diet, and he regained his normal self.

Not long after that, the boy again displayed the same erratic behaviour. Again, the Punjabi woman sought Bhai Sahib's help. Bhai Sahib asked the woman if her son was still taking white sugar, to which she answered no. Bhai Sahib then asked her to write down all the food and drink her son consumed. From the list, Bhai Sahib pointed out that white sugar was present in the biscuits, soft drinks, junk food, etc., that the boy had consumed. At Bhai Sahib's advice, those items were also removed from the boy's diet. Again, the boy regained his normal self. Without Bhai Sahib's power of discernment, the woman and her son would have depended on medical doctors, who would likely have prescribed sedatives or other drugs to treat the boy.

In another incident, a Punjabi woman asked Bhai Sahib for help as her husband was in a moribund state in the Intensive Care Unit of a local hospital. Using the discernment technique demarcated on the chart entitled *Overall Health and Vitality (Physical Body)*, Bhai Sahib discerned that the woman's husband had passed the critical point of no return, and was dying.

The man was the family's sole breadwinner. Bhai Sahib prayed and pleaded with God to show the dying man mercy, because his family would suffer without any source of income. Later, Bhai Sahib again discerned the man's condition and found he had gradually regained consciousness.

On one of his tours to Australia, Bhai Sahib related that a young Caucasian man confided in him that he had great difficulty obtaining good grades in his examinations. Bhai Sahib advised the man to attend his VCM seminar and to practise VCM consistently. The man later called and thanked Bhai Sahib for his help. He had scored distinctions in all his subjects.

A senior VCM practitioner in North America, and now a medical doctor, once called Bhai Sahib for help. The local weather station had forecast an impending hurricane was headed towards where she was living. The practitioner, with Bhai Sahib's help, meditated together online to redirect the hurricane to no man's land. I learned about this incident only because I happened to call Bhai Sahib one afternoon. He sounded very tired over the phone. He presently told me of this incident, in which he had taken on loads of 'heaviness'. He needed to sleep to recover from that task.

Bhai Sahib related another experience in London when he was in his early seventies. It was late at night and he had borrowed a car to get back to where he was staying. On the way there was a heavy downpour. This made driving more difficult, as it was quite dark and he could hardly read the road signs. He then went into a state of surrender and a 'force' within him took over. He was guided to reach his destination faster than usual, as it took a shorter route, which he was not aware of in his normal state of mind. This incident proved that the higher mind has the capability to function like a global positioning system.

Although there are other stories about Bhai Sahib's extraordinary feats, I would like to share several incidents which involved Bhai Sahib and me only. The first is as follows. In 1994 I attended a basic VCM seminar held in the library of Bhai Sahib's residence. Bhai Sahib said that when one is able to realise cosmic superconsciousness one can ask for anything and it would be given. At that moment I retorted at the top of my voice: "Are you sure!" All the participants were stunned with my loud reaction. I remained unconcerned and stood my ground.

The next instant Bhai Sahib moved a step forward and with an outstretched hand asked me what I would like to have. I was thinking to myself that should he fail to deliver the thing that I wanted, I would surely know how to run him down. I then thought of asking for gaming numbers, because that was the fastest way to receive a windfall. Just as I was about to open my mouth, Bhai Sahib interrupted me and exclaimed: "Don't ask me for numbers!" I was shocked. I wondered how on Earth he was able to read my mind. The whole incident took place too quickly for me to change my stance. I kept quiet after this exchange.

Another incident centered on one of Bhai Sahib's sisters, who had just passed on. Bhai Sahib wanted to carry out an akhand jaap for his sister's departed soul. The participation of myself and several other practitioners was needed to make up the numbers required to perform that special prayer. For over a month Bhai Sahib called me frequently regarding the prayer. He would inform me of a date that had been fixed for the prayer, but on another day would call to say it had to be postponed.

One day, Bhai Sahib phoned me to say that the special prayer for his late sister had to be postponed again. At that moment I lost control of myself. I reacted loudly over the phone: "Bhai Sahib, just cancel the jaap! Don't have to pray, lah!" (*Lah*, borrowed from Malay, can be used to soften the tone.) Bhai Sahib responded: "What are you talking about? She is my sister, you know! What are you talking about? She is my sister, you know!"

As Bhai Sahib kept repeating the phrase over the phone, I experienced great pains in my head, as though it was being squeezed tighter and tighter. I cried out aloud: "Okay, Bhai Sahib! I am sorry! Okay, Bhai Sahib! I am sorry!" The next instant, I was back to my normal self, without the pain.

The following day, when I met up with Bhai Sahib, I stared at him from close range, starting from his head to his feet, and from his feet to his head, repeatedly, like I was sending him a message: "What did you do to me yesterday?" But Bhai Sahib, as always, remained humble and acted as if nothing had happened.

I also recall an incident related by Bhai Sahib where a man reacted aggressively towards him over an undisclosed issue. Bhai Sahib said that despite his clarification, the man was still hostile towards him. Bhai Sahib then related that at that critical moment he told God he had done his best. The very next moment, Bhai Sahib said the man in question went down on his knees and begged Bhai Sahib for forgiveness.

I later understood what it meant when Bhai Sahib was categorised as 'God on Earth'. It means he had reached a state of being where, in his normal nature, he could simulate some of the attributes of God. That perhaps explained the experience of my head being squeezed tighter and tighter by Bhai Sahib when I lost my cool over the phone, or in the case of the man who was made to go down on his knees and apologise to Bhai Sahib.

During my years of spiritual practice, I observed that Bhai Sahib, and Bapak (as related by Bhai Sahib), were indeed true Gurus. They taught a similar method of worship, involving total submission and surrender through the inspiration of the higher intuitive self, which would bring about purification and refinement of character, and ultimately oneness with God. I believe it was the same with the prophets of the old. They were simply the humblest and wisest human beings during their times on Earth.

There is no doubt that all the past prophets carried with them the hallmark of being a true Guru. I would like to reiterate that the highest accomplishment and greatest success of any mortal being is when he/she has realised a fully awakened mind, that is, oneness with God. As I ponder when that will happen to all the human community, past, present and future, I recall a saying by prophet Lao Tzu: "Nature does not hurry, yet everything is accomplished." (Feng and English, Verse 29.)

It will be accomplished when humanity has transformed into Divinity. It is then that the Earth will bid goodbye to the current Dark Age and welcome the dawn of the Golden Age. That will be the time when we will make sense of the old adage, of bringing Heaven down to Earth.

Chapter Sixteen

MEDITATION

IN RESPONSE TO A RECEIVING, we were asked to refresh ourselves in our understanding of VCM Basic. The basic course is almost wholly the brainchild of our beloved Bhai Sahib.

WHAT MEDITATION IS AND THE NEED FOR IT

Meditation means different things to different people. To some, meditation is a holy pastime. To others, it has nothing to do with religious or spiritual matters. Why is that so? The word *meditate* can also mean 'to think deeply about', 'to plan or consider mentally', or 'to dwell upon an issue'. According to these definitions, we are already doing meditation in our everyday life. Meditation is therefore something that can be practical, i.e., secular.

Bhai Sahib described meditation as solemn contemplation, a reflecting or dwelling upon, or an engagement in deep concentrated thought, directed towards the Divine. Where does this activity of meditation take place? It must be in our mind. It is only through the vehicle of the mind that the process of meditation can begin.

We may consider the computer as an analogy. We operate a computer more effectively if we understand its features and functions. Like a computer, mind and meditation can also be better understood on a scientific level. With deeper understanding, we enjoy improved use through proper application. So let us explore the makings of the mind.

The human mind may be likened to an iceberg. The tip of an iceberg is visible at sea level. That represents our conscious mind, which is said to constitute about 10% of our total mind capacity, as is commonly acknowledged by scientists and psychologists. The other 90% of the submerged iceberg represents the subconscious level. At one time, this level was described as the unconscious level, a term Bhai Sahib disagreed with. So we shall use the term 'subconscious' in place of 'unconscious'.

Bhai Sahib went further, saying that the mind is made up of not only the conscious, the first level, and the subconscious, the second level, but also has a third level, the superconscious level, also known as cosmic consciousness. The percentage of the total mind used varies from one individual to another. Bhai Sahib said some use as low as 5% of their full mind, but generally it is about 7%. Bhai Sahib also commented that today's inventions and discoveries result from using about 25% of our mind capacity.

Discernment is another VCM tool which facilitates testing to arrive at an accurate percentage of anything. This tool has been meticulously worked out by Bhai Sahib. Let's take the average usage of the mind as 7%, as Bhai Sahib suggested. Since we are only using a very small portion of our mind, the question is how can we use the balance, the 93%? Meditation has a role in enlarging our use of our mind. Science also has a role to play. Bhai Sahib explained that no religious texts state that human beings are using a very, very small part of our mind. Hence, it is necessary to use scientific reasoning. So, where does the 93% or so of the sector of our minds lie?

It lies in sleep. In sleep with dreams. And in sleep without dreams, that being deep sleep. It is said that many of the discoveries that have come about in this world have been intuitively received by inventors and creators, or were received though symbolic dreams.

An illustration is provided by a true story about Elias Howe and his passion for the Lockstitch Sewing Machine. Howe was so obsessed with improving the sewing process that it can be no surprise the idea came to him in his sleep. He dreamed that the sewing process would be improved if the eye of the needle was moved to the front of the needle, instead of its established location at the back. It is reported Howe also dreamed at that time that he was being chased, and was subsequently captured by a foreign tribe. He felt much duress being threatened with death.

Our VCM intermediate level course includes a topic on dream interpretation. Dreaming is described as a language of sleep. Dreams take place at our subconscious and higher levels. They are expressed in symbols. For example, a car or a house in a dream may refer to one's physical body, instead of representing their literal meanings. Howe's dream of being chased, captured and threatened with death, was likely meant to shock him, to help him remember his dream about the needle when he woke.

We know we scarcely remember most of our dreams the moment we wake. We also pay little heed to dreams emanating from our higher mind. But when a dream includes a catastrophic happening, we wake all of a sudden and remember the dream's finer details. The nasty happening in Howe's dream jolted him awake, obviously, which then helped him remember the first part of the dream, about the needle, an innovation that brought convenience to human lives. Albert Einstein wrote in his memoirs that he often slept on his problems. This indicates he received higher inspiration during sleep.

Meditation also helps develop intuition. Often it is the vehicle for conveying messages. A spiritual elder once received a message about combining Siberian ginseng and cordyceps (both are herbs), meant for Bhai Sahib. Months later, I was in Singapore. After a spiritual assignment, I took a break in a busy shopping mall. I was prompted to walk towards a stall displaying herbs. I spontaneously took a bottle of herbs and read that it was a combination of American ginseng and cordyceps. To my surprise, I found that the mixture was similar to what was received by our elder. The only difference was that this comprised American ginseng and not Siberian ginseng. I realised then that the herbalists concerned were likely also receiving intuitively from their higher minds. They may or may not be aware of this.

Through personal learning, I have come to appreciate where the greater part of our mind's capacity lies. This is the sector of the mind that should most interest us. When we are able to use more of our mind, we will function better in our everyday life in every way. Not only will our IQ, EQ and SQ improve, but also our body's health. Using more of our higher mind will also prompt us to make necessary adjustments to our body. A very highly developed mind cannot sit on sordid soil. *Sordid soil* here refers not just to our body and physical health, but to our moral and ethics.

While there may be people who have alert minds, more often than not a diseased body weakens them. We must have a vital physical frame to support a really awakened mind, which we can use at a conscious level to tap into our subconscious and the superconscious states. What is required is going into the 'sleep' state, using the solitude of sleep to access the balance of the 93% of our mind. Meditation enables us to delve into this sleep state.

That is why meditation is all important. It involves people sitting or even standing in a comfortable position, relaxing, then moving into a very, very deep state, a state referred to as samadhi (intense concentration). In this state our higher mind becomes operative. When we are able to practise properly, engaging in regular efficacious and meaningful meditation, we function better, since we start to use more of our higher mind.

In fact, through regular meditation every aspect of our activities will undergo meaningful change. We become happier and blissful, better able to manage ourselves and respond effectively to the world. We will have increased energy, better health, and deeper insight into ourselves. We will not only have improved concentration, better memory, a happier disposition, and the ability to be expressive and relate to others easily, we also gain access to the psychic and clairvoyant powers that are available in a higher state of consciousness.

At this point I wish to revert to a personal experience, during which the higher mind came into play. As mentioned earlier, in 2014 I suffered a heart attack. Prior to the attack, for a week or so, my mind repeatedly told me: "Block, block." This was in a silent mode. I looked into my bathroom mirror and asked myself aloud: "Block? What block?" There was no response. Another day it again silently told me: "Block, block." I spontaneously responded: "Hey, Athan! You are a dead man walking!" If the mind is well awakened, we can definitely use it to our benefit. At that time my spiritual growth was at a rudimentary stage, so I was unable to appreciate my physical condition. Of course, interference from the conscious mind was probably a factor in my inability to grasp and acknowledge the predicament I was facing.

HUMAN ATTRIBUTES

The basic structure of Man includes three principal features: the physical, the mental and the spiritual. The last involves the soul aspect. Bhai Sahib stressed that unless these three principal aspects are developed equally, a person becomes psychosomatic or suffers from mental illnesses, which may potentially also lead to physical illnesses. Common mental illnesses include depression, stress, anxiety and suicidal tendencies. Physical ailments include skin conditions such as psoriasis or eczema, or high blood pressure, etc. As both a teenager and an adult, I suffered from a skin problem on my palm: the skin was always peeling off. Medical treatments did not help at all. These symptoms disappeared completely after I became involved with VCM. Besides skin problems, I also had other ailments, some of which were also resolved via meditation.

There are things we can do to keep our body healthy. These include making the effort to eat good food, performing various exercises, taking up certain sports, and enrolling in fitness centers to develop the physique and to build up strength and stamina. Similarly, there are things we can do to strengthen our mind. We can go to school, to college, to university, attend seminars, or take up courses, to equip ourselves with the latest knowledge, or to acquire certain skills. All these help with developing our physical and mental aspects.

However, we seldom have time for the third feature, which is the most important: the spiritual aspect. You will note that while both the physical and the mental aspects have a lifespan, which means they will eventually die or expire, the third aspect is within, it is eternal, and it never dies. While human beings have devised much for the betterment of our physical and mental aspects, practically nothing meaningful has been done for this third aspect, the cosmic superconscious mind. Its development is not taught in schools or universities.

Meditation is the *only* activity that helps us gain access to this third aspect. When we are able to embrace this third aspect, it should lead to an *awakening*, which we can bring into reality in the mind's conscious level.

MEDITATION TECHNIQUES

This awakening can only be achieved if we know the techniques associated with meditation. They involve surrender and submitting to the innermost core within us, where the 93% of the mind's capacity lies. This deep meditation resembles a sleep state. As we are now into the third aspect, that being the soul aspect within us, we are now reaching the *subliminal*. From this point, science and medical knowledge cannot help us venture any further in our understanding of this Divine aspect. In other words, scientific reasoning and explanation, as we know it today, will have to end here. From this point, spirituality begins.

What standard texts we may refer to, which will assist us to develop the correct meditation technique and help us connect with the sublime and Divine nature within? Clearly, it must be in *all* the world's holy scriptures. It must be in the gospels of *all* the religions. The Almighty has also, from time to time, sent down prophets, for example, Elijah, Abraham, Moses, Lao Tzu, Buddha, Jesus, Mohammad, Krishna, the Sikh prophets and, of course, Bapak Subuh of the Subud Movement, and our beloved Bhai Sahib. These great prophets, when they were on Earth, presumably had one main mission: to show humanity the way to merge with the Creator, The Infinite, within.

VCM practitioners have great faith in Bhai Sahib, who they consider to be a prophet. During his sojourn on Earth, Bhai Sahib's mission was to integrate and synthesise the essence of all the scriptures of all the world's religions. He was commissioned by The Infinite to reveal a consummate technique of meditation to help humanity realise God while in human form.

With correct understanding and appreciation of this technique, people of all races, religions, nationalities, colours, caste and creed, and of whatever diverse nature, will, in time, gather together to carry out this common and profound worship before the Almighty. Humanity will eventually transform into Divinity, as we move on from the current Dark Age towards the coming Golden Age. This is only achievable through regular practice of a Divinely authenticated technique of meditation, that being of *deep surrender and submission to the Divine within oneself.*

People often wonder that if such a technique is found in all the scriptures, why have the custodians of the various religions not revealed the technique that can help one connect to the Creator. Bhai Sahib commented that although the languages of the various scriptures may be simple, they are couched in allegories and metaphors, which may not be easily understood when reading them in either an ordinary or academic fashion. Misinterpretation leads to wrong understanding, to wrong practices, and to wrong actions. This is the major cause of the severe and increasing religious differences that have affected humanity for so long.

It was stated earlier that, on average, human beings use about 7% of their mind's capacity. What is glaringly present in this 7% of our mind at the conscious level is the ego. *In every VCM seminar, Bhai Sahib always emphasised that the greatest stumbling block between Man and God is the ego!*

Incidentally, the word *ego* is also a suitable acronym for *Edging God Out*. So when ego is in action, God cannot be present. The Infinite once said: "Only the meek and mild shall rule the world." That is why it is also important for us to acquire and manifest wisdom and humility. During meditation, we have to humble ourselves to the point of courting death, to be in a state of deep and complete surrender and submission to the Divine within.

Besides ego, other vices are also mentioned in the Sri Guru Granth Sahib. They are obstacles to achieving a higher level of Divine awareness. For easy recall, I have coined an acronym for these vices, EGALA, which is: E–Ego, G–Greed, A–Anger, L–Lust, A–Attachment.

Prophet Lao Tzu wrote: "The clarity of the sky prevents its falling, the firmness of the earth prevents its splitting, the strength of the spirit prevents its being used up ... therefore the humble is the root of the noble, the low is the foundation of the high." (Feng and English, Chapter 39) To be 'low' is to obliterate or subdue one's ego, to the extent that one achieves clarity, firmness and strength, and an awakening of the Divine aspect within. *The awakened Divine aspect* refers to one having arrived at the high state of oneness with God within.

This is similar to what Jesus Christ taught: "Die unto yourself and be reborn!" (See John 3:3-7) *Die unto yourself* refers to the humbling of oneself in deep surrender and submission to the Divine within. This brings about an awakening, which will be the new reborn you. It refers to the realisation of the Oneness with God within. This is the practice. This is the Way.

We also have to acquire wisdom and humility in our interactions with one and all, and with our surroundings. When the Lord said, "Only the meek and mild shall rule the world", (Matthew 5:5), he meant that only those with humble attributes have a chance of attaining communion with the Creator through their higher mind.

Prophet Lao Tzu wrote: "Knowing others is wisdom, knowing the self is enlightenment. Mastering others requires force, mastering the self needs strength." (Feng and English, Chapter 33.) When one is able to master or conquer one's own self (ego), it means one has succeeded in winning over the sublime aspect within oneself, at the cosmic superconscious level, that is the kingdom of God within. It also means a two-way link with the Creator has been established via one's higher mind. Clearly, the grace of The Infinite is also imperative if one is to achieve such a status.

Lao Tzu's saying finds a parallel in a verse from the Sri Guru Granth Sahib: "He alone is called a warrior who is attached to the Lord's love in this age. Through the Perfect True Guru, he conquers his own Soul, and then everything comes under his control." (p. 679) The phrase, *this age* refers to the current Dark Age, in which Satanic forces are predominant. Humanity is trapped and greatly affected by powerful and subtle opposing forces. To appreciate this, we just have to observe ourselves, our relationship with our fellow humans, and examine the world at large, which is mired in so many negativities. How can humanity respond to these ugly and powerful opposing forces? The answer lies solely in stubbornly pursuing meditation, which can help us awaken and develop our higher mind.

We need to realise that the God we are talking about is located inside us. It is our Super Cosmic Mind. Bhai Sahib once declared it is not a God who is up in the sky, looking down on us, with a rod in hand, judging us, deciding whether we should go to heaven or hell.

The Bible often characterises Man as being made in the image and likeness of God. So there must be something godly in *every* human being. Again, Christ said: "Seek ye first the Kingdom of God that is within you and all else shall be added unto you." This means that every one of us is carrying an aspect of God within us. Similar pronouncements are found in the world's other scriptures.

The great Guru, Adi Sankara, expounded the Advaita Vedanta philosophy (non-dualism) of Hinduism, which fought against ritualism and advocated the unity of atman (soul) with Brahman (The Infinite). He discouraged even ritual worship of God, as such ritual assumes that atman is different from Brahman (God). His advaita philosophy emphasised the guidance of a Guru for gaining knowledge.

Those who do not believe in God probably do not want a God that is judging them all the time. They carry an emptiness, because it has been ingrained into them that God is out there, in the sky, in heaven, judging us as sinners, and so on. But if they realise that they are carrying God in their higher mind, their higher cosmic consciousness, and that the kingdom of God is within them, then it is likely all will act more conscientiously.

And since this higher mind is inside me, and is inside you, and is in everyone, it is therefore also outside Man. The net result is that God is a Pervading Presence which is both within us and envelops us from without. It pervades the entire Universe. It is known as a Power, a Force. In the Holy Sri Guru Granth Sahib it is known as the Naam. The kingdom of God is inside us! It is in every human being, regardless of what their belief system may be.

PRIMORDIAL COSMIC POWER: NAAM, THE HOLY LIFE FORCE

Naam, as Bhai Sahib pointed out, is also found in other scriptures. Some examples are as follows:

Dao (Tao), in Dao De Jing;
Aath Paraa Shakti, in the Bhagavad Gita;
Zat Allah, Roh Ilahi, in the Holy Qur'an;
Holy Spirit, in the Holy Bible;
Hukam, in Hindu parlance;
Yasod or Shin, in the Jewish Cabalistic tradition;
Manna, for the Polynesian and Hawaiian Kahunas;
Samadhi, in the Buddhist Dhammapada.

Bhai Sahib said that this powerful, all-pervading kinetic energy is generally known as the Primordial Cosmic Power. This Holy Life Force is also equated to what we call Divine Love ... God is Love ... and Love is God. Bhai Sahib taught that while Divine Love is within reach of every individual, the Naam Kallaah (the inner Holy Life Force) is the privilege of a few fortunate practitioners. The reason is that experiencing this Naam Power is a rare phenomenon. Only a fortunate few are permitted to experience the presence of the Divine awakening within. A verse from the SGGS says: "Naam rung sarab sukh hoeh. bad bhaagee kesai praapat hoei" (p. 279 Sukhmani Sahib), which means the experience of the awakening (arousal) of Naam Power gives complete peace and solace. Only the fortunate few attain the experience of this state.

This particular verse also offers a clue regarding how to achieve Sarab

Sukh, which is 'complete peace and solace'. But before experiencing Sarab Sukh, one must first experience Naam Rung, which is 'the reactive state of ecstasy in prayer/meditation'. Another verse of the SGGS describes this phenomenon: "The euphoric experience of the awakening of Naam brings about all manner of peace and solace, but only a fortunate few can imbibe and receive such a treasured Gift." (p. 271, Sukhmani Sahib) As the Holy Bible emphatically states: "Many are called, but few are chosen." (Matthew 22:14)

Practitioners with a strong will and desire to experience The Infinite are the fortunate few. But even more fortunate among the fortunate few are the very, very few who are blessed with a two-way communication link with the Creator via their higher minds. Bhai Sahib says that only 1:10,000,000 receive such a gift. He termed this Senkadei Cho Ek.

Bhai Sahib once related an episode when a wealthy man drove all the way from Singapore just to meet him. In the early days, with little infrastructure development, it took many hours to travel on the old and narrow trunk road from Singapore to Kuala Lumpur. This wealthy man had heard so much about Bhai Sahib that he wanted to learn meditation from him. Bhai Sahib was willing to meet him without any prejudice, considering that this man was extremely wealthy. Bhai Sahib asked the man why he wanted to learn meditation. The man replied that he did not have any problem. He just wanted to learn meditation because he had a lot of free time. Bhai Sahib then told him that it would be better for him not to learn this meditation. The lesson to be learned from this episode is that VCM is capable of clearing up the dross from one's present and past lives, which may find expression during meditation. I surmised that the wealthy man probably did not appreciate the possible reactions that could arise after taking up VCM meditation. He could possibly even end up having a negative impression of VCM. Much later, this episode with the wealthy man related by Bhai Sahib led me to appreciate the Biblical verse: "It is easier for a camel to enter the eye of a needle than for a rich man to enter My kingdom." (Matthew 19:21-24)

The trappings of wealth are difficult to overcome. Attachment to money is one. Bhai Sahib clearly stated in his writings that any soul on its journey towards ultimate self-realisation must experience the lowest point in its life at least once. I can only deduce that one has to be truly humble to have any chance of walking the straight and narrow spiritual path. For this wealthy man, detachment from his worldly standing may have been an issue. As such, there would be no positive outcome from his desire to learn meditation.

As we are still at the peak of the current Dark Age, the powerful subtle satanic forces also obstruct many from learning the true path towards God-realisation. As a matter of fact, there will be practitioners who will also leave this practice after a considerable period of involvement. That is why it can be very challenging. These are likely some of the reasons why many are called, but only a few are chosen.

Back to the concept of Naam. Bhai Sahib said it is an exuberant Power that is always in ascendancy, always expansive, always in a re-creating mode. This phenomenon is described as Chardee Kalaah. In one of Bhai Sahib's articles, he describes Chardee Kalaah as a powerhouse of limitless energy that can never be depleted, being ever ascendant, i.e., always exuberantly self-replenishing. It never diminishes. It is always complete. It is always perfect. Only God, the Primordial Creator, can actuate this Power. The Qur'an describes this: "And it is We who have built the Universe with our Creative Power and keep expanding it." (Sura 51:47) This concept is also mentioned in Dao De Jing: "Great accomplishment seems imperfect yet it does not outlive its usefulness. Great fullness seems empty, yet cannot be exhausted." (Feng and English, Chapter 45)

Developments in science and technology offer an insight into Chardee Kalaah. In the latter half of the 1990s coloured photographs of a region in deep space taken by the Hubble Space Telescope began to appear in public. Each picture contained countless numbers of colourfully brilliant identical tiny dots. Scientists said each tiny dot represented a galaxy. It took a long time to count them all. Some time after, it was reported that the Hubble Telescope had taken another picture of that same spot in deep space. This time, after another round of counting the tiny brilliant dots, they found the number of galaxies were even greater in number than previously recorded! Again, this lends credence regarding the extent to which Chardee Kalaah is self-replenishing and expansive.

An article in the Malaysian newspaper, The Star, titled *300,000 new possible galaxies detected* (20 February, 2012), confirmed that the Hubble Telescope had indeed looked far deeper into space to produce more detailed pictures than those previously taken by the Paris Observatory. The number of galaxies mentioned is just phenomenal. The discovery by NASA scientists, based on two photographs taken by the Hubble Telescope, confirms Bhai Sahib's explanation that the creative power known as Naam is always exuberant and in ascendancy, always expansive and in a re-creating mode, never diminished, always complete, always perfect.

This Power, Naam (Holy Life Force), is comprehensively described in the SGGS: "The all-pervading Naam is the support of all Thy beings, Oh Lord. Various worlds and universes are supported by It (Naam Power). Naam is the motivating power in the compilation of the *Smritis*, the *Vedas* and the *Puranas* (Hindu scriptures). Naam invokes and propels the highest wisdom and intuition. All continents, the spheres, the nether regions, the galaxies and the firmaments, are supported by and kept precisely in their allocated places by the power of Naam. By hearing of Thy attributes and that of the Naam, all are saved and those on whom, through Thy Grace, the Gift of Naam (The Holy Spirit) is made manifest, obtain salvation by reaching the fourth state of transcendence and superconsciousness (*Turiya*) in bliss." (p. 284)

Naam, therefore, must be a very great power, for It supports the entire creation. Bhai Sahib said this Naam Power must be much more powerful than trillions of hydrogen atomic bombs exploding together. This Naam Power gets even more fascinating, even more amazing, for it is also inside us, as pointed out by Bhai Sahib: "The most treasured nectar, Naam is also resident inside of the human frame, but in a state of dormancy and quiescence." (SGGS, p. 293) *Dormancy* refers to inactivity, a temporary state, while *quiescence* refers to a state of inactivity and quietness. Naam, which is in a state of inactivity and quietness, is like a sleeping giant inside Man. *It must be awakened before we can tap into the 93% of our higher mind.*

If and when this great sleeping giant is awakened from dormancy and quiescence, we will feel total ecstasy. For example, if there is a severe earthquake in the ocean, a tsunami may occur. The effects of that tsunami are akin to the resulting state of euphoria and ecstasy that we feel at our conscious level if this Naam Power within is awakened, via the practice of a meaningful form of meditation. We will be blasted into an active state of arousal, into ecstasy, into euphoria. We may jump around, spin round and round like a top, start to cry, start to laugh in ecstasy, or simply have to keep moving. We may also undergo emotional experiences, such as visioning, in which we 'see' the unseen, 'hear' subtle sounds, 'smell' submerged smells, feel very light or very heavy, or feel like we are levitating. We may feel hot, or warm; we may make spontaneous utterances. We may sing with joy, or sometimes produce sounds that have no meaning. All these *reactions* constitute our *awakening* through our senses, which come about *spontaneously* and without any effort on our part. We play no part in it. *It is effortless.*

OTHER MEDITATION TECHNIQUES

Various Yoga systems and other forms of meditation have been in practice for a long period of time through human history. Only someone who is similar to Bhai Sahib's status is qualified to determine their level of effectiveness, or to determine the source from which any particular yoga or meditation is derived.

Often my discussions with Bhai Sahib gave me insights into which practice is wholesome and which is not. We know Bhai Sahib's power of discernment had the highest accuracy. I once bought a bestseller book in which the author wrote about his conversations with God. Bhai Sahib asked me to discard it. Bhai Sahib gently remarked that the author in question was not receiving from God. He also ruled out a certain spiritual movement, as its founder had fallen from grace, even though he had earlier received inspiration from a higher source. Many such movements and traditions have fallen from grace as their gurus have tainted themselves.

Bhai Sahib, with his status of a messiah, and with his power of discernment, knows the level of effectiveness of any meditation or spiritual practice. Bhai Sahib noted that most systems are superficial, whereas with VCM, after diligent practice, a practitioner will be able to attain a higher level of consciousness.

Bhai Sahib's thoughts about other systems are clearly denoted in his book, *Vibrant Celestial Meditation*: "In contrast, most other systems of meditation currently practised do not have their origins directly and in detail described in the scriptures and they therefore do not quite meet the above criteria set by the Divine for man. Hence, they can be dubbed as mainly man-devised contrivances, although they may in their own right benefit humanity to varying degrees. All these are invariably and subtly effort-orientated and not spontaneous. Their tangible features are stated here for better insight into their man-devised leanings:

"Fixation of attention at various parts of our body/brain structure; too prolonged repetition and chanting of set phrases, mantras or sutras; rigidity in postures and particular positioning of hands and fingers in what are called mudras; control of breath; ceremonial rituals and symbols; picturing of forms of masters, demi-god, goddesses and deities; calling upon masters and guides in channeling processes; over-disciplined dietary requirements; turning of beads and other mechanical artifacts; taking artificial stimulants and going into deep trance states; guided and self-imposed techniques; physical (mechanical) doings and contrivances." (Sri Bhai Sahib Ji, p.166/7)

The designs and features of other systems noted by Bhai Sahib may have limited effect, but are burdensome and not as natural and effortless as VCM techniques.

THE VCM TECHNIQUE AND THE PRACTICE OF MEDITATION

Bhai Sahib's infallible guide into the technique of true meditation is that it must have the stamp of the Divine. It must also fulfil certain basic criteria. Therefore, the technique of worship/meditation that is meant to be genuine, efficacious, and meaningful, requires the following attributes, which must follow somewhat the sequential order shown here:

1. Simple.
2. Natural.
3. Effortless.
4. Loving. (Clear of any hate or hurt feelings; forgive and forget.)
5. Spontaneous. (Automatic.)
6. Deep submission/self-surrender ... and total obeisance to the Divine within whereupon must arise (you will receive) the ...
7. Dwelling of Grace ... as a gift from God Almighty resulting in ...
8. Arousal/Vibration ... which could be termed an awakening, euphoria, or an experience of ecstasy and rapture.

This constitutes the essence and the main body of the worship/meditation actuated by the Divine from within, leading in time to ...

9. Transcendence, superconsciousness, leading to consummation, culminating in a higher spiritual development, followed by ...

10. Self-Realisation ... and ultimately attaining salvation such as satori, nirvana, jiwan mukti.

Any right worship/meditation, which does not conform or comply to some degree with each of the first eight criteria listed above, is without God's blessings. It is usually devised by human thinking and conjecture. Even if it is claimed it comes from higher sources, such as from the revelations of an ascended master, archangel or saint, but still does not conform to the eight criteria, then that revelation is not from the highest Divine source, even though it may be couched in all manner of useful and even noble goals. No doubt such systems can be beneficial. The individual will have to make a choice, whether to imbibe the fullest range of benefits, or to be satisfied with the limited 'benefits' you are now receiving.

A catchphrase that encompasses the main part of the entire process of VCM is "Let go, let God." This means you are totally relaxed and surrendered, which enables God to induce you into a format of worship which is fully acceptable to Him.

This meditation is akin to going to sleep. You cannot sleep by using effort. You cannot sleep by counting goats. Similarly, you cannot sleep when you keep on chanting or repeating a mantra as recommended by many other systems of meditation. As long as you are doing something, you cannot fall asleep. So, sleep comes naturally, effortlessly, spontaneously.

Therefore, the type of meditation that is going to be efficacious, and meaningful, must have these attributes. It must be *simple*. It must be *natural*. It must be *effortless*. It must be *spontaneous*. You must relax very deeply and surrender to the Self within. You will then touch those states in which 93% of your mind lies.

Naturally, if you sleep, you will have dreams. But when you are carrying out a proper and meaningful meditation practice, *it will not be actual sleep*. In place of dreams, you will get an arousal and awakening, euphoria, ecstasy, a change of state, or experiences that are out of the ordinary, activated neither by your will nor by your ordinary mind. Only then can you imbibe all the higher aspects of your mind. What happens next is that your spiritual psychic nature, what they call the soul, is *awakened*.

So, VCM practitioners must 'sleep', i.e. relax very, very deeply. Any technique that does not tell you about self-surrender, to the extent of obliterating your personality, cannot bring about beneficial results. It is said in the scriptures that the body and mind must be sacrificed on the altar of God. The body and mind must be effaced. This sacrifice means 'to die'. That's what Christ meant when he said: "Die unto yourself and be reborn."

When one 'surrenders unto death', the question then arises: "Who is going to do the meditation for you?" "How is it going to proceed?" Divine help is forthcoming at this point. The SGGS scriptures state: "Jeevat merai, merai phun jeevai, aisaa sun sumaaya" (p. 332), which means: While living, 'die'. If you have caught this 'death' (deep surrender), and are in this state of death (merai, allegorical for deep submission), then, I (God) will awaken you (phun, jeevai), and this constitutes merging into a state of communion with God in voidness (aisaah sun sumaaya), the superconscious fourth state of transcendence, known as Turiya. The verse continues: "It is that meditation which I (God) shall will into you; that meditation which I will actuate into you. I will inspire you through the soul. I will start the process in you through the inspiration of the soul." (p. 332)

The samadhi of an awakening is required. You need the experience of the awakening of the Holy Spirit. It is through the vehicle of the Holy Spirit that we can communicate with God, that we receive directions from God.

The Divine within us starts the process through the inspiration of our soul. That is why it is effortless, spontaneous and automatic. We have no part to play with our core senses, our will, or our volition. So, meditation has to come by itself spontaneously and effortlessly *and that is how we sleep*.

God directs the meditation, moment by moment, inside and through us. Because He is directing: "Whatever actions and reactions occur, do not stop them." Because sometimes the actions and reactions may be very awkward, very strange, very mystical. It is said in the scriptures that when you go into this state of euphoria, of awakening and ecstasy, you are being cleansed of all the 'dross' and 'dirt'. The process must feel awkward, occasionally even hideous. That is why people sometimes shout and scream during meditation. It is understood that screaming is one of the manifestations of hurt feelings, hate feelings, trauma, and signals the release of neurosis.

Only when all these are released does a practitioner become fully functional in this world. If people are weighed down by all sorts of hurt and hate feelings and trauma, not only from this life but from past lives, they cannot operate in this world normally and in a fully efficient mode. Hence, meditation is also a state of cleansing. The cleansing of self is pertinent, and the practice is rightfully called, Vibrant Celestial Meditation. The word *celestial* connotes a spiritual gift, a Divine gift from God. This gift reaches us because we have totally surrendered; we have nothing left in us to start the process. So He bestows upon us a grace, a gift.

Reactions and movements in meditation are aspects we can apply to our daily life. We receive solutions to our daily problems through feeling a reaction, a movement, or strong post impressions (the way artists depict lights and colours) etc., where answers to these problems are not ordinarily forthcoming. As followers of this movement we enjoy improved mental and physical health through the innate ability to utilise vibrations as a prime mover, causing our molecular structure to realign and change for the better.

SCRIPTURAL VALIDATION ON THE NEED FOR SURRENDER AND SUBMISSION

The following are some pertinent validations from the scriptures regarding the need for us to surrender and submit.

THE BIBLE

"Die unto yourself and be re-born." (John, 3:3)

"Be still, all mankind, before the Lord, for He is raised up (awakened) out of His holy dwelling." (Zechariah, 2:13)

SRI GURU GRANTH SAHIB

"We are spontaneously led to worship and meditation in an egoless, desireless state, when we sacrifice our body, mind, soul and the very breath of life on the altar of God." (p. 742)

"The highest form of meditation (Bhagti) is achieved by total self-surrender in worship. Nanak liveth in a state of animation by complete effacement of the self in meditation." (p. 268)

HINDU SCRIPTURES

The Narada Bhagti Sutra advocates bhagti, devotional love, as a way to completely surrender to the Divine.

The Bhagavad Gita contains several texts on this aspect of worship:

"With your heart full of love and devotion, worship God by annihilating and surrendering your entire body, mind, and soul. Having thus become wholly absorbed in Me, to Me you will surely arrive." (9:34)

The self and soul of a yogi begins to be purified once he has not only surrendered unconditionally, but has also offered his very soul in sacrifice before the altar of God." (5:11)

"This Divine energy of Mine, consisting of the three modes of material nature, is difficult to overcome. But those who have surrendered unto Me can easily cross beyond it." (7:14)

DHAMMAPADA (BUDDHISM)

"With the self (ego) well subdued in self-surrender, one can then find total refuge within, which otherwise is difficult to obtain." (Verse 160)

"Empty this boat (one's body) mendicant. When emptied (completely effaced in deep surrender), it will move unimpeded (shortest and swiftest path to the Divine within). Lust and hatred (egocentric qualities) are thereby more easily removed, paving the way to nirvana." (Verse 389)

THE HOLY QUR'AN

"Lo! The religion before Allah is the Surrender (Al-Islam) ... If they surrender, then truly they will be rightly guided in prayer." (Surah 3:19-20)

"Ye who believe, completely efface yourself in self-surrender when worshipping your Lord, and do good, that happily ye may prosper." (Surah 23:77)

Bhai Sahib pointed out that the technique of efficacious prayer is already spelt out in the very word, *Islam*. The Arabic term literally means: "With love in your heart, submit and surrender to the will of Allah." He further pointed out that the word *Muslim* is pregnant with meaning. It comes from the word *muslimin*, which means, to surrender. Hence, a Muslim is one who surrenders to the will of Allah.

DAO TE JING

"Empty yourself of everything, let the mind become still ... Being at one with the Tao is eternal, and though the body dies, the Tao will never pass away. (Chapter 16)

"Those who know do not talk ... Guard the senses, temper your sharpness, simplify your problems, mask your brightness, be of one with the dust of the Earth. This is primal union ... This therefore is the highest state of man. (Chapter 56)

NONHANGMUN

In the Nonhangmun, a scriptural work of Ch'ondogyo, the native religion of Korea, the founder Ch'oe Suun sums up that the way of Muwi Ihwa is to still one's heart, enter into an inert inner state, and ensure a spontaneous connection with the absolute energy found within oneself.

SCRIPTURAL VALIDATION OF VIBRANT, EUPHORIC AND ECSTATIC REACTIONS

SRI GURU GRANTH SAHIB

"A God-guided devotee may burst into a state of laughter or crying. When this happens through the scriptural injunction, then it is a sure sign of truthful meditation." (p. 1421)

"In whom the Holy Life Force (Naam) has stirred into manifestation, he may begin to utter a medley of strange sounds." (p. 917)

BHAGAVAD GITA

"The stage of perfection called trance ... is characterised by one's ability to see the self by the pure mind and to relish and rejoice in the self. In that joyous state, one is situated in boundless transcendental happiness." (6:20-23)

THE HOLY BIBLE

"Praise ye the Lord. Sing unto the Lord a new song, and His praise in the congregation of saintly people ... Let them praise His Name in the dance ... Praise Him with the timbrel and dance ... Praise Him upon the loud cymbals ... Praise Him upon the high-sounding cymbals." (Psalms 149, 150)

THE HOLY QUR'AN

"Only those who believe in our revelations, who when they are reminded of them, at once get emptied in body and mind, with spontaneous vocalisation in adoration of Him, and they are thus humbled and left devoid of pride." (Surah 32:15 – Sajdah: The Prostration)

"Saying 'Glory to our Lord,' verily the promise of our Lord has been fulfilled, they fall down again limp and weeping. This increases the earnest humility in them." (Surah 17:108)

"When the angelic hosts descend upon the chosen ones, as the blowing of a soothing winnowing wind, or of the falling of manna as like heavy rain, they glide, they sway and move in ecstasy, affirming the truth of the benevolent grace promised by the Great One." (Surah 51:1-5)

ACTUAL TWO-WAY COMMUNICATION WITH THE INFINITE

Bhai Sahib taught that correct meditation must meet at least eight out of the ten criteria that define what a true meditation should be, as recounted earlier. *Only then will one be able to experience vibrant, euphoric and ecstatic reactions while in meditation.* Nevertheless, for one to establish a two-way communication link with The Infinite, one has to attain the ninth criteria, which involves transcendence to cosmic and superconsciousness, and beyond. This is when one is able to communicate with the all-knowing Divine Source that is resident within oneself. Clearly, the grace of The Infinite is imperative before a practitioner is blessed with such a gift.

A verse from the Sri Guru Granth Sahib, pointed out by Bhai Sahib, confirms the above assertion: "When God grants His blessings and His grace, ecstatic arousal takes place within us. It is only through the experience of such happenings and reactions that we can feel the Presence of God, and thus achieve oneness with Him." (p. 490)

THE SCIENCE OF VIBRANT CELESTIAL MEDITATION

VCM was originally known as Vibrant Charismatic Meditation. Bhai Sahib later changed the word *charismatic* to *celestial*, since *charismatic* is commonly used by a Christian sect. Bhai Sahib was adamant that this meditation should not be associated with any organised religion.

Bhai Sahib asserted that true meditation practice cannot be static, inert or rigid, since everything is perpetually in motion and vibrating. In addition, with the awakening of the Holy Life Force within, various reactions and responses may be vibrantly experienced through the five or more senses in various vibratory modes, such as physical movement, visioning, spontaneous utterances, laughing and/or crying, yawning, feeling light or heavy, and various other feelings of exaltation or ecstasy. This explains the word *vibrant*.

Celestial relates to the heavenly or Divine. The ultimate goal in VCM practice is to attain God-Realisation. The grace of the Infinite is crucial before one may be blessed with a two-way communion with the Creator.

The word *meditation* in VCM has an extra dimension to it. Most of us are only able to experience three states of consciousness, namely:

∞ Waking state
∞ Dreaming state
∞ Deep sleep state

The VCM technique of meditation enables one to spontaneously go beyond the three states to reach the fourth state, the superconscious. It is in this state that one has access to the creative power of the Universe. Once this power resident within has been awakened, one can then say that true meditation has been initiated. To better understand the various states of consciousness, refer to the *Chart Of Brain Activity* (see opposite page) introduced by Bhai Sahib. You will also learn of the different brain activities that take place at the various levels.

Bhai Sahib taught that when the human brain functions at various levels of awareness, it produces certain rates of pulsation that are measurable in cycles/second (c/s) using an electroencephalograph instrument (EEG). The lowest brain frequencies (pulsations) recorded are in the range of 0.7 c/s. They are known as delta and theta waves. When EEG registers zero c/s, it indicates the brain is dead. When one is in a deep sleep state and not dreaming, pulsation may also be near zero.

In the beta region, the range is 14-30 c/s. That is our waking state. It is the location of all our outer conscious day-to-day activities. Those activities are categorised as occurring in the material world. The next highest range, 7 to 14 cycles, is constituted of alpha waves. Alpha, together with theta and delta, constitute the inner conscious levels. This is generally considered the region of the spiritual realm where creativity takes place. Meditation takes place in the alpha, theta and the delta regions. When one is able to submit and surrender very deeply within, the resultant low pulsating frequency renders one's meditation profound and beneficial.

Bhai Sahib once related an incident that occurred in a shopping complex. It involved one of his retired subordinates. This former colleague was then selling EEG instruments. He tested the instrument on Bhai Sahib.

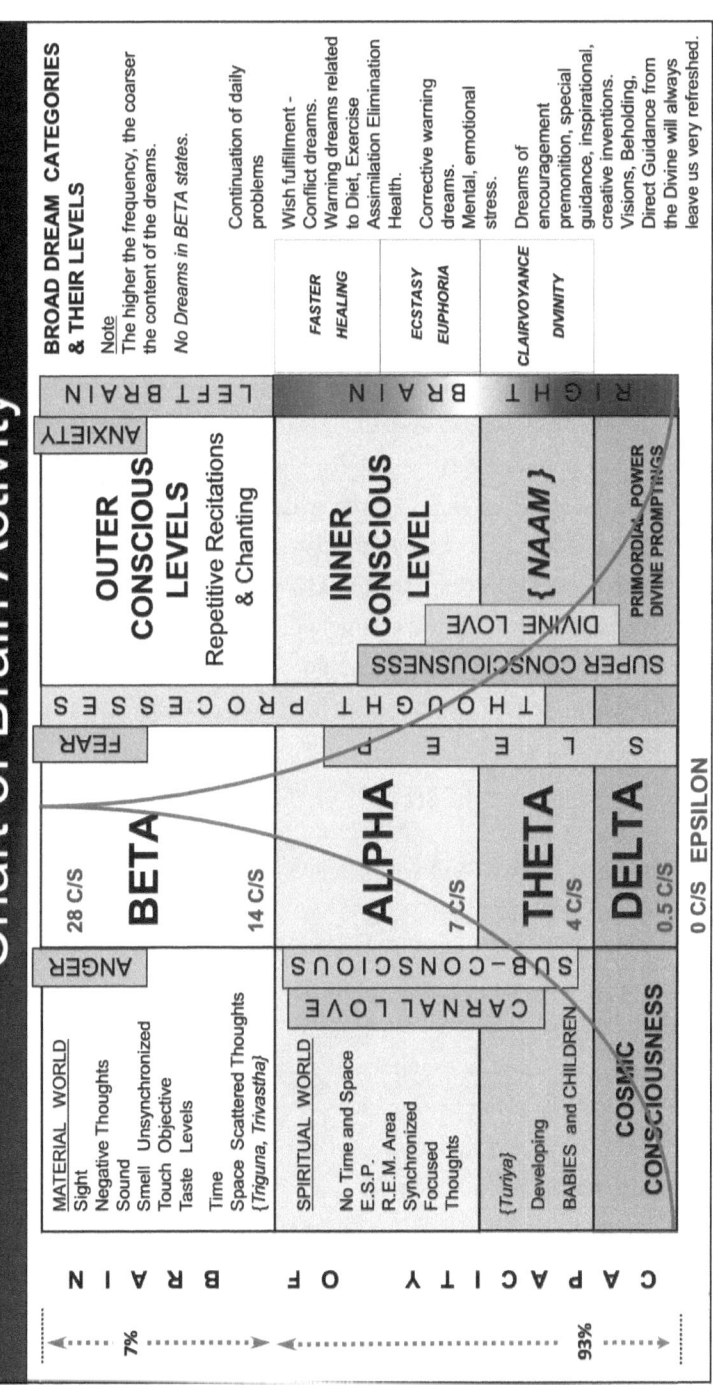

Bhai Sahib noted that he was having a conversation with him even as the EEG Instrument was strapped on. When the instrument began to register a lower and lower frequency, his former subordinate kept repeating anxiously, "Sir, don't talk! Sir, please don't talk. You are at sleep state!"

What happened was that the EEG instrument had been registering a frequency of the delta region and beyond. His ex-subordinate's understanding was that upon reaching that frequency one is literally in a deep sleep state. Yet it showed that with VCM Bhai Sahib was able to reach a deep state, the superconscious level, and still remain awake and aware. It showed that with VCM one who is gifted can go into deep meditation anytime and anywhere, while simultaneously performing another task.

This is a spontaneous message we received from The Infinite which reinforced the precepts that identify what a true meditation involves: "To meditate is to sleep. To sleep is to let go. You must not control yourself. You must let go so that I can express Myself through you. Sleep. Sleep. Cry if you must. Do not hold back. How will you progress if you do not surrender to Me? I am love. I will always guide you for your well-being. Do not doubt Me. I am your Creator."

THE BENEFITS OF VCM IN BRIEF

Below is a list of benefits one may acquire by practising VCM:

∞ Slow down the aging process.

∞ Help with dream interpretation. Virtually all dreams are about the dreamer and surface to provide guidance. VCM helps one understand and interpret dreams.

∞ Acquire an awareness that astral travelling is a risky activity. It offers no progress and does not contribute to spiritual advancement.

∞ Be guided directly how to choose the profession most suitable for one's inner harmony and talent.

∞ Be more easily able to receive useful visions and other directions from God.

∞ Speak more effectively.

∞ Sing and act better in drama and similar performance arts.

∞ Dance and perform callisthenic movements more gracefully.

∞ Drive motor vehicles defensively, in a spontaneous and effective manner, automatically and without recourse to normal logic. When confronted by a sudden emergency, on the spur of the moment you will be capable of taking evasive and remedial action.

∞ Be alert to all manner of impending dangers in an impromptu and unpremeditated manner.

∞ Acquire a better chance of being saved, sometimes miraculously, in emergency situations.

∞ Be able to utilise the movement of hands and fingers and all limbs in a more effective way in various daily duties.

∞ Obtain marked improvement in the way we normally walk (our gait).

∞ Greatly reduce or contain minor ills, stresses and strains of daily life.

∞ Achieve rapid healing for our own selves and when helping others through empathetic processes.

∞ Receive immediate and meaningful indications with respect to the suitability or otherwise of foods laid before you.

∞ Be guided to eat just the right quantity of food and no more in a natural automatic manner.

∞ Be able to assess the spirituality of anyone at an instant.

∞ Have the opportunity to remove the trauma of present and past lives.

∞ Improve the chance of embracing God-realisation.

The benefits one may receive from practising VCM is by no means limited to the above. There are many other benefits that can and have been acquired by different VCM practitioners.

THE ELECTRO-MAGNETIC FREQUENCY SPECTRUM OF NATURE

Bhai Sahib integrated scientific knowledge with his understanding of spirituality. He showed how the human brain's vibrations, specifically its electromagnetic frequency (EMF) spectrum, can be synchronised with the electromagnetic frequency spectrum of nature. (See page 217.) In this spectrum, the brain waves occupy the lower frequency segment and resonate at near zero cycles per second, while very high frequency waves, such as cosmic waves and Divine energy vibrations, occupy the other end of the spectrum.

Bhai Sahib stressed that when one is in a state of profound meditation of a variety like VCM, where one surrenders and submits very deeply, the Holy Life Force within is awakened. As a result, the brain waves slow down considerably to an *extra low frequency*, nearing zero cycles per second. It is at this stage that one is able to achieve stillness of mind.

While in this state, another wave is generated by the brain, oscillating at a very high frequency rate, which reaches out and moves at a speed that is much faster than the speed of light. This *super high frequency* resonates beyond the cosmic ray region into the etheric and Divine realm, which is the abode of the archangels and The Infinite.

A verse from the Holy Bible corroborates the need to surrender and submit very deeply to the Divine within: "Be still (naught), and know I Am God." (Psalm 46:10) When one is able to achieve a state of stillness, ("Be still"), one's brain waves would be resonating at an extra low frequency. If and when one advances further to experience the state of "know I Am God" within, that is when another wave would be generating at a super high frequency, speeding towards the etheric and Divine realms, as shown on the extreme right of the spectrum.

Only the fortunate few, who succeed in moving beyond the eighth level of true meditation, are able to experience the super high frequency wave speeding towards the etheric and Divine realm. (Note: Refer to the topic, *The VCM Technique and Practice of Meditation*, described earlier.) It is at this level that one succeeds in establishing a two-way communication link with the all-knowing Divine Source. Maam Sahib is one of the fortunate few.

The following message is an example of the outcome of VCM in action. It was received from The Infinite by Maam Sahib, and was uttered in a spontaneous and effortless manner: "I am God. I am your Creator. I am always with you, even if you sometimes forget Me. I am always here for you. Seek Me when you are in doubt. I shall save you. I am not beyond your reach. I am in you. I am Infinity. Do not forget to pray, for that will help you to improve, to grow, and come home to Me. You will have no more suffering. But now you have to carry on to learn your lessons in life. Do not forget Me. I am always with you. I am Infinity, your God."

A devoted practitioner in this profound state of meditation is actually in a dual mode: first, in a conscious mode, living an earthly life, and two, in a superconscious mode, possessing the ability to communicate with The

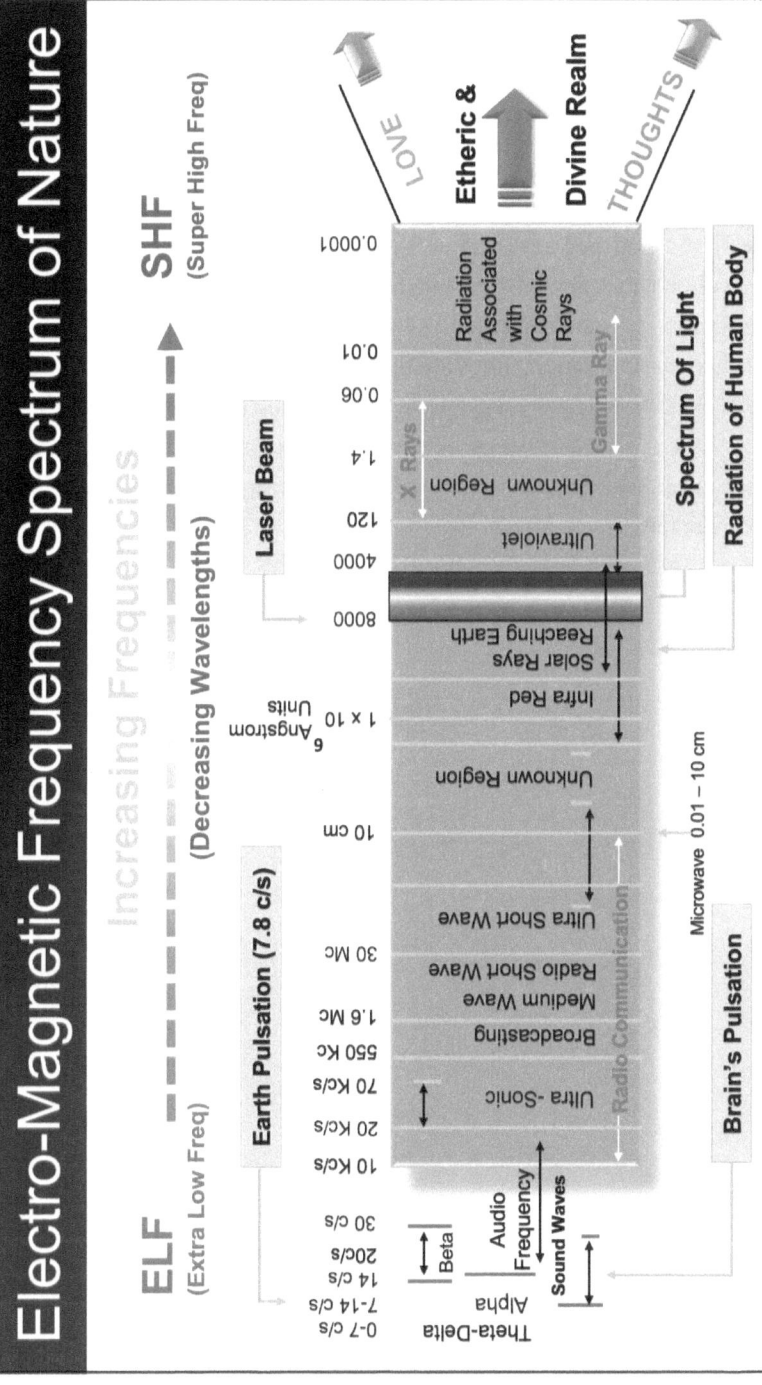

Infinite. It is in this dual mode that one can discern or receive replies and guidance to any question, which our normal mind and senses are not able to furnish.

I end this chapter with two relevant quotations that Bhai Sahib selected from the SGGS to support his findings that everything in the universe is in a state of pulsation and movement, and therefore in vibration. The first: "God pervades the entire Universe as a vibration, and by His benevolent Grace alone He is realised *within*, as a vibrational feeling in deep meditation." (p. 921) The second extract says: "He (the Divine) operates everywhere as a vibration, and only through the feeling of a subtle vibration *within one's self* is His Presence *realised* and *discovered*." (p. 1291)

Without a doubt, the grace of God is necessary for a practitioner to experience the movement of super high frequency towards the etheric and Divine realm.

Chapter Seventeen

CONCLUSION

I AM ALMOST AT THE END OF MY STORY describing my experiential journey in search of the Creator, The Infinite. I wish to express my apologies in advance should any part of what I have written in this book offend anyone.

It has been challenging for me to write in detail of certain revelations and events that seem incredibly out of the ordinary. It is likely an even greater challenge for the overwhelming majority of humanity to appreciate these Divine truths, particularly those deeply entrenched in other belief systems. Increasingly bitter religious differences, reinforced by the consequences of conflicts, have dominated human history. We should be sufficiently courageous to genuinely explore beyond our present religious doctrines and dogmas, including beyond the orthodox religious beliefs and traditional practices we have inherited from our predecessors. There is an urgent need for us to re-examine what beliefs are sustainable, in the face of what we have experienced and what we have consequently learned.

I urge everyone to reconsider the nature of the life they are currently living. Contemplate whether you wish to venture further and seriously explore the Divine Power, which is primordial and universal in nature, and whether you know it or not already plays a dominant role in your life.

If we are able to imbibe the essence of all the world's scriptures with right understanding, followed by right practice, then the outcome should also be right, initiating a vibrant awakening, an experience of universal consciousness. The world would then be a much better and more meaningful place in which to live.

I am aware of and respectful of the right of everyone to find their own path, even if one is walking down one of the world's many alleyways and byways. One will eventually have to extricate oneself from the illusive haze and maze to find the highway that leads to a state of ecstatic awakening.

I was reminded of the above mentioned 'right' when Quin, my third daughter, received the following message one evening in 2008. It was the first of the two messages she has received thus far. It is as follows:

"*The Road to Heaven.* The path of the road to heaven may seem a long journey to those who are going through difficulties in their lives, but they must not let their fear, anger, pain, suffering and confusion stand in their way. They must be strong, calm, patient and never blame others or be envious of the types of life others lead. It is their life, the path they have chosen, that cannot be chosen by others.

"If a person needs help, one must help. And if that person does not ask for help, it is because that person wants to prove that he/she can find or walk his/her path. That person believes in himself/herself. Therefore, he/she can find *the road to heaven*. God will be there waiting for those who can find their way to heaven. They must never lose hope. But if they do lose hope, God will be there to show them the way. So you must not lose hope. Always believe in what you can do in your life. This is a message for you from Above."

My spiritual experiences led me to wander through numerous alleyways and byways before I reached some form of stability. Readers who want to explore are advised to focus on the what and why of true meditation, as well as on its technique and actual practice. One should also dwell on the scriptural validation of the need for total surrender and submission to the Divine within, as well as the scriptural validation of the manifestation of vibrant, euphoric and ecstatic reactions when a true meditation is in progress. A proper understanding will help better prepare you to appreciate the various reactions and responses you may experience when you are involved in VCM meditation, or when you witness this happening to fellow practitioners.

Clearly, the journey of life is very challenging. It is not easy for anyone to be born as a human being. It is even harder to live a life as a human being. Most of us will have to be reborn again and again (reincarnate) as humans beings to continue our lessons in life, until final liberation is realised. Bear in mind the possibility that one may regress to other lower life forms.

Let us therefore carry out the all-important task in our lives, which is to elevate our souls. Bhai Sahib said that all the world's scriptures and Divine doctrines have clearly counselled us that the purpose of life is primarily to develop our spiritual nature through profound meditation. So great is the emphasis on profound meditation that Bhai Sahib also mentioned that the scriptures have declared in unison that even life-sustaining activities, such as eating and drinking, must take second place to meditation.

Human beings have put great effort towards developing their physical and mental aspects, while practically nothing has been instituted to develop their soul aspects. Let me reiterate that while both our physical and mental aspects have a lifespan, the soul is eternal. This explains why, when we do not get our priorities right, which is to develop our soul aspects first, psychosomatic diseases increase. When the well-awakened soul is set in motion, the mental and the physical aspects of our being naturally follow suit, and with much better prospects. This will be so since any manifested volition will be soul-directed from within.

Bhai Sahib quoted some poignant verses from scriptures on why one should first elevate the soul:

"Thou hast by His Grace obtained a human frame. Now alone is the opportunity to attain to thy Lord. Of no avail are thy other works. Join the society of the holy and become absorbed in bhagti." (SGGS p. 12, Raheraas)

"Thy innate inborn nature is to seek oneness with the Divine in meditation. All other works are dross unto thee and so of no avail." (SGGS p. 199, Gauri M.5)

"But seek ye first the Kingdom of God and His righteousness that is within you, and all other things shall be added unto you." (Matthew 6:33)

"I love them that love Me. Those that give Me first-place before everything else shall find Me." (Proverbs 8:17)

"Oh God, thou art my God, and to seek Thee is my first and primary task."(Psalms 63:1)

Bhai Sahib said there are many identical injunctions enshrined in the world's scriptures. They are too numerous to be recorded here.

Let us, therefore, be regular with our practice, deaden our ego, and reduce its continued reign over us. Let us not be too obsessively consumed with mundane activities such as accumulating assets, pursuing success in our career, raising a family, or seeking self-glorification, etc. No doubt these secondary activities do teach us useful lessons, but let us also be aware that the primary purpose of life is to realise our true nature, by being awakened spiritually in order to be one with God, The Infinite.

WHAT IS OUR TRUE NATURE?

The following verse, pointed out by Bhai Sahib, reveals our true nature: ""Oh mind of Man, you are a manifestation of Godhood; recognise your primordial heritage." (SGGS p. 441)

Another message from The Infinite, titled *Within Your Being*, presents a more elaborate description of the human being's true nature: "Arise, put on the whole armour of God and reflect that love in the whole of your being. Look not for love without; find it within, and then reflect it out. *Within your being you hold Me, the Lord, your God.* This is a staggering thought. Stop for a moment and consider it. You have life within you and I AM life. You have love within you and I AM love. You have Spirit within you and I AM Spirit. All is within you—you as an individual. Therefore, I AM within every individual. Therefore, you are one with Me and one with your fellow humans, because I AM within every living soul and all souls are living. As you think on these lines, you become closer and closer to your fellows and closer and closer to Me. You realise that there is no division, no separation. As you realise this, you feel a great joy well up within you and you become aware of Me and of My presence. Dwell on these thoughts. They expand and raise your consciousness, bringing you, in a complete circle, to the realisation of My wonder and My perfection of your oneness with Me. My child, eventually all will have to complete that circle, all will have to come back to the beginning, will have to find their relationship with Me, the Lord their God. Unless you become as little children and are born again in Spirit and in Truth, you cannot enter into the Kingdom of Heaven. This is a very humbling thought—and this is why humankind, with all its knowledge, finds it so difficult." (*God Spoke to Me* by Eileen Caddy, pp. 88-89)

As mentioned earlier, we human beings ordinarily use only about 7% of our mind. As for all the inventions and discoveries that have been made thus far, Bhai Sahib estimated they involved using only about 25% of our mind's capacity. The experiences related in Chapter Seven, and the descriptions of feats performed by Bhai Sahib, are mere glimpses into the infinite possibilities and the even more amazing breakthroughs that may unfold when good meditation practice is incorporated into one's life.

We should therefore focus on augmenting our mind. By doing so, we will be able to bring into reality even more amazing inventions that are beyond our present mental capacity. The human mind can be augmented by using VCM technique to achieve a higher percentage of mind usage. (The percentages of the brain's capacity in relation to levels of consciousness are depicted in the diagram below.)

Baird T. Spalding, in his book *Life and Teaching of the Masters of the Far East* (Volume 5), under the heading, "Is there a God?", draws attention to the scientific discovery of a Universal Force, which he terms Universal Energy. This is a primal Energy that pervades the entire Universe and fills infinite space. He wrote that this Energy is the very substance and principle in which we live and move and have our being. This Energy is given to all and so is resident within, but in a state of sleep. I wish to add that this inner being can only be awakened through the regular practice of meditation that thrusts *surrender and submission to the Divine* to the highest possible level. Spalding concluded: "We fail to realise Divinity if we keep seeking from *without*. We have to realise Divinity from *within*."

To conclude, let me share with you extracts of two messages received during VCM meditation. Although they were 'spoken' to the practitioners

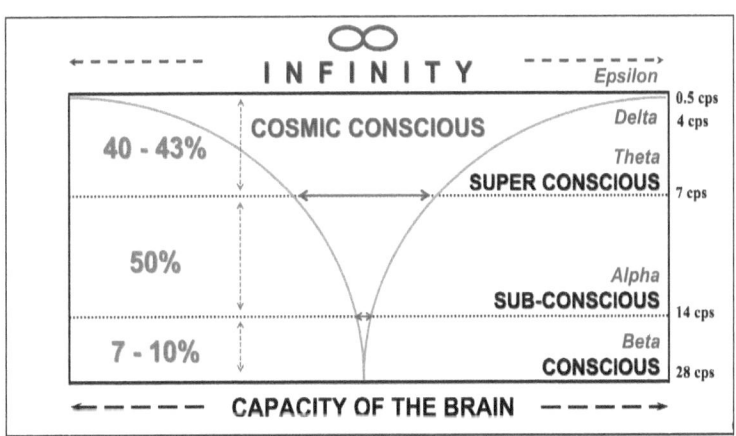

who were present, they may also be useful for you to ponder as you live out the remaining years of your present life:

"Do not look at happiness as being created by money. Anyone can earn money by finding a job. But values ... they come from the Divine. Can you earn the Divine? Can you earn the Divine's deep values? Everyone claims to be religious. Everyone claims to be spiritual. Only I (God) know!"

"To those who know, and to those who still do not know but eagerly seek to know:

I Am The Light.

I Am The Way.

I Am your Salvation.

Walk My Path."

REFERENCES

BOOKS AND ARTICLES REFERENCED IN THE TEXT
[In the order they are cited]

A.J. Russell, (ed.) (2005), *God Calling*. John Hunt Publishing, New Alresford, UK.

Swami Prabupada Bhaktivedanta (1989), *Bhagavad Gita: As It Is*. Los Angeles, Bhaktivedanta Book Trust.

H. Lynn Cayce (1968), *The Edgar Cayce Collection*. New York, Wing Books, USA.

Eileen Caddy (1971), *God Spoke to Me*. Deift Cottage, Dyke: Findhorn Press, UK.

George Cronk (2003), *On Shankara*. Wadsworth, Thomson, USA.

Gia Fu Feng and Jane English (translators) (1991), *Lao Tzu: Tao Te Ching*. Wildwood House, USA.

John W.C. Wu (translator) (2005), *Tao Te Ching*. Shambhala Publications, USA.

Balakrishnan Ramaneyah (2019), *Vedanta Science and Immortal Consciousness*. Vedanta Science Resources: Kuala Lumpur, Malaysia.

Coleman Banks, with John Moyne, A.J. Arberry and R.A. Nicholson (translators) (2011), *Rumi: Selected Poems*. Penguin:UK.

Baird Spalding (1955), *Life and Teaching of the Masters of the Far East*. Marina Del Rey, CA., DeVores & Co. Publishers.

Sri Bhai Sahib, Bhai Kirpal Singh Ji Gill (2002), *Vibrant Celestial Meditation*. World Spiritual Foundation, National Book Organisation, New Delhi, India.

Singh Sahib Sant Singh Khalsa (translator), *Sri Guru Cranth Sahib* (n.d.):

Sentence by Sentence English Translation and Transliteration. Hand Made Books. Tucson, Arizona, USA.

Swami Chimayananda (2005), *Narada Bhagti Sutra.* Central Chinmaya Mission Trust.

Acarya Buddharakhita (translator), *The Dhammapada: The Buddha's Path of Wisdom.* Buddhist Publication Society, BCBS edition.

The King James Bible. Vision Street Publishing, USA.

The Holy Qur'an: English translation of the meanings and commentary. Revised and edited by the Presidency of the Islamic Researchers, IFTA, Call and Guidance, King Fahd Holy Qur'an Printing Complex, Saudi Arabia.

The Star, "Singapore Malays the Unhealthiest," December 22, 2014, Kuala Lumpur, Malaysia.

The Star, "300,000 new possible galaxies detected," February 20, 2012, Kuala Lumpur, Malaysia.

Brian Walker (2009), *Hua Hu Ching: The Unknown Teachings of Lao Tzu.* Harper One, San Francisco, USA.

E.H. White (1999), *The Source of all our Strength.* White Eagle Publishing Trust, New Edition, USA.

Paramahansa Yogananda (1986), *The Divine Romance.* Self Realization Fellowship, Los Angeles, USA.

DIAGRAMS

The diagrams on pages 213, 217 and 223 are copyight © VCM.

TO CONTACT THE AUTHOR

athaneast1@gmail.com

FOR FURTHER INFORMATION

https://vibrantcelestialmeditation.com
https://timelessmind.org
https://spiritualityismedicine.com

TO THE READER

Small publishers rely on the support of readers to tell others about the books they enjoy. To support the author and *In Search of The Infinite*, we ask you to consider placing a review on the site where you bought this book. Feel free to contact the author and pass on your response.

Attar Books has published a number of books that explore issues related to the topics explored here. They include:

Where Do I Go When I Meditate? Keith Hill
The Lantern in the Skull Hugh Major
Prophecy on the River Judith Hoch
The Luminous Nun Kerryn Levy
The Matapaua Conversations Peter Calvert and Keith Hill
The Bhagavad Gita: A New Poetic Version Keith Hill

These books, like *In Search of The Infinite*, are available in paperback and ebook versions. Some are published in hard covers. All may be previewed on the Attar Books' website and on your favourite online store. While our publications are not stocked in bookstores, they may be ordered from bookstores worldwide. And, of course, they may be purchased through all online stores.

If you wish to be updated on Attar Books' latest publications, join the email list at https://attarbooks.com.

www.ingramcontent.com/pod-product-compliance
Lightning Source LLC
Chambersburg PA
CBHW030435010526
44118CB00011B/640